Habermas and Politics

THINKING POLITICS
Series Editors: Geoff M. Boucher and Matthew Sharpe

Politics in the twenty-first century is immensely complex and multi-faceted and alternative theorisations of debates that radically renew older ideas have grown from a trickle to a flood in the past twenty years. The most interesting and relevant contemporary thinkers have responded to new political challenges – such as liberal multiculturalism, new directions in feminist thinking, theories of global empire and biopolitical power, and challenges to secularism – by widening the scope of their intellectual engagements and responding to the new politics. The thinkers selected for inclusion in the series have all responded to the urgency and complexity of thinking about politics today in fresh ways.

Books in the series will provide clear and accessible introductions to the major ideas in contemporary thinking about politics, through a focus in each volume on a key political thinker. Rather than a roll-call of the 'usual suspects' it will focus on new thinkers who offer provocative new directions and some neglected older thinkers whose relevance is becoming clear as a result of the changing situation.

Each book will:
- Provide a summary overview of the thinker's contribution
- Position the thinker within the contemporary political field and their intellectual contexts
- Explain key concepts and events
- Balance accessibility with a serious critical treatment of the thinker
- Expose the thinker's ideas to robust tests of empirical and conceptual evidence
- Focus on ideas and debates in relation to real-world politics and contemporary political questions with empirical examples
- Include text boxes to highlight key concepts and figures

Published titles
Agamben and Politics: A Critical Introduction
Sergei Prozorov

Foucault and Politics: A Critical Introduction
Mark G. E. Kelly

Taylor and Politics: A Critical Introduction
Craig Browne and Andrew P. Lynch

Habermas and Politics: A Critical Introduction
Matheson Russell

Forthcoming titles
Irigaray and Politics: A Critical Introduction
Laura Roberts

edinburghuniversitypress.com/series-thinking-politics.html

HABERMAS AND POLITICS
A CRITICAL INTRODUCTION

Matheson Russell

EDINBURGH
University Press

Edinburgh University Press is one of the leading university presses in the UK. We publish academic books and journals in our selected subject areas across the humanities and social sciences, combining cutting-edge scholarship with high editorial and production values to produce academic works of lasting importance. For more information visit our website: edinburghuniversitypress.com

© Matheson Russell, 2019

Edinburgh University Press Ltd
The Tun – Holyrood Road, 12(2f) Jackson's Entry, Edinburgh EH8 8PJ

Typeset in Sabon by
Servis Filmsetting Ltd, Stockport, Cheshire.

A CIP record for this book is available from the British Library

ISBN 978 1 4744 2021 1 (hardback)
ISBN 978 1 4744 2029 7 (webready PDF)
ISBN 978 1 4744 2028 0 (paperback)
ISBN 978 1 4744 2030 3 (epub)

The right of Matheson Russell to be identified as the author of this work has been asserted in accordance with the Copyright, Designs and Patents Act 1988, and the Copyright and Related Rights Regulations 2003 (SI No. 2498).

Contents

Acknowledgements vi

Abbreviations of Habermas's Works vii

Introduction 1

1 The Liberating Power of Reason 5

2 Critical Perspectives: Power, Ideology and Communicative Reason 38

3 The Origins and Transformations of Political Power 54

4 Critical Perspectives: Power and Domination in Contemporary Society 101

5 Deliberative Democracy 123

6 Critical Perspectives: Power, Conflict and Deliberative Politics 174

References 198

Index 207

Acknowledgements

I owe a debt of gratitude to Geoff Boucher and Matthew Sharpe for inviting me to write this title for the Thinking Politics series. Their encouragement and support over the course of the project have been unflagging. I am also grateful to the editorial staff at Edinburgh University Press who have been gracious and patient at every turn.

The chapters of the book dealing with criticisms of Habermas would have been considerably less well-informed were it not for the excellent research assistance provided by Andrew Mathieson.

Finally, I'd like to thank my family, especially my wife, for their patience and support over the years since I agreed to take on this project.

Abbreviations of Habermas's Works

BFN *Between Facts and Norms: Contributions to a Discourse Theory of Law and Democracy*. W. Rehg (trans.). Cambridge, MA: MIT Press, 1996.

BNR *Between Naturalism and Religion*. C. Cronin (trans.). Cambridge: Polity, 2008.

BNS 'Beyond the nation state?' *Peace Review* 10(2) (1998): 235–9.

CD 'Constitutional democracy: A paradoxical union of contradictory principles?' *Political Theory* 29(6) (2001): 766–81.

CES *Communication and the Evolution of Society*. T. McCarthy (trans.). Boston, MA: Beacon Press, 1979.

CEU *The Crisis of the European Union: A Response*. C. Cronin (trans.). Cambridge: Polity, 2012.

DW *The Divided West*. C. Cronin (trans.). Cambridge: Polity, 2006.

EFP *Europe: The Faltering Project*. C. Cronin (trans.). Cambridge: Polity, 2009.

FR 'Further reflections on the public sphere'. In C. J. Calhoun (ed.), *Habermas and the Public Sphere* (pp. 421–61). Cambridge, MA: MIT Press, 1992.

HA 'Hannah Arendt's communications concept of power'. *Social Research* 44(1) (1977): 3–24.

IO *Inclusion of the Other: Studies in Political Theory*. C. Cronin and P. DeGreiff (eds). Cambridge, MA: MIT Press, 1998.

JA *Justification and Application*. C. Cronin (trans.). Cambridge, MA: MIT Press, 1993.

LT *The Lure of Technocracy*. C. Cronin (trans.). Cambridge: Polity, 2015.

MC *Moral Consciousness and Communicative Action*. C. Lenhardt and S. W. Nicholsen (trans.). Cambridge, MA: MIT Press, 1990.

NO 'The new obscurity: The crisis of the welfare state and the exhaustion of utopian energies'. *Philosophy and Social Criticism* 11(2) (1986): 1–18.

OPC *On the Pragmatics of Communication*. M. Cooke (ed.). Cambridge, MA: MIT Press, 1998.
P '"The political": The rational meaning of a questionable inheritance of political theology'. In E. Mendieta and J. VanAntwerpen (eds), *The Power of Religion in the Public Sphere* (pp. 15–33). New York: Columbia University Press, 2011.
PC *The Postnational Constellation*. M. Pensky (ed. and trans.). Cambridge, MA: MIT Press, 2001.
PDM *The Philosophical Discourse of Modernity*. F. G. Lawrence (trans.). Cambridge, MA: MIT Press, 1987.
PS 'The public sphere: An encyclopedia article (1964)'. *New German Critique* 3 (Autumn 1974): 49–55.
PT *Postmetaphysical Thinking*. W. M. Hohengarten (trans.). Cambridge, MA: MIT Press, 1992.
PT2 *Postmetaphysical Thinking II*. C. Cronin (trans.). Cambridge: Polity, 2017.
R 'A reply'. In A. Honneth and H. Joas (eds), *Communicative Action* (pp. 214–64). Cambridge, MA: Polity, 1991.
RCP 'Reflections on communicative pathology'. In *On the Pragmatics of Social Interaction*. B. Fultner (trans.). Cambridge, MA: MIT Press, 2001.
RR *Religion and Rationality: Essays on Reason, God, and Modernity*. E. Mendieta (ed.). Cambridge, MA: MIT Press, 2002.
STPS *The Structural Transformation of the Public Sphere*. T. Burger and F. Lawrence (trans.). Cambridge, MA: MIT Press, 1989.
TCA1 *The Theory of Communicative Action*. Vol. I: *Reason and the Rationalization of Society*. T. McCarthy (trans.). Boston, MA: Beacon, 1984.
TCA2 *The Theory of Communicative Action*. Vol. II: *Lifeworld and System*. T. McCarthy (trans.). Boston, MA: Beacon, 1987.
TJ *Truth and Justification*. B. Fultner (trans.). Cambridge, MA: MIT Press, 2003.

Introduction

Jürgen Habermas (born 1929) is a unique thinker, an heir to the Enlightenment legacy, a champion of reason and democracy, a social theorist of unusual sophistication and breadth, and an astute commentator on contemporary politics. He has come to be viewed as the unofficial philosopher laureate of the European Union. But what is his distinctive contribution to contemporary political theory? And why has his work commanded such attention?

Habermas's childhood was marked by the experience of war. Not old enough to be a solider, fate spared him the guilt of active participation. But history did not spare him from the responsibility of thinking through the significance of the period. What did these catastrophic events mean for German intellectual life? And what would be required in order to ensure that the forces of cultural chauvinism and political exclusion are tamed by a democratic ethos in Germany (and Europe) in the post-war period? To his credit, Habermas has not shied away from addressing these questions, and he has taken the opportunities available to him to engage as a public intellectual in a variety of controversies and public debates.

After the war, Habermas felt the strongest intellectual affinity with those German intellectuals who had stood against Nazism, among them Wolfgang Abendroth (who would become his habilitation supervisor), Hannah Arendt, Karl Jaspers, Hans Kelsen, Max Horkheimer and Theodor Adorno. But, significantly, Habermas's distrust of the prestige of the German philosophical heritage also motivated him to look outside the German tradition for new intellectual paradigms. His reading of the American pragmatists (Peirce, Dewey and Mead) and ordinary language philosophers (Wittgenstein, Austin and Searle) – and more recently of Rawls and those who have continued his style of political philosophy – has left a permanent mark on his thinking. Inevitably, these and numerous other encounters with foreign philosophical perspectives have motivated many developments and refinements in Habermas's thinking (see Müller-Doohm 2016).

Nonetheless, throughout his long career, Habermas has displayed a commitment to a remarkably stable set of principles: (1) history must not be repressed; (2) the failures of Nazi Germany cannot be treated as exceptional; (3) the new beginning gifted to Europe after the war must be grasped to promote an inclusive cultural ethos supported by carefully designed and implemented democratic political institutions; (4) the political methods for this transformation should be non-coercive and non-violent (there must be no replication of the logic of fascism within the project of democratisation); (5) the tradition of social democratic thought must evolve, informed by Marxism but conceptually reconstructed around the core values of equality, freedom and democratic participation; (6) the project of social democracy must be advanced, but not without critical self-reflection on its own tendencies towards bureaucratic dehumanisation and illiberal exclusion, and not without critical reflection on the 'indissoluble' tension between democracy and capitalism (TCA2 345).

This book offers a critical introduction to Habermas's political thought. The book is intended to be introductory, so I presuppose no knowledge of Habermas's work and I do my best to explain the key concepts and arguments in detail from the ground up. But the book is also a *critical* introduction, and I have dedicated chapters to surveying some important 'critical perspectives' that one finds in the secondary literature. In addition to outlining the criticisms, I offer my own assessment of the criticisms and indicate which of them I believe name genuine oversights and theoretical problems with Habermas's work, and which of them are open to plausible rejoinders from a Habermasian standpoint.

I have chosen not to recount the development of Habermas's thought in this book. In some cases, it has been impossible to avoid a discussion of his intellectual development. But, on the whole, I have tried to present a synoptic view of Habermas's considered, mature political theory. I have taken this approach because I assume that, first and foremost, readers of this book will to want know what Habermas brings to contemporary political theory.

Another distinctive feature of this book is that it is guided by an interest in Habermas's theory of power. Broadly speaking, Habermas is concerned to understand how relationships of exploitation and domination can be overcome through the institutions and practices of a democratic form of life. The democratic form of life is one in which a collective empowers itself to be co-authors of the laws that govern the shape of its social life, and in which relations of domination are overcome through the liberating power of reason and the freedom-preserving rule of law.

The theme of power provides a useful lens through which to approach Habermas's contributions to political theory. But a second motive for taking power as a theme in this book is that the relationship between power and reason remains a hotly contested topic in contemporary critical theory (see Allen, Forst and Haugaard 2014). Habermas's contributions on this topic are still among the most sophisticated and formidable in the literature, and they continue to be a touchstone for contemporary debates.

The book is organised in three parts. Three long expository chapters form the backbone of the book. Chapter 1 introduces the philosophical perspectives and Chapter 3 the sociological perspectives that are the essential background to Habermas's political theory. Chapter 5 draws on these philosophical and sociological perspectives to articulate the main lines of Habermas's normative political theory. Each main chapter is followed by a 'critical perspectives' chapter which surveys the critical literature related to the preceding chapter.

Chapter 1 lays out Habermas's theory of 'communicative rationality' with a focus on how communication is both a site of domination and a source of liberating power, the power of reason. First, I describe the moving parts of Habermas's theory of communicative action (1.1). Then I elaborate on the conception of freedom that emerges along with his theory of communicative action (1.2). Finally, I show how these components inform Habermas's analysis of the concept of power (1.3).

But can reason really serve as a liberating power, or is reason itself complicit in systems of domination? In Chapter 2, I engage in a critical discussion of Habermas's theory of communicative rationality, freedom and power. The critical discussion is framed by the debate between Habermas and Foucault, whose ideas concerning the relationship between knowledge and power Habermas uses as a foil when articulating his own theory of communicative rationality.

Chapter 3 provides a retelling of Habermas's story of the 'unfinished' project of modernity with a focus on his analysis of the historical transformations of political structures in the West. It weaves together the story that Habermas himself occasionally tells in a synoptic fashion but which he typically articulates in such a technical and/or shorthand fashion that it is barely intelligible even to educated readers. The chapter includes a discussion of Habermas's famous analysis of the public sphere (3.2). But it also traces the broader historical transformations that: (1) led to the emergence of the capitalist economy, (2) consolidated political power in the modern nation-state, (3) gave rise to the literary and political public sphere, (4) tied the state apparatus to the functioning of the market economy and the family, and (5) precipitated the distinctive 'legitimation problems' of the liberal-democratic welfare state. Since the publication of his landmark *The Theory of Communicative Action* in 1981, Habermas has continued to investigate and commentate on the subsequent transformations of social and political institutions in Europe and globally, among other things analysing the changing fortunes of the European Union, the 'lure' of technocracy, globalisation, the challenges of post-national democracy, and US militarism post-9/11. These recent social and political developments are discussed in Chapter 3.4.

How adequate is Habermas's conceptual framework for understanding the power structures of modern societies? Chapter 4 addresses criticisms of Habermas's social theory from a variety of perspectives including feminist, Marxist and postcolonial perspectives.

Chapter 5 reconstructs the major lines of Habermas's contributions to normative political theory against the backdrop of the philosophical analysis of Chapter 1 and the sociological analysis of Chapter 3. Chapter 5.1 introduces the tension between the principle of sovereignty and the principle of consent which Habermas attempts to navigate in his constructive political theory. Chapters 5.2 and 5.3 survey the basic components of Habermas's discourse theory of law and democracy. In particular, I examine Habermas's model of the circulation of communicative power in relation to administrative power, with a focus on the question of how power is exercised by the people within the public spaces of modern liberal democracies. Attention is given in Chapter 5.4 to the debate between Rawls and Habermas, and to the vexed question of how to understand the place of religious discourse in modern secular democracies. Chapter 5.5 considers Habermas's attempts to show the applicability of his model of deliberative democracy in the context of emerging transnational and global formations of political power.

Habermas is deeply motivated by the desire to develop a theory of constitutional democracy and cosmopolitanism that overcomes the pernicious legacy of Carl Schmitt. But how successful are his efforts? Chapter 6 surveys some criticisms of Habermas's theory of constitutional democracy and his cosmopolitanism that place its success in question.

1
The Liberating Power of Reason

Jürgen Habermas's theory of democracy has at its core the belief that reason is a liberating power. A society that is organised by a shared rationality can overcome relationships of domination ('power over'). Shared reasons reached through unconstrained agreement give us rational motivations for social action and form the basis for non-dominating solidarity with each other ('power with'). In this chapter, we will look at how Habermas's understanding of rationality (1.1), freedom (1.2) and power (1.3) are grounded in his theory of communicative action. In later chapters, we shall see how this philosophical perspective yields a distinctive conception of democratic politics, one in which free and equal citizens harness the power of reason against the influence of money and power in order to build a democratic form of life.

1.1 *Communicative Rationality*

Habermas's political thought is grounded in his theory of 'communicative rationality'. Indeed, all of his intellectual contributions are grounded in his theory of communicative rationality: his theory of society refers back to the shared 'lifeworld' which is continually reproduced and reformed through dialogue; his theory of morality is grounded in the claim that disagreements among individuals over practical matters can be oriented by universally binding rights and obligations; and his theory of law and democracy reframes the familiar motif of the social contract – i.e. the idea that basic social arrangements are supposed to be endorsed by the citizens who are subject to them – in terms of the rights citizens have to contribute to the democratic project through public discourse. Dialogue, disagreements and public discourse are all forms of communicative reason. So, what then is Habermas's theory of communicative reason, and how does it support his core thesis that communicative reason is a liberating power?

The Rational Basis of Our Lives

To introduce Habermas's theory of communicative reason, it will help to first consider how he understands human agency, its rational basis and its connection to language. As human beings, our relationship to the world has what Habermas calls a 'validity basis'. That is to say, our relationship to the world is mediated by a set of assumptions or beliefs about what is true, what is right and what is valuable.[1] 'My office is on the 4th floor'; 'My neighbour's cat is called Poppy'; 'Tackling obesity should be a priority for public health policy right now'; 'Taking the motorway will be the fasted route to the airport.' We act on our assumptions and beliefs as we live our lives each day. What's more, for the most part, we find that the world conforms to our assumptions and that the people we interact with share our understanding of the world. These shared understandings of the world enable us to coordinate our action with others; shared understandings stabilise a shared world of action. At the same time, what we take to be true, right and valuable is largely affirmed and reinforced through our everyday action in the world and our interactions with others. As a result, we have confidence that the 'validity basis' of our relationship to the world – our assumptions about what is true, right and valuable – is secure.

We don't develop our ideas about what is right, true and valuable from scratch. All of us are socialised into the cultural beliefs and values, social practices and the languages of our contemporaries. These provide us with a readymade worldview. Heidegger calls this 'thrownness' (*Geworfenheit*) (Heidegger 1962: 174–5). Habermas accepts the fact of our 'thrownness' (PT 41). But he also emphasises that from our 'immanent' starting point we are motivated to ensure that our lives have a sound 'validity basis'. None of us enjoys a privileged position from which to make any definitive judgements about the truth of a belief, the justifiability of a moral norm or the value of a conception of the good life. Our judgements on such matters are always fallible and revisable. Nonetheless, it is possible to revise our assumptions or beliefs about the world when we discover that they are false or indefensible (indeed, this is a common experience for us). What the rational person does is seek to take responsibility for how his or her beliefs and convictions evolve. Habermas calls this a 'pragmatic' or 'procedural' conception of rationality (TCA1 8–22; OPC 307–17).

Rationality on this view requires self-critical attitudes and practices:

- being open to correction and not maintain beliefs in the face of substantial counter-evidence;
- reflectively considering how tasks might be accomplished more effectively when an attempt to achieve something in the world is inefficient or fails;
- acting towards others in ways that are morally justifiable;
- conscientiously asserting only what we have good reason to believe is true or rationally justifiable;
- conscientiously believing what we are told only when we have reason to believe it is true or rationally justifiable;
- being willing and able to provide justifications for our beliefs, actions and speech if required to do so.

Philosophers have not always understood rationality in this way. But, according to Habermas, it is no longer plausible to think that rationality rests upon a foundation of divine revelation, metaphysical insight or formal logic. Rather, we must view reasoning as a contextually situated, fallible and social activity – in short, as a learning process. Human understanding and reasoning do not fall from the sky but are constructed by us collectively using the means available to us as acting, speaking and thinking beings. Because it denies a transcendent foundation for knowledge, Habermas calls his a 'postmetaphysical' conception of reason (PT 34–51). In epistemology, this 'pragmatic' and 'postmetaphysical' approach allies him broadly with the pragmatism of Richard Rorty, Hilary Putnam and Robert Brandom.[2] In moral and political philosophy, it allies Habermas with the 'Kantian constructivism' of John Rawls, Onora O'Neill, Christine Korsgaard and T. M. Scanlon.

COMMUNICATIVE ACTION

Let's now focus on the *communicative* dimension of this picture. The assumptions we make about the world and the beliefs we hold about what is true, right and valuable are structured in such a way that they can be articulated in propositions. 'My office is on the 4th floor'; 'My neighbour's cat is called Poppy'; 'Tackling obesity should be a priority for public health policy right now'; 'Taking the motorway will be the fasted route to the airport.' In sentences such as these, we can assert what we already tacitly take to be the case, or what on reflection we are convinced of. Habermas calls the assumptions and beliefs that we can put into sentences 'validity claims'.

Habermas emphasises that validity claims are raised in conversation all the time. When Terri informs her mother that 'The traffic in town this morning was awful', her mother understands that Terri is attempting to share with her what she found to be the case. And Terri anticipates that what she says will be received by her mother as a statement of fact, i.e. as true. Similarly, when Terri warns her boyfriend that 'You shouldn't eat so much deep-fried food', he recognises that she is recommending a rule of action that she wants him to adopt for reasons she would happily lay out for him. The point of these examples is to illustrate that speakers generally assume that what they say reflects what is true (in the case of 'truth claims') and/or can be backed up with reasons that are compelling (in the case of 'normative claims' or other kinds of validity claims). Habermas calls this 'the validity basis of speech' (OPC 21–5).

On this view, what makes an assertion function *as* a sharing of knowledge is not merely that it happens to be true, but that the speaker is able to stand behind the claim in a particular fashion. In asserting that 'The traffic in town this morning was awful', Terri is claiming *knowledge* and is inviting her mother to accept what she says as such.[3] She is presenting herself (1) as saying something that is in fact *true* in the sense that it describes a state of affairs which obtains in the world independently of its being believed or stated, and also (2) as having *justification* for the claim that she makes in the sense that she will be able to show why it is worthy of belief if required to do so.

In general, when a speaker makes a validity claim it falls to the hearer to decide whether the claim is acceptable. It is not enough that the hearer understands what is said, he or she must also accept it; a speech act succeeds only if there is 'uptake' on the part of the hearer. For example, when Dan says 'I will meet you for lunch tomorrow at the café across the road' and Edgar replies 'Okay', a promise is made and a shared commitment between them is established, enabling them to coordinate their expectations and actions. If the hearer accepts the claim that is offered as valid, then the speaker and hearer are said to have achieved a 'mutual understanding'. When speakers engage with each other with an orientation towards reaching a mutual understanding, then the speakers are said to be adopting a 'communicative attitude'. Philosophers of language typically have had little to say about the hearer's role in speech acts or they portray it as entirely passive. Yet it is the hearer's *acceptance* of claims raised in speech acts that enables speaker and hearer to coordinate their action: e.g. a promise is made, a command is received, a request is acknowledged. It is important to note, however, that the coordinating effects of language use are not confined to a narrow set of performative utterances such as promises, commands and requests. The 'illocutionary force' of speech is also felt, for example, when Terri simply *tells* her mother that 'The traffic in town this morning was awful' and her mother believes her.

When Terri's mother believes her daughter, she comes to share her daughter's understanding of how the world is, thus reinforcing the solidarity between them at a cognitive level. Language has the power to bind people together cognitively and practically. Habermas refers to these interpersonal consequences of successful communication as the 'binding and bonding' effects of language (OPC 220-3). Speakers who reach agreement with one another in language weave together a common world, a shared 'lifeworld' (OPC 239-46). Speakers who belong to a shared 'lifeworld' share (1) a stock of knowledge and ways of interpreting the world ('cultural paradigms'), (2) a repertoire of action types, roles and social relationships seen to be permissible or valuable ('legitimate orders'), and (3) abilities, dispositions and motives that enable them to participate in the shared world and to gain a sense of their own identity through it ('personality structures') (OPC 246-55).

Importantly, the power of communication to bind us together in a shared lifeworld helps to explain how individuals gain a sense of identity and how individuals coalesce into social groups:

> ... communicative action is not only a process of reaching understanding; in coming to an understanding about something in the world, actors are at the same time taking part in interactions through which they develop, confirm, and renew their memberships in social groups and their own identities. Communicative actions are not only processes of interpretation in which cultural knowledge is 'tested against the world'; they are at the same time processes of social integration and of socialization. (TCA2 139)

Belonging to a shared lifeworld matters to us. If we do not share rich 'communicative' relationships with others and we lack that reservoir of shared understandings, we suffer. Our ability to make sense of the world and to secure knowledge of it withers. Our sense of solidarity with others is undermined, and we find ourselves in a social world where shared norms and non-coercive coordination of action cannot be assumed. Finally, as individuals, our sense of identity loses its support. To the extent that we are not held to standards of morally acceptable behaviour, our moral agency atrophies. And, we are more susceptible to psychopathologies, especially experiences of alienation (TCA2 141–3).

> Individuals acquire and sustain their identity by appropriating traditions, belonging to social groups, and taking part in socializing interactions ... They do not have the option of a long-term absence from contexts of action oriented toward reaching an understanding. That would mean regressing to the monadic isolation of strategic action, or schizophrenia and suicide. In the long run, such absence is self-destructive. (MC 102)

We will discuss the relationship between individuality and sociality, autonomy and solidarity, in more detail below in Chapters 1.2 and 1.3. Later, in Chapter 3.3, we shall consider how commodification and bureaucratisation threaten our shared lifeworlds in modern capitalist societies and give rise to distinctive 'social pathologies'.

Shared lifeworlds are a resource that makes communication possible. When we achieve mutual understanding with each other through speech, that achievement takes place on the surface of a deep reservoir of shared knowledge and convictions that we largely take for granted. As Hans-Georg Gadamer argued, misunderstanding and disagreement presuppose a background of understanding and agreement.

> Misunderstanding and strangeness are not the first factors; thus, avoiding misunderstanding cannot be regarded as the specific task of hermeneutics. Just the reverse is the case. Only the support of familiar and common understanding makes possible the venture into the alien, the lifting up of something out of the alien, and thus the broadening and enrichment of our own experience. (Gadamer 2007: 87)

For this reason, Habermas describes the lifeworld contexts that we share as a *stabilising factor* that protects us against the risk of disagreement inherent in attempts to achieve mutual understanding:

> If communicative action were not embedded in lifeworld contexts that provide the backing of a massive background consensus, such risks would make the use of language oriented to mutual understanding an unlikely route to social integration ... The constant upset of disappointment and contradiction, contingency and critique in everyday life crashes against a sprawling, deeply set, and unshakable rock of background assumptions, loyalties, and skills. (BFN 22; see also OPC 237)

Even so, the background consensus of a shared lifeworld does not guarantee agreement or cooperation between individuals. Disagreement and conflict can still occur. When they do, we have several options for navigating our way through the breakdown. We can (1) suppress the disagreement, (2) withdraw from interaction with the other party entirely, (3) try to resolve the disagreement through argumentation, or (4) engage in 'strategic action', using threats or inducements to get the other to act in ways that cohere with our own practical interests (BFN 21; OPC 236). Before we look at the path of argumentation, let's first consider the path of strategic action.

Strategic action

We do not always interact with others out of a sense of mutual understanding or with an intention to establish a mutual understanding. In some cases, we operate in an attitude that Habermas dubs 'strategic'. In the strategic attitude, we still seek to coordinate our action with others, but not by allowing the illocutionary force of speech to determine the outcome of communication. Instead, we attempt to use speech as a means to influence others to do what we want them to do. Strategic action 'instrumentalises' speech to achieve a desired outcome. For instance, Terri calculates that she can get her housemate to do the dishes if she offers to clean the bathroom. The achievement of her goal requires that she offer her housemate an inducement sufficiently attractive to motivate him to do what she wants him to do. Take another example: Carl wants the money in the till. He calculates that brandishing a cleaver and yelling 'Give me the cash!' will provide the shopkeeper with a sufficient threat to motivate him to hand it over. Terri uses a carrot. Carl uses a stick. But both aim to get another person to line up with *their* plan of action through the exertion of influence.

It might seem that, as in the examples of communicative action given above, the examples that I have just given involve an *agreement* being reached between two individuals. Does Terri not make her housemate an offer which he in turn *accepts*? And does Carl not issue a command to the shopkeeper which he in turn agrees to comply with? In both cases, not only do we appear to have an agreement, we seem to have agreement on the basis of *reasons*, since the threats and inducements offered to the shopkeeper and the housemate respectively give them reasons to accept the proposals presented to them. This makes clear that strategic action, whatever it is, isn't simply an application of force; it operates in the 'space of reasons' (Forst 2015: 115–16). In both of these respects, it is initially unclear how to differentiate communicative from strategic action.

Habermas nonetheless insists that there is a crucial distinction to be made between communicative and strategic action, and he emphasises two points of contrast. First, it is true that strategic action can be described as a form of an agreement, even a form of *rational* agreement: an offer is made and it is freely accepted on the basis of compelling reasons. However, the agreement is not reached on the basis that the hearer regards the speaker's speech act (request, command) to be reasonable. The shopkeeper does not regard it to be morally acceptable to simply give money from the till to Carl. This is what differentiates a threat from a command; a speaker who issues a command assumes the right to issue the command and the hearer *recognises* that right and feels obliged to carry out the command.[4] The hearer of a command who recognises the speaker's authority to issue the command finds the speech act rationally acceptable. But Carl has no authority to demand the money, and so rather than relying on 'illocutionary force' he substitutes the threat of violence. The reason that the shopkeeper has for acting in compliance with Carl's threat has nothing to do with the 'illocutionary force' of the utterance; it is simply that, faced with a threat to his well-being, his own self-interest gives him reason to act. The strategic action is successful from Carl's point of view because it effectively mobilises the shopkeeper's practical orientation towards self-preservation to achieve Carl's goal (OPC 302–4, cf. 321–9).

This last point explains why the deal struck between Terri and her housemate is not an instance of mutual understanding either. While the two strike a bargain that is mutually acceptable, it is mutually acceptable only in the sense that each has reason to accept it from their own standpoint. The deal is accepted by each party on the basis of personal reasons, whose validity they do not seek to justify to each other. Each party may be able to appreciate the reasons the other has for agreeing – their 'agent-relative' reasons are 'publicly intelligible' – but they need not regard these as *generalisable* reasons – they need not be 'publicly acceptable' (OPC 322). Hence, there is no *communicative* agreement, based on the intersubjective recognition of validity claims, but merely a 'confluence of the egocentric perspectives of self-interested actors' (BFN 346).

Having said that, it is true that one or the other party to the housemates' bargain could seek to justify the *appropriateness* of the deal on the grounds, say, that it is a *fair* arrangement. If they did so, this would be an attempt at communicative agreement, because a justification that both could recognise as valid is offered as a reason for the acceptability of *the act of bargaining* that they are both participating in. And, as we shall see, the possibility of a reflective justification of bargaining and other strategic behaviours will prove to be important for Habermas's social and political theory (see Chapter 5.3). Nonetheless, such reflective justifications would at best establish a mutual understanding about the moral permissibility of the deal, not its desirability from the standpoint of the parties. The reasons that motivate each party to accept the offer of the other remain 'personal'. (Habermas sometimes contrasts 'private' with 'public' reasons to underscore this distinction.)

Of course, the fact that individuals act for 'personal', 'private', or 'egocentric' reasons does not prevent social coordination from occurring. On the contrary, strategic action often leads to patterns of social interaction that are quite orderly and predictable. When individuals act according to their self-interest and interact with others under the expectation that they will do the same, 'social systems' are the result. These systems are unintended consequences of interaction, yet they represent a distinct aspect of social order (R 252). Social sciences such as classical economics are able to generate models of social systems, such as markets, by assuming that individuals will act 'rationally' according to a strategic attitude (OPC 219–20). In these interactions, a 'medium' such as money or power allows the transmission of 'signals' or 'codes' that agents use to make practical decisions. In the medium of money, the asking price is either accepted, enabling a transaction, or it is rejected. In the medium of power, the threat is heeded, leading the threatened party to acquiesce to the will of the threatening party, or it is countervailed.

But Habermas emphasises that human beings do not only interact strategically. We also act in the world and interact with each other communicatively. Social action coordinated via 'codes' (called 'media-steered' interactions) can be contrasted with 'communicatively mediated' interactions, which rely upon mutual agreement about what is right, true or good. What's more, according to Habermas, the strategic attitude and the communicative attitude – the orientation towards success and the orientation towards mutual understanding – are mutually incompatible. To engage communicatively with another person, we must break from our egocentric attitude, and vice versa. Communicative and strategic action take place in 'different constellations' even though they may be intertwined in practice (OPC 220).

This observation leads Habermas to embrace a 'dual aspect' approach to social theory (R 250–60). We can analyse social life from the perspective of the *lifeworlds* that we inhabit or the *systems* that emerge unintentionally as a result of our instrumental or strategic behaviour. The 'lifeworld' perspective makes sense of the fact that human actions, as well as social institutions and cultures, are *intelligible* to us; we take actions that we can understand and justify to others, and we can understand and reflect upon cultures and social institutions from this 'communicative' standpoint. The 'systems' perspective makes sense of the observable patterns of human society that are the result of countless 'rational' actions taken by individuals in response to their environment: the ebbs and flows of traffic on the motorway, the daily peaks and troughs of energy use, property cycles, or the seasonal spike in the price of avocados. The most important social systems, for Habermas, are those that emerge from interactions steered by money (markets) and the systems that emerge from the rule-governed deployment of coercive power (the administrative state).

Discourse

If we want to re-establish a mutual understanding in the face of disagreement, the only option available is to reason with each other, a practice Habermas calls 'discourse'.

In many conversations, we do not find ourselves having to argue over the truth or acceptability of what is said. We simply accept what is said on trust. I trust that my friend is speaking truly when she tells me that there are no more copies of the book in the bookshop. I assume that she is telling me what she sincerely believes to be true, and that she has good (enough) reasons to believe it is true. When we trust that someone is a reliable source of knowledge or practical judgement, we usually see no need to test whether they can back up what they say with evidence.[5] Nonetheless, there are occasions when we find ourselves unwilling to accept what we are told without additional justification, and rightly so. Perhaps what we are told sounds improbable, or we suspect the speaker is trying to deceive us (or gild the lily), or we are sceptical about the speaker's knowledge or judgement in the given topic area. In such cases, we can call on the speaker to justify the things they say. When we do so, the conversation shifts into a new 'reflexive' register, and we engage in a procedure of argumentation or 'discourse' until we are satisfied that there is sufficient reason to accept or reject the disputed claim (MC 100). Habermas views such interludes as a kind of 'court of appeal' whose purpose is to resolve questions of justifiability.[6]

What then does the procedure of argumentation involve? Habermas characterises argumentation as both a 'ritualized competition for the better argument' and a 'cooperative search for the truth' (TCA1 25–6). In argumentation, we face one another as 'proponents' and 'opponents'; but we play the game together in order to ascertain whether some claim is supported by good reasons (TCA1 36). Each participant in the game of argumentation is called upon to produce logical and relevant arguments that will move an opponent towards the goal of rationally motivated agreement by providing reasons to accept or reject some claim. Discourse proceeds via turn taking, with evidence or justification being offered for a claim that has been made, followed by attempts to provide reasons to accept or reject the evidence or justification provided. And so it continues, with participants batting the ball back and forth.

It is up to the participants themselves to determine whether they are satisfied that a claim has been justified. In doing so, participants will consider the merits of particular arguments ('logical' considerations). They will also consider the way the game itself is being played ('dialectical' and 'rhetorical' considerations) (TCA1 26; see also MC 87–9). For instance, has the debate proceeded in a sufficiently exacting fashion? Has each party made relevant contributions? Have they responded to challenges? Have they met the burdens of proof laid upon them? Other considerations have to do with whether the exchange has been sufficiently guided by reason. For instance, has anyone who could have made a relevant contribution been prevented from being heard? Has everyone who has a relevant contribution to make had an equal opportunity to contribute? Have the participants been sincere and forthcoming in their contributions? Has the debate been constrained by relationships of domination or coercion? If these conditions are not satisfied, or not satisfied to a sufficient degree, then participants might question whether the outcome of the discourse is determined more by extrinsic factors and contingencies than by 'the force of the better argument' (TCA1 25; BFN 103). Participants are liable to point to any such deficits as reasons why they remain unconvinced by the argument. This in turn gives the opponent motivation to make good on the deficits and thereby make their case more compelling for their opposite number. Feedback mechanisms such as these make discourse a 'self-correcting learning process' (BNR 84).

It would be easy to assume that inclusivity, equality, truthfulness and absence of coercion are presented by Habermas's discourse theory as *ideals* to be aspired to. But Habermas does not present them this way. Rather, he calls them 'unavoidable pragmatic presuppositions' of argumentation (BNR 82; also TJ 106–7). They describe not so much the conditions that we should strive to approximate when we argue as the conditions that we must assume *have been satisfied* to a sufficient degree. Only when we believe that the argument has been sufficiently inclusive, egalitarian, truthful and non-coercive can we believe that the dialectical process of argumentation has tested the claim in question and proven its worth. If the competition for the better argument isn't felt by the participants to be sufficiently rigorous then participants cannot assure themselves or one another that it has fulfilled any meaningful purpose in weighing arguments. What is supposed to be a competition for the better argument collapses into a farce. As a consequence, it fails to mobilise the motivating force of reason. It might be possible to get an opponent to say that you are right by bullying them or by excluding inconvenient counter-arguments, for example. But, by doing so, you rob yourself of the prize you seek: to win the recognition from another that your claim is rationally justified (i.e. true, right or valuable) (TJ 106–9).

Discourse, the practice of arguing, plays a central role in Habermas's theory of communicative action. Just as there is no substitute for the role communication performs in preserving shared conviction between individuals, so there is no substitute for the role that discourse performs in resolving disagreements between individuals over facts or norms (IO 43). According to Habermas, there is no way to systematically refuse the practice of justification and at the same time expect to help oneself to the 'binding and bonding' energies of the communicative use of language. If speakers consistently refuse to provide justification for their claims when it is required, the intersubjective recognition of the legitimacy (and hence acceptability) of those claims can no longer be assumed. Interpretations of the world diverge, the shared lifeworld withers, and this leads to a diminished sense of solidarity between social groups. Social coordination can still be achieved – e.g. the 'strategic' deployment of power and money can channel individual behaviour into a kind of social order – but social life can no longer continue on the *rational* and *non-coercive* basis of shared conviction (MC 100–102). Both communicative action and discourse are therefore indispensable if our social lives are to retain their basis in shared conviction.

However, Habermas recognises that the process of argumentation can be burdensome and unsettling. In the modern world, where nothing is sacred, there is no limit to what can be brought into question. In an ever-widening swirl of contestation, it is easy to feel threatened and disoriented as one's core convictions about what is true, right or good are brought into question. What's more, there is no guarantee that an agreement will be reached on the far side of discourse and that the ruptures caused by disagreements will be repaired. Social networks built on shared convictions are therefore fragile. They are subject to disruption and potentially a collapse of confidence if their basic convictions are brought into question (BFN 35–6). As we shall see, Habermas argues that in modern liberal societies *the mechanism of law* steps into this breach, providing relief from the burdens of communicative agreement but also saving us from the nihilism of purely instrumental social relations (BFN 36–8). Political and legal institutions play a vital role in protecting and harnessing the liberating power of reason. But we shall delay our discussion of the role of law until Chapter 3.1, and the role of rational discourse in democratic politics will be discussed in Chapter 5.

CONCLUSION

Habermas's conception of communicative rationality is an attempt to explain how, in a 'postmetaphysical' era, we are able to achieve rational agreement about theoretical and practical claims. For Habermas, the sources of rationality and normativity are not found in a philosophy of history (Hegel), nor in the retrieval of tradition (Gadamer), nor in the nature of human beings (Max Scheler, Arnold Gehlen). They are found rather in 'the linguistic medium through which interactions are woven together and forms of life are structured' (BFN 3–4). As an achievement that occurs in the medium of language, rationality is not the possession of any individual, nor of any particular society. Instead, it is 'inscribed in the linguistic telos of mutual understanding' and is 'expressed in a decentered complex of pervasive, transcendentally enabling structural conditions' (BFN 4). This conception of rationality underpins Habermas's conception of human freedom (Chapter 1.2) and his conception of the social dimension of power (Chapter 1.3).

1.2 Communicative Freedom

At the heart of Habermas's philosophical outlook is a claim about the internal connection between reason, autonomy and solidarity. We enjoy autonomy insofar as we identify with and contribute to a rationalised lifeworld; but, equally, the rationalised lifeworld enables us to enjoy relationships of solidarity and cooperation with others. It is this picture of a non-coercive shared life constructed through the use of reason that underwrites Habermas's discourse theory of law and democracy. In what follows, I flesh out this picture and argue that Habermas's conception of freedom is best understood as a 'social' conception of freedom as described by Frederick Neuhouser and Axel Honneth.

The idea of social freedom

A 'social' conception of freedom holds that individual freedom cannot be attained apart from social relationships (Neuhouser 2000; Honneth 2014: 42–62, 2017a, 2017b).[7] There are two closely related arguments given to justify this claim.[8]

The first line of argument begins with the observation that many of our intentions and desires cannot be realised as individuals. Let's say I set out to a catch a fish. I can plausibly expect to accomplish this goal acting entirely by myself. But I cannot build a modern house as an individual. Even if I have the skills to undertake the labour myself, the preparation of the materials and tools requires the work of others. I am 'free' to build a modern house only as someone who acts within a network of agents whose actions enable me to fulfil my intention. Similarly, let's say I desire to live in a just society. Not even the most capable, charismatic and virtuous individual can *make* a just society. It is possible only as a collective project. Insofar as my intentions can only be fulfilled within a network of relationships, my ability to act (hence my freedom) is contingent upon the cooperation of others.

But there is a second reason to think that freedom ought to be conceptualised in social terms. In the examples I have just given, we have started from the image of an individual whose intentions and goals are entirely their own. But consider the following example. Priya's daughter wants to learn to ride a bike and she asks if she can have a bike for her birthday. As someone who cares for her daughter and wants to see her happy, Priya decides that she will save the money to buy her daughter a bike. In so doing, she has allowed her own intentions and plans to be formed by the desires of another, her daughter. Now her intentions are not simply her own, as it were; they are formed as part of an interpersonal relationship. Her desires and plans are not in competition with her daughter's; they are intertwined with them. The daughter's desire is 'completed' through the provision of the bike by her mother, as in the examples above. But, crucially, Priya does not experience her daughter's demands upon her as a curtailment of her freedom since she desires to act *for* her daughter. When she wills and acts to provide the bike for her daughter, she wills and acts freely. Indeed, in procuring a bike for her daughter she acts upon her own deepest goals and values, even though the desire for a bike was not her own. That's because caring for her daughter and helping her flourish is part of what she freely accepts and embraces as a part of the relationship of love and care between a mother and daughter.

Relationships of love are not the only context in which this pattern of intertwined intentions and desire occurs. Similar patterns can be seen in many arenas of life – in clubs and societies, political parties, corporations, friendship circles, families, and so on. In each of these arenas, we form intentions and desires that only make sense within a shared form of life in which we freely participate.

What we experience when we experience 'social freedom' is not the annihilation of our individuality but the freedom of living and acting as an individual within a social space where the projects and practices of others reflect our own values and goals – a social space in which we see in the intentions and actions of others a *complement* to our own intentions and actions, and vice versa. Hegel tries to capture this experience in the idea of 'being at home with oneself in one's other' (Hegel 1991a: §24, addition 2; see also Hegel 1991b: §7 addition). When we experience social freedom, to use Hegel's idiom, the 'subjective' freedom of each individual supports and is supported by the 'objective' organisation of society, e.g. family, market and the state. Hence, for Hegel, the ethical substance (*Sittlichkeit*) of a concrete historical community serves as the *social medium* in which it is possible to live a free life.

The Hegelian idea of social freedom is said by Honneth to be carried forward in the socialist tradition (especially in the works of Pierre-Joseph Proudhon, Karl Marx and John Dewey), in the work of Hannah Arendt, and to be taken up again in his own work (Honneth 2017b: 184–8). But, according to Honneth, the approach taken by Habermas (and Karl-Otto Apel) merely 'refers' to the concept of social freedom; it does not in fact 'cross the threshold to a social concept of freedom' (Honneth 2014: 43). Habermas (and Apel) think that a social medium is necessary for freedom, to be sure, but only because they hold that a social medium is necessary for *discourse* and discourse is required, in turn, for *autonomy* (Honneth 2014: 42).

I think this criticism is misleading. Discourse is no doubt a realisation of social freedom. But, for Habermas, discourse is only one of many social practices in which we can experience freedom in a realised fashion. This claim requires further explanation. First, we will examine how the concept of lifeworld and theory of communicative action give Habermas a non-Hegelian framework for articulating a social conception of freedom. Then we shall examine the conception of individual freedom that dovetails with this social picture. Finally, we will focus on the pivotal notion of communicative freedom, which lies at the root of both social and individual freedom.

Social Freedom and Communicative Action

Like Hegel, Habermas argues that individual freedom can only be made intelligible and be realised in a social form of life. However, for Habermas, this is understood to mean that individual freedom can be attained only through participation in a 'shared lifeworld' and through participation in the practices of communication and discourse. Why?

First, we owe our ability to act in concert with others to the 'binding and bonding' powers of language that are harnessed when we reach agreement with each other on the basis of shared meanings and reasons. Social solidarity is mediated by judgements of validity. We see value in social practice or institution x because it fulfils a legitimate need y; hence we endorse it. That judgement of validity places us in reciprocal agreement with all others who see value in social practice or institution x for the same reasons, and hence establishes the basis for action coordination between us.[9] Mutual recognition between individuals is established via mutual recognition of validity claims. This is Habermas's first distinctive contribution to a theory of 'social freedom': namely, the insight that if social freedom is to be achieved in a given social context, it must be grounded in the free and un-coerced intersubjective recognition of the validity (i.e. legitimacy) of social arrangements by those who participate together in them.

Second, it follows from this that social solidarity is dependent not simply upon shared practices but also upon discourse. Because disagreement and social conflict can only be resolved (in a way that preserves conviction) if parties to the dispute come to agreement on the basis of reasons all can accept, the practice of argumentation plays a fundamental and uncircumventable role in the preservation of social freedom. This is Habermas's second distinctive contribution to a theory of 'social freedom'.

For these reasons, Habermas will argue that freedom within a political context can only be realised on a *democratic* basis. As we shall see in Chapter 5.1, this is not an expression of some prior commitment to the value of democracy but rather follows from the fact that the basis of conviction on which social freedom is predicated can only be preserved if everyone has the right and the ability to contribute to the discourses through which the common life is negotiated. The basic point is in fact made well, in fact, by Honneth:

> ... in the case of social freedom, one's own contributory actions must fulfill the autonomously generated wishes or intentions of one's fellow participants. This assumption can remain valid only so long as I concede to the other the opportunity to place the negotiated scheme of cooperative action into question when her individual needs, interests, or positions have changed. Because such a claim must be reciprocally acknowledged, so that all participants can understand their contributions as fulfilling the autonomous wishes of others, the exercise of social freedom must be bound to the assumption of the recognition of the claim of every other to codetermine the commonly practiced schema of cooperation. Though social freedom can be exercised only in the pursuit of common aims, the determinate content of these aims always remains open for revision and contestation by the members of the 'We.' (Honneth 2017b: 190)

In summary, the conditions of social freedom (especially the kind of relationship between the individual and others that it requires) are cashed out in connection with the practices of communication and discourse. Only within the medium of language, and within the shared lifeworlds that language constructs, is social freedom possible.

Individual freedom and communicative action

The social practices of communication and discourse are essential for establishing and maintaining a shared lifeworld, the context in which we can enjoy *social* freedom. But the social practices of communication and discourse are also essential for the realisation of *individual* freedom. Why?

Habermas endorses Kant's conception of individual freedom as autonomy or self-determination: I am free insofar as I am able to act according to rules that I give myself (TJ 95). For Habermas, autonomy has cognitive, practical and communicative aspects (OPC 312–16):

- Cognitively, it implies the capacity for impartiality, the ability to liberate oneself from the 'egocentric perspective' of immersed agency in order to consider matters from a reflexive point of view.
- Practically, it implies the ability to orient one's actions by validity claims.
- Communicatively, it implies the capacity to articulate and justify one's beliefs and action in language.

In thought, action and speech, autonomy implies a relationship to reasons. Here I would like to focus on the practical aspect of this conception of individual freedom.

In Habermas's account, individual freedom has three aspects. Each aspect relates to a different kind of reasoning (JA 1–18; OPC 311):

(1) *'Freedom of choice'* is the agent's ability to make intelligent judgements about how to achieve ends by using the available means. Making 'free' choices in this sense relies upon a 'pragmatic' use of practical reason. When we determine our action by free choice, we exercise the ability to decide and act in accordance with our desires and intentions. One does not act 'freely' if one's actions are involuntary, i.e. not intended or willed.

But self-determination in this first sense is compatible with 'heteronomy', i.e. being ruled by something other than ourselves. An addict employs a pragmatic use of reason when he or she searches for a way to access drugs in a locked cabinet. A slave employs practical intelligence in order to fulfil the request of a master. In these cases, the action is willed by the actor and a goal is achieved, but it is not willed autonomously. Truly free action, therefore, as Kant famously argued, requires not mere self-determination but self-determination according to norms that are given to oneself and recognised by oneself as rationally binding. Hence, Kant proposed the more demanding idea of freedom as autonomy:

(2) *'Free will' or autonomy* refers to 'the capacity for binding one's will on the basis of moral insight'. 'Moral insight' is the ability to judge whether rules for action are capable of being seen as valid and binding *for all*. This requires a 'moral' use of practical reason. The will is 'free' in this sense when it is directed *solely* by the insights of moral reason, and not by the will of another or by psychological inclinations, habitual dispositions, life history or personal identity.

Against Kant, Hegel famously contended that the fundamental goal of living a good life, a life that is valuable and is not a failure, cannot be guided by the moral law alone. At best, the moral law can articulate the *form* of a life that is free; but the moral law cannot supply the *content* of such a life. To decide what is to be done in the course of a life requires the ability to form a sense of the meaning of one's life and to judge what would be good (or bad) to do or to be. This 'ethical' content can only be supplied by the individual's own values and practices, which are inextricably linked to the traditions of the human community to which the individual belongs. Habermas accepts Hegel's critique of Kant and agrees that, in addition to Kantian autonomy, a genuinely free life requires the capacity for 'ethical self-understanding' and the ability to resolutely pursue a worthwhile life in the context of a community of shared value. Hence a third mode of self-determination is required for the individual to attain freedom:

(3) *'Ethical freedom'* refers to the capacity for 'self-realisation', for pursuing the good as you understand it. It consists in the capacity for committing yourself to a life project in light of reflections upon your sense of who you are (identity) and who you would like to become (purpose). Ethical freedom requires the 'resoluteness' to pursue the life project to which you have committed yourself, and the 'reflectiveness' to review one's life project in light of changing circumstances so that it remains authentic. Ethical freedom is directed by the 'clinical advice' derived from the 'ethical use of practical reason'.

According to Habermas, utilitarianism privileges the pragmatic use of reason, Kantian deontology the moral use, and Aristotelian virtue ethics the ethical use. Each tradition presents a truncated vision of practical rationality and, at the same time, limits our understanding of what individual freedom amounts to. Habermas's analysis suggests that all three modes of practical reason – the pragmatic, the moral and the ethical – play a role in making a life of rational self-determination and self-realisation possible. Individual freedom requires the exercise of practical reason in all three modes.[10] (We shall consider the role of pragmatic, moral and ethical reasoning in political discourse in Chapter 5.2).

But I can be convinced that my pragmatic, moral and ethical judgements are rationally justifiable only via the practice of reasoning. On the same basis, we require the medium of communication in order to 'stabilise' our identities as individuals and 'reassure' ourselves of the validity of our individual beliefs and actions:

> In communicative action, the suppositions of self-determination and self-realization retain a rigorously intersubjective sense: whoever judges and acts morally must be capable of anticipating the agreement of an unlimited communication community, and whoever realizes himself in a responsibly accepted life history must be capable of anticipating recognition from this unlimited community. Accordingly, an identity that already remains mine, namely, my self-understanding as an autonomously acting and individuated being, can stabilize itself only if I find recognition as a person, and as this person. (PT 192)

That is to say, communication and discourse support my sense of autonomy or individual freedom. Communication is thus not only socialising but also individuating.

Without the ability to act together with others on the basis of mutual understanding within a shared lifeworld and the ability to reason with others about questions of validity, we are thrown back onto a purely 'strategic' relation to the world and to others. The result is an impoverished experience of individual freedom, in which the self is reduced to a 'worldless' actor who is only able to orient him- or herself by egocentric wishes and desires:

> Under conditions of strategic action, the self of self-determination and of self-realization slips out of intersubjective relations. The strategic actor no longer draws from an intersubjectively shared lifeworld; having himself become worldless, as it were, he stands over and against the objective world and makes decisions solely according to standards of subjective preference. He does not rely therein upon recognition by others. Autonomy is then transformed into freedom of choice (*Willkürfreiheit*), and the individuation of the socialized subject is transformed into the isolation of a liberated subject who possesses himself. (PT 192)

In short, individual freedom is made possible by a shared lifeworld and, ultimately, by communication and discourse through which the shared lifeworld is maintained. Without a shared lifeworld not only meaning but also freedom is impossible.

Communicative freedom

We are now in a position to appreciate the role of 'communicative freedom' in Habermas's philosophical framework: the freedom to say 'yes' or 'no' to speech acts. Habermas calls communicative freedom the 'anarchistic core' of social order (and of deliberative democracy, as we shall see) (BFN xl, 186). But does this not mean that communicative action (or deliberative democracy for that matter) lacks rules and norms. On the contrary, communicative freedom brings with it a package of entitlements and obligations.[11]

Communicative freedom entails entitlements because it implies a liberty to say 'yes' or 'no'. This is the liberty to accept an invitation to dinner or reject a proposal of marriage. But it is also the liberty to disagree when a speaker asserts something you take to be false, the freedom to ask for reasons when you are not convinced by an argument, or to require evidence when you suspect your interlocutor is speaking untruthfully. In general, it is the freedom to say 'yes' only when one is satisfied that what is offered is acceptable.

But communicative freedom brings with it obligations as well. Speakers and hearers expect each other to exercise their freedoms as interlocutors *in order to* reach a mutual understanding with each other. This requires that speakers speak truthfully and that hearers respond conscientiously. A hearer's conscientious attempt to judge the validity of what another says cannot lead to a mutual agreement if the speaker is not asserting what they believe, or is asserting a belief they could not justify if asked to do so. Conversely, a speaker's attempt to reach mutual understanding will be frustrated if the hearer won't play their part and respond to speech offers with a rationally motivated 'yes' or 'no'. Illocutionary success can 'be achieved only cooperatively and is never, as it were, at the disposal of an individual participant in interaction' (OPC 204). Furthermore, participants expect each other to go on in the discussion or subsequent action taking account of what has been said and following through on what has been agreed to. In these two ways, the freedom to agree or disagree is coupled with 'illocutionary obligations':

> With his 'yes' the speaker accepts a speech-act offer and grounds an agreement; this agreement concerns the *content of the utterance*, on the one hand, and, on the other hand, certain *guarantees immanent to speech acts* and certain *obligations relevant to the sequel of interaction*. (TCA1 296)

These entitlements and obligations are neither 'moral' nor 'legal' entitlements and obligations in the first instance. They are simply the set of rights and responsibilities that make the social practice of communication the practice that it is, in the same way that the rules of chess govern the game of chess and make it the game that it is (BNR 82–3). If participants did not grant each other to enjoy communicative freedom, they would not be able to seek mutual agreement with another about something on the basis of rationally motivated agreement. The granting of communicative freedom to another is therefore not so much a matter of individual caprice as it is a condition of entry into the social practice of communication.

To enter into a 'communicative attitude' towards each other, speakers must assume that their interlocutors are capable of taking a 'rationally motivated' stance on validity claims (see TJ 58–9, 162–6; LT 128–32):

> ... the interacting parties must consider themselves mutually accountable, hence they must presuppose that they can orient their action according to validity claims. As soon as this expectation of rationality turns out to be false, the participants – just like the sociological observer in the role of virtual participant – drop their performative attitude in favor of an objectivating one. (BFN 20)

Habermas calls this a presupposition of 'rationality' or 'rational accountability' (TJ 93–9; also OPC 310). This is a rich presupposition; it involves a complex set of assumptions and attributions. As Klaus Günther explains, there are at least four main assumptions or attributions implied in it. First, it implies the attribution of the physiological and psychological capabilities and dispositions needed to *form intentions* and to *realise* these intentions in actions. Second, it implies the attribution of *authorship* in relation to these intentions and action: 'it presupposes that it will be she, and nobody and nothing else, who does it – no demons, no fate, not the social milieu, nor psychic tension' (Günther 1996: 1047). Third, it implies the attribution of *responsibility* for actions. To consider an agent the author of actions means to interpret the action as something done for reasons, upon which the agent has acted, and not merely acted from motives. Unless one demonstrates the capacity to overrule counter-motives and to act on reasons, then one cannot be held responsible for doing so or failing to do so in any particular instance. Fourth, implicit in the recognition of authorship and responsibility is an attribution of 'communicative freedom' (BFN 119). 'Without any right to say "no," the subsequent action does not count as an action of an author who is responsible and who can be held accountable for her behavior' (Günther 1996: 1048). The flipside of this communicative freedom to say 'no' is the freedom to say 'yes' and thus to freely and publicly take on illocutionary obligations to which one can be held accountable.

Taken together, these assumptions and attributions amount to a *recognition* of the other as a practical agent who enjoys the freedom to act according to reasons and the responsibility for that action.[12]

This is a basic form of recognition, not the recognition of an individual as a *person*, but the recognition of an individual as a *rational being*, i.e. of their capacity for rational 'accountability'. The status of the individual as free in this sense, i.e. exercising practical rationality, is not a metaphysical thesis. It is communicatively constituted. It emerges out of the linguistic practice of performing illocutionary acts and being responsible and accountable for the positions one takes as a hearer and speaker. In other words, our rational agency is something we discover and sustain in the medium of language. Free rational agency, at this basic level, is made possible by a social context – specifically, by the social practices of linguistically-mediated interaction and accountability.[13]

CONCLUSION

The communicative attitude, in which 'I' and 'you' address one another in an orientation towards mutual understanding and grant each other communicative freedom, lies at the root of individual and social freedom. It is the basis of autonomy in the Kantian sense, since it is in the intersubjective process of moral discourse that we learn what is morally required of us. It is the basis of freedom as self-realisation, since ethical discourse is the medium in which we work out who we are and what we should strive for. It is even the basis of freedom of choice, since our goal-directed action requires practical deliberation, which in turn is based on criticisable assumptions about what is true and what is effective. What's more, the communicative attitude is essential to the realisation of social freedom, since social freedom is made possible by participation in shared lifeworlds with which we can identify, and shared lifeworlds can only be sustained through communication and repaired through discourse. From Habermas's point of view, 'these structures set the conditions of normalcy for human existence, indeed for an existence worthy of human beings' (HA 8).

Habermas's discourse theory of law and democracy can be seen as an attempt to work out what it required to attain the goal of individual and social freedom in the context of late modernity. As we shall discuss, his theory attributes a prominent role to legal and political institutions. These institutions have an essential role to play in preserving and enhancing freedom, but only on the condition that they are themselves founded on the liberating power of communicative reason.

1.3 Communicative Power

The counterpart of Habermas's concept of communicative freedom is his concept of communicative power. In this part of Chapter 1, we shall situate the concept of communicative power in the context of Habermas's general theory of power. The basic conceptual distinctions made by Habermas in his general theory of power will be applied when we look at the historical development of modern Western societies and of the social systems and political institutions that characterise them (Chapter 3). Later, we will consider how the circulation of power should be regulated in order to institutionalise the principle of democracy (Chapter 5.3).

THE CONCEPT OF POWER

Habermas does not dwell on the general concept of power.[14] His interest is rather in analysing the social dynamics of power and understanding the ways in which power is exercised. He wants to understand how power emerges within social contexts, and how the use of power shapes social contexts. With these questions in mind, Habermas considers power from at least four distinct perspectives.

(1) *Social power*. First, following Max Weber and Robert Dahl, Habermas considers power from the perspective of an individual's (or group's) ability to fulfil their desires in the world by getting others to do what they would not otherwise do.[15] Political philosophers sometimes call this 'power over', but Habermas calls it 'social power' (BFN 175). What are the bases of power in this sense? Habermas distinguishes two kinds of social power. On the one hand, social power can be 'prestige based' (BFN 138–43, 175). Those recognised as a having special social standing – e.g. royalty, priests, prophets, elders, or in more recent times, experts – can expect deference (and even obedience) from others to some extent *without relying on sanctions*. On the other hand, social power can be based in an ability to issue credible threats or offers. For example, monetary rewards or the threat of violence can be used to attach costs or benefits to the options faced by another agent.[16] ('Economic power' is therefore a 'special form' of social power; see EFP 168.) Often both bases of social power are found together, so that individuals possess both social prestige and material resources, and the two are mutually reinforcing.

The deployment of social power can be reciprocal or non-reciprocal.

In the practice of bargaining, for instance, parties reciprocally deploy social power in the form of threats and inducements in an attempt to achieve an outcome that serves their interests. From a theoretical point of view, we can imagine an ideal situation in which a bargain is reached between parties in a non-coercive fashion, since the 'bargaining power' of the parties is balanced (BFN 166–7). However, market interaction and bargaining processes are rarely non-coercive (and the mere absence of 'manifest violence' does not indicate absence of coercion) (BFN 17). In most cases, one party will enjoy greater bargaining power than the other, a greater ability to exercise influence over another than the other enjoys with regard to them. When this is the case, we might say that the former stands in a relation of 'domination' over the latter.[17] Hence, 'free' market interactions and bargaining processes are best understood as occupying a spectrum ranging from reciprocal, non-violent and consensual at one end to non-reciprocal, manifestly violent and dominating at the other.[18]

(2) *Administrative power*. Habermas recognises that an analysis of power cannot merely treat the level of interactions between strategically-oriented individual actors. It must also consider the impersonal structures of social and political systems. In particular, politically organised societies are able to vest *the power of command* in offices, and to use this resource of power to resolve conflicts and organise collective action to achieve goals. Habermas calls this form of power 'administrative power' (BFN 39–40, 137–44).[19] Administrative power is the capacity to rule: it is the capacity to make legally binding decisions and issue commands, to determine whether these decisions and commands are being complied with, and to compel compliance through coercion (BFN 142–3).

Administrative power is like social power in that it is a power *over* individuals and groups to compel them to act in ways they would not otherwise do. But administrative power differs from social power insofar as it is a capacity that belongs to a political system, not to an individual or group. Whereas prestige-based social power accrues to specific individuals, administrative power is impersonal and accrues to offices. The administrative power of political institutions is administered through the decisions and actions of individuals who hold positions within those institutions. But the ability of these individuals to wield power over others has its basis in the authority of the office, not in the authority of the individual as such. The administrative power of officeholders should therefore not be confused with the social power of individuals.

Habermas's idea of administrative power is indebted to Talcott Parsons. On Parsons's theory, the capacity of the political system to get things done in pursuit of collective goals relies on a number of variables. These include (1) the resources that the system has at its disposal, (2) the means it has at its disposal to ensure obedience, and (3) the level of consent and support for the political system. Depending on these variables, administrative power can expand or contract. The generation of mass loyalty or support is thus an imperative of the system in order to maintain and expand its functioning. Indeed, Habermas will adopt this insight and insist that the 'organized extraction of mass loyalty' is a tendency of the self-reproducing character of the political subsystem (BFN 483).

Nonetheless, following Hannah Arendt, Habermas emphasises that mass loyalty or support must be motivated by reasons and grounded in conviction. Conviction can be manipulated, of course, but it cannot be unilaterally engineered by a political actor through the deployment of material resources or the use of coercion (HA 6). This points to the limitation of both the 'action-theoretic' and the 'systems-theoretic' conceptions of power discussed so far. In both Weber's action-theoretic account of power and Parson's systems-theoretic account, 'what is specific to the power of unifying speech, what separates it from force, is lost' (HA 5). This anticipates the third concept of power, 'communicative power', which is neither the social power of actors nor the administrative power of political systems.

(3) *Communicative power.* The third concept of power refers to the ability of groups to achieve collective goals through acting together on a basis of non-coerced agreement. In the literature, this kind of power is sometimes called 'power with'. Habermas is concerned not so much with understanding the structure of collective action *per se*, but with the ability of groups to generate and sustain the shared opinions and practical convictions that are the basis on which collective action can be organised and carried out. He calls this 'communicative power'. I will discuss this concept of power in more detail below.

(4) *Media power.* Finally, Habermas considers power from the perspective of the ability of individuals and organisations to influence the medium of communication itself. In particular, Habermas is concerned with the ability of those who work in mass media to filter sources of news and opinion, and to decide how the content that is published will be presented. Through their powers of selection and

presentation, agenda setting and issue framing, the media affect the distribution of opportunities to influence public opinion. Habermas calls this 'media power' (FR 455; EFP 169).

Needless to say, media power itself can be influenced by powerful social agents. Likewise, those with social power are often in a position to gain privileged access to the media, as are, for example, representatives of government and spokespeople for businesses and financial institutions. For these reasons, sociologists of mass communication tend to depict the public sphere as 'infiltrated by administrative and social power and dominated by the mass media' (BFN 379). On the other hand, media power can be placed in the service of the development of communicative power.

Having briefly introduced the main concepts of power that Habermas deploys, we will now focus on the idea of communicative power since this concept of power is central to Habermas's theory of constitutional democracy.

COMMUNICATIVE POWER

Habermas's understanding of communicative power takes its lead from Hannah Arendt, who viewed power as 'the human ability not just to act but to act in concert' (Arendt 1970: 44). Arendt's model of power can be summarised in five theses: (1) power is the ability to act 'in concert'; (2) the ability to act in concert is the property of a group, not an individual (Arendt 1958: 200); (3) the power of a group rests upon shared public conviction among its members, upon 'an opinion upon which many publicly are in agreement' (Arendt 1963: 71); (4) the power of a group to act in concert can be actualised through empowering individuals to act in the group's name (Arendt 1970: 44); (5) the power of the group can also be actualised through empowering institutions, including legal and political institutions (Arendt 1970: 41).

The fifth thesis recalls Parsons's acknowledgement that political power rests on the consent and support of the people. Indeed, this is what links power to politics in Arendt's analysis:

> It is the people's support that lends power to the institutions of a country, and this support is but the continuation of the consent that brought the laws into existence to begin with ... All political institutions are manifestations and materializations of power; they petrify and decay as soon as the living power of the people ceases to uphold them. This is what Madison meant when he said 'all governments rest on opinion', a word

no less true for the various forms of monarchy than for democracies. (Arendt 1970: 41)

Inspired by Arendt's work, Habermas attempts to spell out in detail how the authorising or legitimating force of communicative power can be channelled into legal and political institutions, and how this relationship of empowerment can be protected through the system of rights and sustained through procedures of public deliberation and democratic lawmaking. But Habermas's appropriation of Arendt's concept of power is not uncritical. To prepare the way for the discussions ahead, let's consider what Habermas takes from Arendt's concept of power (a), then consider his criticisms of her analysis of power (b).

(a) Habermas's appropriation of Arendt's concept of power

Fundamentally, Habermas agrees with Arendt that power can 'spring up' between people on the basis of their publicly sharing a conviction. The 'communicative power' that is generated in this fashion is interpreted as *'motivating* force' (BFN 147). In the first instance, 'motivating force' refers to the fact each individual takes him- or herself to have 'good reasons' for action. But this 'weak' motivating force of good reasons is strengthened when the good reasons that individuals recognise are discerned through communication with others and when these reasons are shared with others through an intersubjective agreement that is publicly expressed. The intersubjective recognition of validity claims is *autonomous* from the standpoint of each actor, since the reasons are one they themselves recognise as reasons. Yet, the *shared* acceptance of validity gives rise to shared expectations regarding belief and behaviour, and rational conviction is supplemented by accountability within a social network.

More specifically, Habermas traces the link between communication and motivating force to the fact that a hearer's acceptance of a speech act produces 'illocutionary obligations' to which interlocutors hold one another. Klaus Günther plausibly fleshes out the connection between reason and motivation described by Habermas as follows:

> When the hearer takes an affirmative position, she is obliged to adopt the reasons justifying the validity claim as her own reasons, and as her own reasons for action. Taking an affirmative position is the turning point at which the speaker and hearer legitimately expect of one another that each act according to the reasons. As a consequence, the illocutionary obligation serves as a bridge between reasons and motives. (Günther 1996: 1041)

As commitments of this kind build up, new 'social facts' are created upon which actors can rely (BFN 147).

Communicative power thus denotes a shared commitment to practical norms and specific obligations that arises through communication and is sustained through relationships of mutual accountability. But, crucially, in communicative power the 'motivating force' does not rest on coercion or violence but on communicative freedom (see Günther 1996: 1041–51). In other words, communicative power is fundamentally different from social power. Whereas the former involves 'the formation of a *common* will', the latter involves the 'instrumentalization of *another's* will' (HA 4). (Habermas thus endorses Arendt's distinction between 'power' and 'violence'.)

Furthermore, Habermas also accepts Arendt's insight that 'Political institutions live not from force but from recognition.' The argument for this is relatively straightforward:

> ... it is not at all clear that someone should be able to *generate* legitimate power simply because he is in a position to prevent others from pursuing their interests. Legitimate power *arises* only among those who form common convictions in unconstrained communication. (HA 18)

Following Arendt, Habermas accepts that communicative action and the power it generates are fragile and need to be stabilised and protected by legal rules and democratic institutions (HA 8–9). Communicative power is a *strong power* because it motivates action on the basis of shared conviction. Yet it is also a *weak power* because the shared conviction is fragile; it can easily be overturned by disagreement or simply by countervailing interests. Hence, communicative power needs to be 'stabilised'. This naturally occurs where there is a shared lifeworld (Chapter 1.1). But in complex and pluralistic modern societies there is also need for mechanisms that: (1) protect the generation of communicative power from being undermined by illegitimate interests and motives; (2) accommodate reasonable dissent without sacrificing the possibility of generating communicative power; and (3) enforce the results of legitimate democratic discourse and decision-making to some extent, so that they have a better chance of overruling wrongful resistance (see Günther 1996: 1051–8). In Habermas's model, these 'stabilising' functions are achieved through the system of laws, as we shall discuss in more detail in Chapter 3.

(b) Habermas's critique of Arendt's concept of power

The introduction of the concept of communicative power enables Habermas to portray the legal and political systems as (potentially, at least) an extension of the 'unimpaired intersubjectivity' of the shared lifeworld (HA 7). It thus provides a perspective from which to challenge the 'realist' vision of politics as either a contest between self-interested individuals and groups or a self-programming system of domination (BFN 330). But, while Arendt's concept of communicatively generated power is indispensable for Habermas's political thought, he regards some of her analyses of political institutions and of political action as dubious. He presents three main lines of criticism, and each of these teaches us something about how Habermas sees the interrelation between the concepts of power we introduced above.

First, politics cannot be equated with the activity of public persuasion. Arendt theorises the way in which political systems are empowered, but she fails to theorise the means by which political systems deploy the power they possess (HA 18–20). The communicative power that supports political and legal institutions must be distinguished from the administrative capacity to make binding decisions and to enforce those decisions (BFN 273). We cannot do without an analysis of the structure and dynamics of administrative power.

Second, Arendt fails to account for the processes by which political power is attained. Competition and power struggles are a normal feature of modern politics. Indeed, to some extent, competitive and oppositional behaviour is seen as legitimate and is institutionalised in the modern political system. Examples include the role of the parliamentary opposition, the contest between political parties for votes, and labour struggles. But this should not lead us to view politics as a whole as a Machiavellian power struggle. 'The *acquisition* and *maintenance* of political power must be distinguished from both the *employment* of political power – that is, rule – and the *generation* of political power' (HA 17). Only in the first of these three dimensions should strategic competition be accepted as a legitimate mode of political action. In the employment of political power and the generation of political power, the unregulated influence of social power is illegitimate (see Chapter 5.3).

Third, Arendt fails to theorise the way in which political rule can rest on irrational and/or ideological foundations. It is true, as she states, that political rule can only last as long as it is *recognised* as legitimate. But, the recognition of legitimacy is rarely generated purely through inclusive and unimpaired discourse in the public sphere. Rather, political rule is liable to be stabilised through what Habermas calls 'structural violence':

> Structural violence does not manifest *as force*; rather, unperceived, it blocks those communications in which convictions effective for legitimation are formed and passed on. Such an hypothesis about inconspicuously working communication blocks can explain, perhaps, the formation of ideologies; with it one can give a plausible account of how convictions are formed in which subjects deceive themselves about themselves and their situation ... They thereby communicatively generate a power which, as soon as it is institutionalised, can also be used against them. (HA 22)

The idea of structural violence sketched in this context is closely connected with Habermas's account of 'systematically distorted communication', which we shall discuss in Chapter 2. Here, the important point is that Habermas acknowledges the need to offer a theory of *ideology*: a plausible account of the way in which apparently free and non-coerced communicative agreement can give rise to convictions which are nonetheless illusory ('illusions that are outfitted with the power of common conviction' (HA 22)). He also acknowledges the need to provide some critical standard by which a merely *de facto* consensus can be distinguished from a rationally justified consensus. Arendt fails to provide any such critical standard since she holds that opinion cannot admit of being true or false.[20] By contrast, Habermas asserts that there is a test of rational justifiability that can be applied in the forum of political discourse: the procedure of argumentation. There is no other court to which we can appeal to resolve disputes over the rational justifiability of a *de facto* consensus. Whether this is a satisfactory approach to adopt we shall consider in the following chapter.

Notes

1. Truth, rightness and value are not the only forms of validity for Habermas. He recognises many other kinds of validity, including judgements of sincerity, authenticity and aesthetic value (TCA1 8–23). However, to simplify matters, I will refer to truth, rightness and value, as a shorthand for factual, moral and ethical judgements.
2. Habermas has critical disagreements with each of these fellow travellers. See his critical discussions in TJ and in OPC 343–82. For discussions of Habermas's 'Kantian pragmatism' and his disputes with

Rorty, Putnam and Brandom on questions of truth and knowledge, see Bernstein (2010: 168–99), Baynes (2016: 82–96), Flynn (2014a), Levine (2010).
3. Habermas shares the conviction that a speaker's assertion implies a claim to knowledge with Michael Dummett and Robert Brandom. See TJ 125 and 143–4.
4. Habermas admits that the bare imperative (threat) and the command are *limit cases*, and it would be more accurate to speak of a *continuum* of possibilities between 'power that is merely a matter of factual custom and power transformed into normative authority' (R 239).
5. Habermas treats this feature of communication in terms of the 'guarantee' that a speaker provides regarding the justifiability of what they say. See OPC 316–17. His account is a version of what has come to be called the 'assurance view' of testimony (Moran 2005).
6. Habermas's theory of argumentation is laid out in TCA1 22–42; see also BFN 225–9 and BNR 81–4.
7. Neuhouser (2000: 5) points out that Hegel himself uses the term 'substantial freedom' (*substantielle Freiheit*) rather than 'social freedom'. But Neuhouser regards the latter term to be more transparent than Hegel's own metaphysical terminology, which renders his position somewhat opaque to contemporary readers. Honneth follows him in this.
8. Similar arguments are made by other Hegel-inspired contemporary philosophers, for example Charles Taylor and Robert Pippin.
9. Admittedly, most of the 'validity claims' implicit in our social lives remain tacit, unexamined, and simply assumed as part of the massive background consensus that constitutes a lifeworld. Only a small portion of these validity claims are ever articulated and subjected to rational scrutiny. Nonetheless, Habermas insists that we assume their validity insofar as we act on the basis of them as 'unthematic knowledge'. See OPC 237–46.
10. Habermas's attempt to integrate these three concepts of freedom into a complex whole is reminiscent of Hegel's *Elements of a Philosophy of Right*. For a discussion of this point, see Baynes (2002).
11. Habermas's account of the normative structures of communicative action is comparable to Robert Brandom's theory of speech pragmatics (Brandom 1994). See TJ 131–74.
12. In his article on 'Recognition' for the *Stanford Encyclopedia of Philosophy*, Mattias Iser refers to this form of recognition as 'elementary recognition'. See section 2.1 of Iser (2013).
13. This interpretation places Habermas in close alignment with a number of contemporary philosophers who consider rational agency to be *inextricably* connected to social practices of accountability. See, for instance, Brandom (1994), Postema (1995), Scanlon (1998), Darwall (2006), Pippin (2008), Honneth (2010), Laden (2012).

14. For a useful overview of the contemporary debates, see Lovett (2012).
15. Max Weber defined power as 'the probability that one actor within a social relationship will be in a position to carry out his own will despite resistance, regardless of the basis on which this probability rests' (Weber 1978: 53). Robert Dahl offered a definition of power that is very similar to that of Weber: 'A has power over B to the extent that he can get B to do something that B would not otherwise do' (Dahl 1957: 202–3).
16. It has been noted that possessing the ability to offer monetary rewards or to physically intimidate another individual will not necessarily make one powerful. Whether it does or not will depend on the context. For a discussion of these points, see Barry (2002: 160–3). Habermas does not consider this important point.
17. I am employing the definition of 'domination' offered by Pettit (1997: chapter 2). On the distinction between 'rule' (*Herrschaft*) and 'domination' (*Beherrschung*), see Forst (2015: 113–14 and 124–5).
18. It is best to interpret Habermas's distinction between 'weak' communicative action and strategic action as describing kinds of linguistically-mediated interaction at different points along this spectrum. See OPC 317–33.
19. In *Theory of Communicative Action*, this form of power is described as 'organizational power'. See TCA2 160–70.
20. Arendt does outline a process of 'representative thought', i.e. thinking from the standpoint of all others. But this is insufficient, Habermas claims, to ground the difference between justified and unjustified conviction (HA 22–3).

2

Critical Perspectives: Power, Ideology and Communicative Reason

Habermas's portrayal of reason as a liberating power has been met with scepticism, most notably by Foucault and those influenced by him. In this chapter, we shall review some strands of criticism that emerge from Michel Foucault's work as well as from the work of Judith Butler and Amy Allen. While there are deficits in Habermas's theory of power and ideology, I shall try to demonstrate in what follows that they hold up reasonably well in the face of criticisms.[1] In the final analysis, communicative rationality is viable as a basis for the critique of power. Indeed, it is the only basis we have.

The Subject and Power

Foucault's challenge is not motivated by a denial of reason *per se*. Foucault himself regarded rationality to be 'indispensable' (Foucault 1984: 249). Nor is his scepticism motivated by a rejection of the project of emancipation. Foucault describes his own project as 'seeking to give new impetus, as far and wide as possible, to the undefined work of freedom' (Foucault 1984: 46). Rather, the challenge is motivated by the conviction that reason and power are more thoroughly intertwined than Habermas would like to admit. If this is so, then it raises serious questions about the emancipatory potential of reason in Habermas's social and political theory.

What then is the substance of the Foucauldian challenge? It emerges from Foucault's own complex and multifaceted conception of power and its relation to reason. In a series of famous studies, Foucault investigated a variety of historically determinate social contexts, from the mental asylum to the doctor's clinic, the prison to the confessional.[2] Foucault's goal in each of these studies was to expose the ways in which power circulates via social techniques of discipline and personal techniques of self-discipline, and to examine how competent subjects are produced and constrained by these techniques of power.

For Foucault, subjects are constituted by what it is possible for them to do, think and say. Competent subjects have developed the rational capacities of reflective thought, purposeful action and language use. But their competency as subjects is both produced and constrained by the contingent cultural norms, social practices and 'technologies of the self' to which they are subject and which they adopt. On the one hand, cultural norms and social practices limit the horizon of possible actions, thoughts and speech. On the other hand, these same norms and practices are enabling: by means of them, the subject is constituted as a subject with the power to act, think and speak. Foucault thus regards power 'as a kind of quasi-transcendental locus of productivity' (Ingram 2005: 262). Hence, as Judith Butler clarifies, the Foucauldian conception of the 'constituted' character of the subject does not at all mean that the subject is a passive victim:

> To claim that the subject is constituted is not to claim that it is determined; on the contrary, the constituted character of the subject is the very precondition of its agency. For what is it that enables a purposive and significant reconfiguration of cultural and political relations, if not a relation that can be turned against itself, reworked, resisted? (Butler 1995: 46)

A corollary of this concept of subjectivity *as* power is that interactions between subjects are never free of power, but are a field of power relations. This idea of power relations refers to both 'strategically' and 'communicatively' coordinated action as Habermas would understand them. Thus, for example, relationships of love are described by Foucault as a 'sort of open strategic game', and this feature, he claims, is an integral part of the dynamic of passion and sexual pleasure (Foucault 1988: 18). Or, to take another example, for Foucault democracy is not an alternative to relations of power but a formation or configuration of 'power relations'. For instance, in democratic forms of life the power of the majority must be resisted by the counter-power of virtuous subjects. Or, to provide one final example, the activity of the scholar is not above relations of power. The production and legitimation of knowledge is both a social practice and a personal discipline that operates in a medium of power (Foucault 1984: 73). In these and all other social contexts, subjects enjoy 'agency' by virtue of participating in the structured possibilities to act upon others and to be acted upon.

For Foucault, the question then is not whether there is power in a given social context, but how the relations of power are arranged.

No form of power is good or bad in itself. At the same time, Foucault suggests in his late work that power relations can be categorised along a spectrum between (1) strategic play between agents who enjoy the liberty to influence each other's conduct, (2) the use of 'governmental technologies' to constrain the formation of subjects and their activities, and (3) states of domination. The first category is relatively benign, the second more ambivalent, and the third presents a clearly problematic case of power relations (Foucault 1988: 19–20).[3]

Foucault expresses reservations about Habermas's theory of communicative reason by reference to his thesis about the ubiquity of power in social relations (including in communicative interactions):

> The thought that there could be a state of communication which would be such that the games of truth could circulate freely, without obstacles, without constraint and without coercive effects seems to me to be Utopia. It is being blind to the fact that relations of power are not something bad in themselves, from which one must free one's self. I don't believe there can be a society without relations of power, if you understand them as means by which individuals try to conduct, to determine the behavior of others. The problem is not of trying to dissolve them in the utopia of a perfectly transparent communication, but to give one's self the rules of law, the techniques of management, and also the ethics, the *ethos*, the practice of the self, which would allow these games to be played with a minimum of domination. (Foucault 1988: 18)

I would like to make some clarifications in connection with this passage to suggest that the distance between Foucault and Habermas is not as great as it might first appear.

Habermas recognises the ability of subjects to influence each other's conduct, not only in the forms of action he calls 'strategic', but also in the forms he calls 'communicative'. In the context of communication, what Foucault describes as the 'games of truth' might not be so different to what Habermas understands by the pragmatics of communication and discourse. There is a 'power' of a kind at play in the illocutionary use of speech. A speaker makes 'moves' within the language game, for instance, by making promises or accepting illocutionary obligations. Such agency is enjoyed by speakers in their interactions with each other to the extent that they are recognised as competent speakers (see Chapter 1.2). But, from Habermas's standpoint, the agency enjoyed by speakers is not to be conflated with power in the sense of violence or coercion. The 'force' of illocutionary acts is forceful, according to Habermas, only to the extent that the hearer freely accepts the validity of what is said. In discourse, this corresponds to the 'unforced force of the better argument' (BFN 306).

It is possible that Foucault has something similar in mind when he states that 'Power is exercised only over free subjects, and only insofar as they are free' (Foucault 1983: 220). Indeed, in a surprisingly Habermasian fashion, he explicitly applies this thought to the context of dialogue:

> In the serious play of questions and answers, in the work of reciprocal elucidation, the rights of each person are in some sense immanent in the discussion. They depend only on the dialogue situation. The person asking the questions is merely exercising the right that has been given him: to remain unconvinced, to perceive a contradiction, to require more information, to emphasize different postulates, to point out faulty reasoning, etc. As for the person answering the questions, he too exercises a right that does not go beyond the discussion itself; by the logic of his own discourse he is tied to what he has said earlier, and by the acceptance of dialogue he is tied to the questioning of the other. (Foucault 1984: 381)[4]

Foucault apparently recognises that dialogue is not an *unbridled* competition but a *structured* competition between contestants who act in accordance with rules of the game and who are subject to the consequences of their actions and the actions of others within the game. In this kind of 'strategic' interplay – which Habermas would call 'communicative' not 'strategic' – the freedom of the other is preserved; the interaction is non-dominating. What's more, like Habermas, Foucault insists that the freedom of the other is in fact *presupposed* insofar as players within the game attribute to others the power to act and to be acted upon. Hence, in communication, there is a sense in which participants exercise a weak 'power over' each other, but not violence or domination.

Thus, although they begin from different philosophical starting points, Habermas and Foucault appear to converge in their understanding of communication as a language game, and both see the sort of 'power relation' embodied in dialogue as compatible with freedom as non-domination. Habermas would nonetheless insist that it unhelpfully confuses matters to describe language games as 'power relations' since it obscures precisely the non-coercive aspect of the orientation towards mutual understanding. Furthermore, Habermas arguably goes beyond Foucault in his insistence upon the distinction between assumptions of validity and the ability to rationally reflect upon those assumptions of validity in discourse. On Habermas's account, discourse uniquely provides a court of appeal in which truth claims, norms and value-orientations can be subjected to critical scrutiny and their validity weighed. This distinction between communication as a practice (which can be a context of power) and discourse as a practice (within which power must be justified) is crucial to Habermas's philosophical outlook.

But is it plausible to think that discourse can function as an impartial court of appeal? Won't any procedure of argumentation itself be subject to the distorting effects of ideology? To consider these questions, we need to introduce Habermas's theory of ideology, which is found in his analysis of 'systematically distorted communication'.

Systematically Distorted Communication

Habermas accepts that as a matter of fact communication is never 'power free' in the sense of being purified of *coercive* or *repressive* influences. In fact, Habermas recognises at least two ways in which communication itself can be infiltrated by power.

On the one hand, the use of language to reach mutual understanding can be *manipulated*. For instance, by lying a speaker can manipulate the process of reaching 'un-coerced' agreement such that the hearer is led to 'freely' agree to do or to think what the speaker wants them to do or to think. This is a form of strategic action, since it is oriented towards 'success'. But Habermas calls it '*latent* strategic action' because the fact that it is strategic is concealed: on its face, it appears to be committed to free and un-coerced communicative action (TCA1 332; OPC 93). Latent strategic action is *parasitic* on practices of communication oriented to rationally motivated agreement since it only works insofar as it successfully mimics those practices (OPC 301–4).

On the other hand, Habermas acknowledges that, except in the most 'improbable' social situation of complete 'non-repression', what is considered normal and legitimate within a social context will include relations of domination and oppression (R 254). That is to say, Habermas expects that the cultural norms will in fact 'normalise' relationships of violence and domination to some extent. And these features of the lifeworld can have distorting effects on communication itself. Habermas explains how underlying imbalances of power can disrupt communication and create the conditions for their own (unwarranted) justification in his theory of distorted communication.

In general terms, Habermas says that 'distorted' communication occurs when the 'external organization of speech', i.e. the social context, is 'overburdened' and this burden is 'shifted onto the internal organization of speech', i.e. the way the linguistic exchange is carried out (RCP 147). To illustrate the 'overburdened' external organisation of speech, Habermas gives the example of the family in which unresolved conflicts are suppressed so as to be bearable. The tensions and resistances which lie beneath the surface have effects when the members of the family engage in conversation with each other and attempt to negotiate the practicalities of their life together. When they ask questions or make requests of each other, the family members *appear* to interact with an expectation of consensual agreement. But the apparent orientation towards mutual understanding is strained and subverted. Requests are fulfilled and comments are agreed with, but to some extent only because the addressees want to avoid conflict or other psychological threats (even if they do not admit this to themselves). 'Defense mechanisms' (in the Freudian sense) thus subvert the apparent orientation towards mutual understanding, and the apparent 'free assent' to the requests and the comments is illusory (TCA1 332; PDM 419n5). Avoidance and repression may not lead to a 'break in communication' or to 'the transition to openly declared and permissible strategic action'; but they do 'distort' communication (RCP 154).

Similar distorting effects can be seen at a societal level when patterns of domination and discrimination have become habitual (see also Fraser 1992; Olson 2011). For example, the social dominance of men in most contemporary societies (including Western societies) impinges on communication in the expectation that women will defer to men. Thus, for instance, in conversations involving men and women, men reportedly ask for the input of women less frequently than they do for the input of other men, and women are less likely to proactively offer their input than men. This defuses the rational potential of speech and reinforces the cultural or symbolic power of men over women (R 226). The unequal distribution of social power between men and women, and the sublimated violence that the former exercise in relation to the latter, thus stamps its mark on the way men and women interact with each other in the context of communication.[5] The consensus that results from such interactions is, therefore, a 'pseudo-consensus' (RCP 165).

Habermas's account of systematically distorted communication is intended to fulfil the role that the notion of ideology as false consciousness played in classical Marxism. For Marx and Engels, ideology is a cognitive error that scientific consciousness – namely, the critique of capital – can rectify. For his part, Habermas rejects the scientism of Marx's theory of ideology. He argues that there is no scientific point of view from which we can expose ideology once and for all and achieve an undistorted vision of the world. The best we can hope for is the unmasking of ideologies in a fallible and revisable learning process, a clarification of positions in light of reasons. What's more, we should anticipate that ideology will be tricky to spot because it is reinforced by unconscious motivations. We shall return to this theme below.

Although he speaks less frequently of ideology in his more recent writings, Habermas continues to make use of the idea of 'structural violence' to explain conflicts and the breakdown of mutual trust. In *Between Facts and Norms*, he interprets the distortion of communication in terms of 'the repressive and exclusionary effects of unequally distributed social power [and] structural violence' (BFN 307). In *The Divided West*, he likewise notes the ways in which asymmetries of power in social relations (resulting from economic inequalities, discrimination, impoverishment and marginalisation) are reflected *within* communication in the form of distortions: violence, strategic action and manipulation. When communicative action is distorted to a sufficient degree, he argues, the goal of communicative agreement is frustrated, resulting in a 'spiral of mutual mistrust', the breakdown of communication, and eventually violence (DW 15).

How should we evaluate Habermas's theory of ideology? A good deal of empirical and philosophical research on issues related to power and ideology has been carried out in recent years. Examples include the literature on 'adaptive preference formation' (Cudd 2006), 'structural injustice' (Haslanger 2015) and 'implicit bias' (Brownstein and Saul 2016). In light of such recent work, it's not obvious that Habermas has adequately characterised the mechanisms that lead to ideological convictions. At very least, it would have to be admitted that his theory of distorted communication is 'underdeveloped' (Bohman 1986: 340). But, in what follows, I would like to focus on a different issue that presents an even more radical challenge to Habermas's theoretical framework.

The more radical challenge is this: the idea that communication could be systematically distorted represents a potentially serious threat to the very idea of communicative rationality. If the very social interactions that occur within the practice of communication can themselves be distorted, even without the awareness of the participants themselves, then it is possible that the apparently un-coerced competition for the better argument will serve only to justify ideological convictions. If so, then procedures of free and un-coerced argumentation cannot be trusted to lead to valid conclusions. What's more, once we recognise the pervasiveness of 'smouldering' unresolved conflicts between social groups in modern Western societies – for example, between the sexes or between racial groups – it seems plausible to think that many if not most of our communicative contexts will be affected by systematically distorted communication. If this is true, then the 'pathological' case might actually be the norm, and we would do well to suspect that most of our 'rational convictions' rest on potentially shaky foundations. Indeed, under these conditions, one might also be suspicious that the very norms and standards of rationality themselves are manifestations of cultural or symbolic power. As Allen says:

> Once Habermas lets power into the lifeworld in this way, it becomes difficult to see how one can achieve the kind of reflexive distance from one's beliefs, practices, norms, and life projects that is requisite for genuine autonomy and that supplies that notion critical bite. Indeed, it becomes difficult to make sense of systematically distorted communication at all, inasmuch as this notion relies implicitly on the possibility of undistorted communication and subjectivity while simultaneously calling into question the very distinction between communicative and strategic interaction that would make it possible to identify a communication or form of subjectivity as such. (Allen 2008: 106)

Is it plausible to expect that the practice of discourse will be able to correct these distortions, or will discourse remain essentially and inescapably tainted by power? This, it seems to me, is the most radical challenge to Habermas's theory of communicative rationality that emerges from the broadly Foucauldian perspective.

Socialisation and Subordination

Amy Allen and Judith Butler have sought to turn the screws even further by analysing how ideological convictions entrench themselves through the process of socialisation. Superficially, it can be noted that socialisation in the family context involves coercion in the form of threats and inducements used by parents or other authority figures to train children in how to behave as 'mature', 'responsible' and 'rational' subjects. Similarly, educational institutions form 'rational' agents using methods of training and discipline. As Foucault himself remarks:

> The activity which ensures apprenticeship and the acquisition of aptitudes or types of behavior is developed there by means of a whole ensemble of regulated communications (lessons, questions and answers, orders, exhortations, coded signs of obedience, differentiation marks of the 'value' of each person and of the levels of knowledge) and by the means of a whole series of power processes (enclosure, surveillance, reward and punishment, the pyramidal hierarchy). (Foucault 1983: 218–19)

However, the problematic feature of these techniques of discipline and subject formation is not simply that they rely on coercion and violence. As Butler and Allen argue, the problematic feature is more that these techniques of socialisation train people to find their identity and meaning in hierarchically organised social identities such as masculine/feminine or white/coloured. These social norms and values lead to oppression for some and privilege for others (a point mentioned above). But the important point for Butler and Allen is that subjects who are socialised within these formations of value and social identity can become *psychologically attached* to the very identities that subordinate them. The dynamic in view here works as follows. First, love leads to attachment, and then attachment generates a desire to be loved; since 'there is no possibility of not loving, where love is bound up with the requirements for life' (Butler 1997: 8). But, when this occurs, individuals have a reason to desire what the other desires for them. Lucy's mother longs for her to be a proud housewife, and because Lucy desires her mother's love and approval she is motivated to attach to the object of her mother's hope. Her sense of happiness is thereby *affectively tied* to her our ability to realise what she has been taught to value and to fulfil the roles she has been taught to aspire to (Allen 2010: 25–6).

These psychological dynamics have political implications. When an individual's goals and desires for 'self-realisation' are formed within a social context of domination, the motivation to achieve their self-realisation becomes a mechanism for the reproduction of these relations of domination. For subjects in dominant positions, 'self-realisation' requires the exercise of power over others. For example, to fulfil expectations of masculinity, men must desire to exercise power over women. Conversely, for subjects in subordinate positions, 'self-realisation' is contingent upon fulfilling expectations of submissiveness. To fulfil expectations of femininity, for example, women must desire to be submissive to men. As Allen writes:

> ... because power plays an unavoidable role in subjectivation, subjects are vulnerable to becoming psychically attached to and invested in the forms of subjectivity and identity that are subordinating. It is precisely this dimension of subjectivation and the psychic cost of the subjugation that Habermas's account glosses over. Moreover, because the child cannot distinguish between subordinating and non-subordinating modes of attachment, and because she will attach to painful and subordinating modes of identity rather than not attach – for some form of attachment is necessary for psychic survival and social existence – her psychic attachment to subordination may well precede and inform the development of her capacity for autonomy. This is one way of filling out a claim that Butler makes elsewhere: '[P]ower pervades the very conceptual apparatus that seeks to negotiate its terms, including the subject position of the critic.' (Allen 2009: 25; quoting Butler 1995: 39)

In such cases, the critique of power represents not so much a promise of liberation as a threat to the individual's very sense of self. For Allen, this presents a serious challenge to the Habermasian model of communicative rationality since it leads us to expect pervasive *resistance* to critical reflection on questions that threaten our identity:

> [G]ender identity provides an excellent example of this. It is not just that traditionally or stereotypically feminine modes of subjectivity and identity serve to reinforce and reproduce women's subordination; beyond this, having a coherent gender identity, either masculine or feminine, is a requirement for social and cultural intelligibility, thus, for being a subject at all. As a result, taking up a critical perspective not only on normative femininity but also on gender dimorphism itself threatens our very identities and selfunderstandings. (Allen 2008: 105)

Let us now consider how Habermas sees things. To begin with, it is worth noting that Habermas acknowledges the coercive aspects of the process of socialisation. For instance, he describes the development of moral autonomy as following the path from subjection to the arbitrary will of the parental authority figure (backed with 'sanctioning power'), to the internalisation of this will, i.e. the 'reworking' of this will 'into the authority of a suprapersonal will detached from this specific person' (MC 153–4). This process necessarily involves punishment, shame, and guilt (CES 79–81). On these points, as Allen notes, Habermas's account 'overlaps, at a purely descriptive level, with Foucault's Nietzschean account of the role that the internalization of disciplinary power plays in the constitution of the subject' (Allen 2007: 644). However, in contrast to Foucault, Allen and Butler, Habermas does not regard this disciplinary process as entailing any negative consequences for the rational autonomy of the adult subject. Habermas sees no reason to think that the disciplinary formation of rational subjects in any way undermines their capacities or standing as rational subjects, and this is for two reasons (see Allen 2008: 106–21).

First, he assumes that the norms that are internalised by the child are themselves morally justifiable, and that the sanctioning activity of the parents is legitimate. Hence, while social controls may involve repression, they are 'not based on repression *alone*' since they can *also* be seen as valid norms that obligate (TCA2 39). That is to say, the norms and practices that are imposed on the child can in principle be justified, including to the child themselves – notwithstanding that we assume the child does not yet have the capacity to reflectively judge the validity of these norms and the value of these practices. (A similar argument will be made by Habermas regarding the status of the law. The law is backed with a sanctioning power and hence enforces obedience, but it can also be seen to issue a rationally justifiable demand for obedience from the perspective of its addressee. It can be viewed either from the standpoint of the motivating force of sanctions it imposes or from the standpoint of the motivating force of the reasons that justify its demands.) (R 245–6; BFN 29–31). The second reason is simply that, from Habermas's perspective, the role of power relationships in disciplinary processes is benign insofar as it helps to produce competent subjects who are able (retrospectively) to rationally reflect upon the norms and practices into which they have been socialised. Of course, neither of these arguments justifies the cruel treatment of children, and no doubt Habermas would argue that coercion should be minimised wherever possible. But, the point is that the repressive aspects of the socialisation process can be justified, including to those who are subjected to them.

The more complex issue is that of psychological attachment to patterns of social domination. In response, it should be noted first of all that Habermas is not oblivious to these psychological dynamics. In fact, he makes the very same observation that attachment to identities can be a source of the production and reproduction of power in his 'Reflections on communicative pathology'. For example, he describes how threats to one's sense of identity can motivate psychological defences, and how these defences can undermine communication and discourse if preserving one's identity is pursued as a goal (RCP 156).

However, the mere fact that Habermas recognises the problem does not answer the substantive question: do these psychological dynamics undermine the possibility of communicative rationality? Attachment to our identities, whether dominant or subordinate, may well provide obstacles to reflection and promote what today we would call 'motivated reasoning', that is, reasoning mobilised to arrive at conclusions we want to reach (Kunda 1990). But there are two points that can be made in this regard. First, in his early work at least, Habermas suggests that for some oppressed individuals or groups a 'therapeutic' (indeed, clinical) process of dialogue might be required, one that is aimed at the reconstruction of identity so that one's identity is no longer bound up with the very thing one should be critically confronting. Second, independently of this 'therapeutic' work, Habermas could stress that reasoning is a social process. The fact that some individuals or groups are motivated to resist or subvert dialogue on matters that might represent a threat to their identity does not mean that others cannot or will not press the point. The power of reason is not the possession of the individual subject – nor can it be blocked by any individual subject or group. It is the result of a network of social interactions in which a plurality of subjects reason together. Reasoning does not emerge from the hidden depths of our conflicted subconscious but unfolds (fallibly) as each individual contributes to an ongoing public dialogue. And, while every individual has biases and is susceptible to errors of reasoning, the failings of individual reasoners are counteracted by procedures through which each individual's contributions to discourse are subject to critical scrutiny by others (Ingram 2005, 251).

Hegemonic Discourse

Even so, it could be objected that this a naïve conception of reason. Even if 'errors' of reasoning are corrected in the process of public argumentation, the influence that hegemonic discourses have upon the process of reasoning nonetheless leads the 'free' public discourse to endorse certain perspectives that serve the interests of some and not others. How should we respond?

First, we should be clear about what Habermas does and does not claim regarding the power of reason. As already discussed, Habermas fully accepts that reason is historically situated, linguistically mediated and socially constructed (PT 28–53). If human beings possess a capacity for rationality and critical reflection, then this capacity is exercised by human beings within the immanent horizons in which we find ourselves. Our historical situatedness will inevitably mean not only that we are taught falsehoods (as well as truths) but also that we are taught to *see* the world in ways that are misleading or ideological and that we are taught to *reason* in ways that are inadequate for arriving at justified true beliefs. What's more, we will never able to fully transcend these limitations in order to reason from a pure or 'transcendental' standpoint. This observation leads Habermas to embrace a 'weak' concept of 'linguistically embodied reason' which acknowledges that even conscientious reasoning is fallible and prone to illusions (PT 142; also PDM 311–15).

Nonetheless, recognising the situated, fallible and potentially illusory nature of reason need not destroy our faith in reason. After all, if we distinguish between truth and error, appearance and reality, this is because we have discovered procedures of experience and argumentation that can demonstrate the difference between the two. This is why our awareness of the fallibility of reason does not dissuade us from turning to critical reasoning when we suspect error or illusion. Fallible and prone to illusion though it may be, reason harbours within itself the resources for self-correction. Rainer Forst articulates the point as follows:

> If it turns out that a democratic process has gone wrong in some way, this insight is already the (provisional) result of a better and more inclusive exercise of reciprocal and general justification – a result that needs to be validated in further argumentation. There may always be better answers than the ones arrived at in democratic procedures; but the meaning of 'better' is: more justifiable in a process of deliberation and argumentation. Deliberative democracy is, as I said, a self-correcting institution, but *self*-correction means that the authority to question its authority always remains within the realm of reasons among citizens. There is no rule of reasons apart from the self-rule of citizens by justified reasons. (Forst 2012: 186)

Thus, Habermas's 'postmetaphysical' conception of reason stresses fallibility but does not embrace scepticism. Once we recognise that reason is what we fallible human beings are able to construct from where we are, in dialogue with each other and through mutual efforts of knowledge creation and mutual criticism, we recognise the provisional nature of all knowledge. But 'provisional' does not necessarily mean 'false' or 'suspect'; it simply means 'fallible' and 'revisable'. Thus, vigilant self-criticism, not thoroughgoing scepticism, is warranted.

In particular, Habermas argues, we should always consider whether our discursive practice satisfactorily fulfils the presumption that it is inclusive, egalitarian, truthful and non-coercive. Where there is exclusion, hierarchy, any form of deception, or coercion, the cooperative search for truth becomes a mere semblance (BFN 227–9). In the relation to the problem of 'distorted' communication, the subtle coercive effects of power are especially pertinent. But here too the relevant standard is provided by the idealising presuppositions of communications; in particular, discourse must be 'freed from external and internal coercion so that the "yes" or "no" stances that participants adopt on criticizable validity claims are motivated solely by the rational force of the better reasons' (IO 44). And it is not beyond our cognitive capacity to identify patterns of avoidance, repression, or subtle forms of exclusion that violate this norm, even if we are psychologically motivated to ignore them.

For her part, Allen is concerned that the very idealising presuppositions that Habermas sees as intrinsic to the practice of argumentation, including the norms of egalitarian reciprocity, are in fact rooted in the specific historical, social and cultural context of late Western modernity. And, as such, they must be viewed as 'open to contestation and revision' (Allen 2009: 27). I will have more to say about this in Chapter 4. For now, suffice it to say that Habermas admits that the social practices of argumentation that we know today are the result of a social evolution and that they do not fall from the sky readymade. I suspect he would also be quite amenable to the thought that these social practices will need to undergo further revision and modification. (What are developments in scientific method if not revisions and innovations of this kind? And what is intercultural dialogue if not a learning process that enables us to speak and think in new ways?) But whatever revisions are found to be necessary will be justified by reference to the language game of truth and justification itself; they will be justified because they rectify deficiencies uncovered by participants in the course of their attempts to convince one another about what to believe or to do. To this extent, innovations or developments in the norms and standards of rationality themselves already presuppose the basic presuppositions of communication oriented towards mutual understanding. The idealising presuppositions that are the basic constituents of the practice of argumentation cannot be 'historicised' in the same way as other norms and practices. They are 'quasi-transcendentals': that is, they are conditions for the possibility of the practice in which we make truth claims, normative claims, and in which we justify such claims, including the practice of subjecting norms and beliefs to contestation and revision.[6]

Conclusion

Despite claims that he is naïve about the role of power in the process of subject formation and in the processes of communication and argumentation, we have seen that Habermas is well aware of 'the repressive and exclusionary effects of unequally distributed social power' and of 'structural violence', and that he seeks to account for them in his theory of systematically distorted communication. Whatever the strengths or weaknesses of his theory of distorted communication, I have suggested that there is a strong case for accepting Habermas's claim that the 'self-correcting' practice of discourse bears within it the resources to expose and criticise power and its effects.[7]

The questions we shall now consider concern how the liberating power of reason has shaped the evolution of human societies, in particular how it has shaped the legal and political institutions of Western societies (Chapter 3), and what kind of normative political theory can be derived from the theory of communicative reason (Chapter 5).

Notes

1. A similar conclusion is reached by Fraser (1989), McCarthy (1990) and Honneth (1991). For contrary views, see Kelly (1994) and Ashenden and Owen (1999).
2. See respectively, Foucault's *History of Madness in the Classical Age* (2006), *The Birth of the Clinic* (1973), *Discipline and Punish* (1977) and *History of Sexuality, Volume 1: An Introduction* (1978).
3. It is not clear to me how to make sense of these distinctions in relation to Foucault's other remarks about power. According to Amy Allen's reading, the difference between benign 'power' and pernicious 'domination' is that 'power relations are reversible and unstable, whereas in relations of domination, the free flow of power is restricted and some individuals or groups are unable to exercise it' (Allen 2009: 21n76).
4. It is possible that his analysis in this passage is influenced by Habermas with whom he declares sympathy.
5. Habermas's critical perspectives on this point anticipate recent developments in critical social epistemology, notably the recent interest in

theorising forms of 'epistemic injustice', including practices of silencing and motivated ignorance. See Daukas (2006), Fricker (2007), Dotson (2011), Mason (2011), Anderson (2012).
6. There are some indications that Foucault himself arrived at a similar view in his final years. The new 'ethics of dialogue' which he advocated and practised sounds remarkably similar to Habermas's conception of discourse as a 'cooperative search for the truth' (TCA1 25).
7. Although I have defended Habermas's view of discourse as the court of appeal for questions of validity, I do believe that his theory of argumentation is inadequate. Here Michel Foucault and contemporaries such as Pierre Bourdieu and Jacques Rancière have much to teach us. On Bourdieu's model of discourse, see Russell (2016); on Rancière's see Russell and Montin (2015).

3
The Origins and Transformations of Political Power

Habermas's political theory has a sociological strand and a philosophical or normative strand. In this chapter, we examine the sociological strand. In Chapter 5, we examine the philosophical or normative strand. Habermas describes what he supplies in the sociological parts of his political theory as 'a normatively informed reconstruction of the historical development of the constitutional state and its *social* basis' (BFN 65). It is 'normatively informed' by his normative political philosophy. But, just as surely, his normative political philosophy is informed by his sociological analysis. It is, therefore, somewhat artificial to separate these two strands out. And, in Habermas's writings, the sociological and normative lines of argument almost always come intermingled. Nonetheless, I have chosen to try and separate them out in order to show the broad sweep of the sociological analysis and the philosophical analysis respectively.

What then is a 'reconstruction of the historical development of the constitutional state and its *social* basis'? The reconstruction that Habermas provides essentially attempts to portray the major historical transformations of the political organisation of (Western) society. 'Compromises' are reached in each historical epoch between societal forces and the need to legitimise political power. As circumstances change, instabilities in these compromises ('legitimation problems') lead to further transformations in the structures of political power. In Habermas's telling, these transformations are said to bring about evolutionary advances in the internal structure of societies, including in their legal and political institutions.

The most important overarching trend within this history of transformations for Habermas's political theory is the evolution of law as a governing medium. Indeed, Habermas argues that human history can be viewed as a series of 'waves of juridification'. By 'juridification' he simply means *the regulation by law*. The historical processes of juridification involve the extension of legal regulation into new domains of life and the expansion of legal regulation into increasingly detailed specifications and prescriptions (TCA2 357). According to Habermas, each historical 'wave of juridification' has further *domesticated* political power and made it more *rational*.

In this chapter, we will discuss in turn the five historical 'waves' of juridification described by Habermas.[1] The first wave gives rise to the administrative state, and the second to the bourgeois constitutional state (3.1). The third wave culminates in the democratic constitutional state (3.2). The fourth corresponds to the emergence of the welfare state (3.3). A fifth wave of juridification is currently underway in our contemporary 'postnational' world order, and this wave corresponds to the formation of a 'cosmopolitan condition' under the rule of international law. Habermas's recent political writings focus on this current phase of juridification (3.4).

Habermas's overall assessment is that we are inheritors of remarkable legal and political innovations that have enabled humanity to make huge strides forward towards a state of peace, justice and human flourishing. However, he also argues that the contemporary political landscape is plagued by legitimation problems, and that our contemporary political institutions as they currently stand are inadequate to fulfil the social roles they must perform. It is into this situation that Habermas introduces his normative political philosophy.

3.1 The Constitutional State and Liberal Rights

Legitimacy provides the glue that holds a society together. To be stable in the long run, a social order must be maintained by the willing participation of individuals who see it as legitimate. As Max Weber observed:

> An order which is adhered to from motives of pure expediency is generally much less stable than one upheld on a purely customary basis through the fact that the corresponding behavior has become habitual. The latter is much the most common type of subjective attitude. But even this type of order is in turn much less stable than an order which enjoys the prestige of being considered binding, or, as it may be expressed, the prestige of '*legitimacy*'. (Weber 1978: 31; quoted in BFN 68)

But legitimacy alone is not sufficient to 'stablise' a social order. Even legitimate social orders can break down. This can occur, for instance, if some members of the society do not accept the validity of the social order (for whatever reasons). Or, it can occur when desires and interests motivate members of the society to violate norms they nonetheless recognise to be valid. In such instances, the legitimate social order must be stabilised by 'second-order' institutions that are able to shore up perceived legitimacy and to regulate social conflict. Morality and law are second-order institutions in this sense. They are social mechanisms by which the assumed legitimacy of norms is *supplemented* by an 'external guarantee' (BFN 68). On the one hand, moral norms are socially enforced through reactive attitudes of approval or disapproval (social sanctions). On the other hand, laws motivate compliance through the threat of sanctions backed up by administrative power of the political system (legal sanctions) (BFN 68–9). In these two ways, morality and law 'come to the rescue when the stability of institutionalized first-order expectations is in danger' (BFN 73).

This description already gives us Habermas's basic sociological understanding of law: law has the specific social function of 'stabilizing behavioral expectations' and thus of supporting the social integration made possible by all other social and cultural institutions (BFN 133). But Habermas doesn't merely offer a general characterisation of law. He also offers a historicising account which traces the emergence of the mechanism of law at a certain stage in human history and its evolution over time in connection with institutions of political power. Let's now turn our attention to this evolutionary history.

Political Organisation from Tribal Societies to the European Middle Ages

Tribal societies already employ sophisticated social mechanisms for conflict resolution and action coordination. Of particular interest to Habermas is the social mechanism that has certain members of the social group serve as arbitrators or leaders. Typical candidates for these roles are those who possess 'prestige-based *social power*' within the group (BFN 138). Figures such as elders, priests and members of respected families come to hold juridical and political power insofar as they are recognised as having authority to resolve conflicts within the society and to decide questions of collective goals and projects. These basic forms of political organisation might lack the institutional mechanisms of the administrative state: (1) the formality of decision-making taking the form of law (positivisation of law); (2) institutional figures responsible for the interpretation and application of law (legal authority); and (3) the institutionalised means for organised enforcement of law (administrative power) (BFN 138). Nonetheless, members of tribal societies by no means live in a Hobbesian state of nature. They have customs, rituals and symbolic practices that form the social orders of their societies. And, in addition, they possess structures of political power, and even a form of law insofar as the word of the elders, priests or chiefs is taken by members of the group to have a binding authority based on a 'religious worldview and magical practices' (BFN 141).

A step towards the state-organised form of political society occurs when the functions of conflict resolution, collective decision-making and the power to command and judge within tribal societies are monopolised by a 'royal judge' (BFN 141). Habermas supposes that a leader could establish political rule of this kind only to the extent that he 'makes himself the exclusive interpreter of the norms the community recognises as holy and morally obligatory' (BFN 142). In such circumstances, the word of the leader is taken to be *morally binding* because it interprets the sacred law. But, crucially, the leader's authoritative interpretation of sacred law is also backed up by the leader's ability to impose sanctions for disobedience, an ability the leader has at their disposal thanks to their prestige-based social power. Thus, the conversion of social power into 'legitimate' political power rests on the basis of sacred law (e.g. the will of the gods, the traditions of the elders) which is articulated and enforced by the leader as a quasi-divine figure. This pattern, in which political power is coupled with binding law, becomes a defining feature of all subsequent formations of political life, even as it undergoes a variety of transformations over time.

The next stage of political organisation, in which political rule can properly be called a 'state', is reached when administrative organisation – and hence 'administrative power' – is added to the decision-making power of the political ruler (BFN 142). The first centrally organised political systems of this kind emerged in the ancient empires of Mesopotamia, Syria and Egypt. In these societies, the function of social integration was transferred from kinship structures to royal bureaucracies. These became more formalised in response to the needs of social organisation within larger and more complex populations. Three significant innovations followed: (1) The system of laws is made effective by the predictable use of coercive power by the hierarchically organised state bureaucracy. As a result, obedience to laws becomes an established and normal feature of social life for ordinary people. (2) Because laws are enforced by a judicial apparatus and a penal system, law becomes an instrument of coercion by means of which a political ruler can organise subjects and achieve goals. (3) The codification of law becomes indispensable. The decrees of rulers take the form of promulgated statements in order that they can be disseminated, interpreted and applied by officials (BFN 142–3). As a result of this third feature, 'familiar elements of the legal system can develop for the first time', including:

> ... legal norms or programs that pertain to *possible* future cases and safeguard legal claims *ex ante*; secondary legal norms that authorize the generation and alteration of primary norms of behavior; an administration of justice that transforms legal claims into possibilities for lawsuits; an execution of the law supporting the threat of sanctions, and so on. (BFN 74)

Despite the efficacy of codified law as a tool for organising large and complex societies, the right of kings and emperors to make law cannot rest simply upon might. The maintenance of political power relies upon the state system establishing itself as the legitimate source of law. The original forms of consolidated state power coalesced through a successful mobilisation of religious worldviews to this end. The law emanating from the seat of power was presented as having a sacred origin, and the authority of ruling families was given a 'sacred aura' by being linked to mythical narratives. The motivational force of law was tightly bound to mythic sources of 'terror' and 'zeal' (BFN 23–5). By presenting the law in this way, the political powers could establish themselves on the independent basis of religious conviction. Simultaneously, ritual practices were co-opted to serve as 'state rituals', symbolically incorporating the political order into the religious orders of society (P 17).

During the Axial Age (c. 800 BCE–200 BCE), the religious basis of political power became susceptible to critique from influential figures outside the institutions of state power. In Israel, China and Greece, for instance, prophets, monks and wise men systematically elaborated metaphysical and religious worldviews for the first time. These intellectual elites took a detached and critical standpoint with regard to society and its changing fortunes, including with regard to its political rulers. From the perspective of these prophetic figures, the flow of events and relationships making up the temporal world were set off against the 'God's eye point of view'. Projecting themselves into the impartial and transcendent standpoint of the divine opened up the project of philosophy as a quest for knowledge (the attainment of enlightenment) and for salvation (the unification of the individual with the mind of the eternal God). But it also opened up a new critical perspective from which to describe and criticise mundane affairs. If the human lawmaker claimed to 'represent' the divine will, then reflection on the divine law, which emanates from God, provides a standard by which to judge human laws.

> Once this transformation has taken place the political ruler can no longer be perceived as the manifestation of the divine but only as its human *representative*. From now on, he, as a human person, is also *subordinated* to the *nomos* in terms of which all human action must be measured. (P 18–19)

Thus, while religious symbols are effectively deployed to legitimate political power, these religious symbols are not entirely at the disposal of political rulers. The sacred power to which they lay claim is always transcendent.

The result of these developments is a social order in which 'the political' equates to 'the symbolic order of the collective self-representation of political communities in the mirror image of rulers whose authority is legitimated by some sacred power' (P 19). This configuration of 'the political' persisted throughout the European Middle Ages, a period in which the tension between the temporal and the eternal sources of law was institutionalised in the relationship between the emperor and the pope. Political structures in Europe continued to draw authority from their legitimate role as 'temporal' powers within the kingdom of God well into the early modern period. Nonetheless, this configuration of 'the political' was dealt a series of fatally blows with the transition into the modern era.

Secularisation and capitalist modernisation

Starting in the sixteenth century, major shifts in the social, cultural and economic landscape led to a different kind of state organisation. The most important developments for Habermas's narrative are (a) the process of secularisation brought about by the Reformation and (b) the emergence of the capitalist mode of production.

(a) Religious pluralism and secularisation

The hegemonic power of the Roman Catholic Church was undermined by the Reformation and the subsequent fracturing of Europe through sectarian conflicts. The climate of religious conflict incentivised a privatisation of religious belief, and laws of religious toleration were gradually adopted throughout Europe, establishing for the first time a legally recognised space of 'private autonomy' for all citizens as individuals (not as households). This was an important early milestone in the evolution of modern liberal rights. The Church retained a hegemonic position as a moral and religious authority in the social landscape, but over time its hegemonic position eroded until it came to be seen as one moral authority among others and as one legally recognised form of association among others.

As the power of the Church to convincingly present itself as the inner-worldly representation of the perspective of God on society diminished, political rulers were less able to rely on the implicit authority of religious institutions to legitimate their power. The long-standing duality of the 'two kingdoms' of sacred and secular law slowly faded as an organising principle, and with it the assumption of 'the hierarchical subordination' of human law to 'a higher law' (BFN 71). The situation of religious pluralism and sectarian conflict created the need for a state that is able to accommodate a diversity of religious communities and to adjudicate disputes between social groups impartially. This imposed an imperative upon the political and especially legal structures of the state apparatus to strip themselves of symbolic attachment to any particular creed, and to generate and enforce laws in a way that demonstrably transcended sectarianism. In short, the social phenomenon of religious conflict created a structural imperative towards secularisation in the systems of political power.

> The relation between church and state in modern Europe assumed different forms either side of the Pyrenees, north and south of the Alps, and west and east of the Rhine. The religious neutrality of the state took on different legal forms in different European countries. However, within civil society, religion everywhere assumes a similarly apolitical role. (DW 46)

In the pre-modern paradigm, the spellbinding authority of the divine insulated norms and values from problematisation, and they were entrenched through 'a prescriptive choice of themes and the rigid pattering of reasons' (BFN 36–7). What's more, factual acceptance of the legal and political order was not distinguished from its claim to legitimacy; these were 'fused' in the conviction of the members of the society who were overawed by the authority of the sacred ruler. But, as religious legitimations of political power began to lose their unproblematic character, we observe a freeing up of the potential for rational self-criticism. Justifications of political authority and of laws relied more and more on appeals to natural law and to the use of practical reason.

> After the canopy of sacred law had collapsed, leaving behind as ruins the two pillars of politically enacted law and instrumentally employed power, reason alone was supposed to provide a substitute for sacred, self-authorising law, a substitute that could give back true authority to a political legislator who was pictured as a power holder. (BFN 146)

The disenchantment of religious worldviews gradually shifted efforts to legitimate political authority onto a 'post-conventional' basis (BFN 71). It is not just that political discourse relies increasingly upon mundane reasoning as opposed to religious or metaphysical reasoning; it is also that it is understood that legitimacy must be grounded in the interests and the consent of the governed. The early modern social contract tradition reflects this changing basis of political legitimation, as we shall discuss below.

(b) Capitalism and the market economy

In the centuries following the Reformation, dramatic changes in the structure of the economy were driven by the development of techniques of industrial production, the establishment of capitalist markets, colonial expansion and innovations in banking and finance. The fundamental innovation, however, was the organisation of productive labour in the form of capitalist enterprise. In this new paradigm, economic production was taken out of the hands of feudal estates and given over to the 'private sphere' of 'civil society' in which individuals would contract with each other to fulfil needs. Work would no longer be organised according to the rights and responsibilities of estates, but according to the principles of supply and demand for labour. The symbolic organisation of the society around the hierarchy of church, princes and nobility broke down under the pressure of these economic and social changes (STPS 5–12, 57–78).

Workers and consumers in the capitalist economy are expected to make rational choices based on calculations of utility. The 'language' of money facilitates a simplified decision-making process, in which the orientations provided by values and norms are eclipsed by self-interested evaluations of the costs and benefits attached to available options. As participants in the capitalist economy, individuals do not entirely abandon their value-orientations, but they do 'detach themselves from lifeworld contexts and adapt themselves to formally organized domains of action' (TCA2 321). The result is what Habermas describes as the 'uncoupling' of the economic 'system' from the 'lifeworld':

> Actors have always been able to sheer off from an orientation to mutual understanding, adopt a strategic attitude, and objectify normative contexts into something in the objective world, but in modern societies, economic and bureaucratic spheres emerge in which social relations are regulated only via money and power. Norm-conformative attitudes and identity-forming social memberships are neither necessary nor possible in these spheres; they are made peripheral instead. (TCA2 154)

The 'uncoupling' of the economic system from the lifeworld in the form of 'bourgeois civil society' represents the emergence of the market economy as a self-regulating, quasi-autonomous social system.

From the bourgeois 'absolutist' state to the 'constitutional' state

The pressures of religious pluralism and the emerging bourgeois market economy shaped (a) the modern absolutist state, which was in turn domesticated by (b) constitutional frameworks guaranteeing basic liberal rights.

(c) The bourgeois 'absolutist' state

The cultural and legal infrastructure of Western societies had to develop to a sufficient extent before the institutionalisation of the administrative state and the market economy could be achieved (TCA2 173). The form of political organisation in which this took place, Habermas claims, was the bourgeois 'absolutist' state famously depicted in Hobbes's *Leviathan* (1651) (TCA2 359).

According to Hobbes's famous argument, a sovereign with 'absolute' (i.e. irresistible) power is instrumentally valuable for enforcing law and thus establishing and maintaining a state of civil peace. Since all people share an interest in transcending the war of each against all and entering into a state of civil peace, the sovereign's monopoly on power can be said to be legitimate on the basis of an original 'social contract' and not merely on the basis of the divine right of the sovereign to rule. In reality, the absolutist state was established through a modification of existing political structures along two axes.

On the one hand, public law enshrined the state as the sovereign power, holding a monopoly on coercive force and the sole legal authority. The institutions of public administration and the military were taken out of the direct control of princes and officeholders within the royal courts and were reorganised under new legal and bureaucratic structures. The authority of the nobility was transformed by the legal oversight of government so that it became a part of the administrative function of the state itself, or else receded into a private existence. The trades and professional guilds were likewise transformed into associations within the private realm of civil society (PS 51).

On the other hand, civil or private law provided legal sanction and protection for the sphere of private exchange, in which individuals were permitted to contract with each other in the pursuit of personal goals. Through its enforcement of law, especially the enforcement of contracts under private law, the sovereign state provided the means to embed the market economy. The new bourgeois legal order constituted 'civil society' as a private sphere of exchange that was 'emancipated' from the feudal lifeworld (DW 47). And, indeed, the emergence of the economic sphere as a sphere of action 'uncoupled' from the lifeworld was experienced by the bourgeois class in the eighteenth century as a gain in *freedom*. However, the 'emancipation' of wage labourers from the feudal system also meant social dislocation, exploitation and impoverishment. The bourgeois freedoms of capitalist society, as Marx so perceptively observed, amounted to a freeing of capital accumulation from the fetters of moral constraints and its elevation to the status of a quasi-spiritual power holding humanity in its thrall. The emancipation won by the bourgeois state was an ambivalent achievement to say the least (TCA2 361).

In the bourgeois 'absolutist' state, what had been symbolically and functionally fused together within an encompassing metaphysical and religious worldview in pre-modern societies had come to be 'functionally differentiated' into the 'private' and 'public' spheres. The 'public authorities' would play a specialised regulatory role in society alongside 'civil society' which would take care of the material needs of society. And, as the political system receded to become one social subsystem alongside others, society as a whole was 'depoliticised' to a certain extent (P 20). At the same time, the state began to take on a role in regulating markets as well as enforcing contracts. The influx of tax revenue from increasing economic output made possible new and previously unimagined possibilities for expansionist and state-building activities, eventually extending to the state-sponsored provision of health care and pensions.

(d) The constitutional state

After Hobbes, it becomes widely accepted that, if social institutions need to be justified on the basis of rational principles, then the fundamental problems of law and politics have to be resolved at the *constitutional* level (BFN 144). Corresponding to this new sensitivity to the self-regulation and legality of the political system, Habermas describes a process of 'constitutionalisation' which occurred in different ways and at different speeds across Europe from the seventeenth to nineteenth centuries. The process of constitutionalisation was driven by the imperative for self-legitimation. This imperative necessitated that the administrative state be organised and be perceived to be organised according to legitimate legal principles from the ground up. Self-limitations and 'precautionary measures' were introduced to preserve the standing of the state as an institution of justice and as a servant of the public good (BFN 39). This extended to a diverse set of public institutions – including the permanent administration, the standing army, and the bodies responsible for making law (parliament) and applying law (courts) – all of which came to be more formally regulated by law. As a result, the absolutist state transformed itself into the constitutional state (*Rechtsstaat*), in which the absolute and unbridled power of the sovereign is domesticated under law.[2]

A consequence of this second 'wave' of juridification is that citizens acquired new actionable rights against the sovereign, especially against the sovereign's interference in the freedom of private persons.

> The guarantees of life, liberty, and property of private persons no longer arise only as functional side effects of a commerce institutionalized in civil law. Rather, with the idea of the constitutional state, they achieve the status of morally justified constitutional norms and mark the structure of the political order as a whole. (TCA2 360)

A further step is thus taken towards establishing the legitimacy of the state upon the recognition of the standing of citizens as free and equal. However, such liberal rights do not yet amount to a share in the activity of government itself. (The establishment of democratic rights of political participation is the topic of Chapter 3.2.)

THE STABILISATION OF POST-CONVENTIONAL MORALITY THROUGH LIBERAL RIGHTS

Earlier, I said that Habermas has a thoroughly historicising view of law. In this final section of Chapter 3.1, I would like to summarise how Habermas views the distinctive social function of law in the modern context.

In the modern era, as we have noted, traditional forms of life have been critically dissected and have fragmented; they no longer command the common assent requisite to secure social solidarity. This development has had numerous ramifications. First among them, according to Habermas, is that being able to rely less on the pre-established consensus of a shared tradition has had a 'rationalising' effect on the lifeworld itself. The very existence of a shared lifeworld is now 'saddled upon the interpretative achievements of actors themselves', and our worldviews have increasingly become the subject of *rational reflection* (TCA2 145). Similarly, society has been progressively rationalised in a *self-determining* fashion as new norms are negotiated. And, finally, without the rigid guidance of traditional roles and norms, individuals have come to expect each other to pursue a life that is freely shaped according to each individual's sense of what is right and valuable. Habermas describes these changes as a shift from a 'conventional' to a 'post-conventional' basis for social life (TCA2 176–8).

Under these conditions, morality remains as a second-order 'normative resource' for social integration. However, in the post-conventional context, all received moral orientations are open to possible criticism, and everything risks becoming drawn into 'the whirlpool of problematization' (BFN 113). The risk of dissent is heightened by the fact that communicative agreement is no longer underwritten by the 'spellbinding' aura of divine authority, and agents cannot rely on the resources of a shared ethical life. Hence, within the modern context, the moral agent faces unprecedented cognitive, motivational and organisational demands: (1) it is hard to apply the highly abstract and generalised norms of morality to real-life situations; (2) the impartial judgement of what is right ('good reasons') does not necessarily supply the motivations that lead to moral action; and (3) the more that moral consciousness attunes itself to universalistic value-orientations, the greater are the discrepancies between uncontested moral demands, on the one hand, and organisational constraints on the other. In a surprising twist, moral reasoning has thus become increasingly *unsuited* to the task of resolving conflicts and other problems of social integration. Indeed, post-conventional morality itself requires 'stabilisation'.

According to Habermas, the stabilisation of morality is provided for through the system of modern law. Law can play this role because 'legal norms have an immediate effect on action in a way that moral judgments do not' (BFN 80). Provided that the system of laws can itself be seen to be normatively binding, it rescues the 'overburdened' mechanism of social integration based in communicative agreement: (1) the cognitive burdens of forming moral judgements in situations of uncertainty are 'absorbed' by the fact that legal rules set parameters for action (BFN 115); (2) the law supplements moral motives 'with threats of sanctions in such a way that addressees may restrict themselves to the prudential calculation of consequences' (BFN 116); and (3) the moral demands for system-level reform can be formulated and implemented through the means of positive law (i.e. legal regulation) (BFN 117–18). The law remains, as always, a mechanism for stabilising behavioural expectations. But, in the modern context, law presents to us a new face as 'a mechanism that, without revoking the principle of unhindered communication, removes the tasks of social integration from actors who are already overburdened in their efforts at reaching understanding' (BFN 38).

> ... the state's guarantee to enforce the law offers a functional equivalent for the stabilization of behavioural expectations by spellbinding authority. Whereas the archaic institutions supported by worldviews fix value orientations through rigid communication patterns, modern law allows convictions to be replaced by sanctions in that it leaves the motives for rule compliance open while enforcing observance. (BFN 37–8)

Liberal rights create a framework for social action steered through the medium of law (i.e. coercion), and, like the economic system, the legal system relieves the burdens of action coordination based on mutual agreement. However, the system of laws cannot simply displace communicative agreement in general nor the system of morality in particular. If it is to serve the function of 'institutionalising' the economy and the administrative state and stabilising post-conventional morality, the system of laws must itself be seen to be legitimate from the perspective of modern subjects, and that judgement of legitimacy requires the use of practical reasoning (BFN 28–33). In short, the validity of laws and political institutions is tied to the practices of communication and discourse. Or so Habermas argues in his discourse theory of law and democracy (see Chapter 5).

3.2 The Process of Democratisation and the Role of the Public Sphere

With the establishment of the constitutional state and liberal rights, a shift occurs in the balance of power in modern societies. Bourgeois civil society establishes a degree of autonomy from the state. But the limitation of the sphere of state action and the legal institutionalisation of capitalism did not as such bring about a democratisation of political institutions. Indeed, there is no necessary connection between liberalism and democracy. This is clearly illustrated by the experience in Germany, where the constitutional arrangements put in place following the failed revolutions of 1848 and 1849 established the rule of law, civil liberties, and a separation between private and public law *without* democracy:

> The state put individuals and society into a condition of civil liberty, and it maintained them in this condition through the creation and enforcement of the new legal order. Yet individuals and society did not attain *political* freedom, that is, no share in the political decision-making power concentrated in the state, and no institutionalized possibility to exert an active influence upon it. (Böckenförde 1991: 153; quoted in FR 431)

Nonetheless, throughout Europe, citizens who enjoyed 'private autonomy' were able to assume an active political role once they organised themselves as a 'public' who spoke as representatives of the popular will. The 'public' coalesced as a politically relevant entity in this way thanks to two complementary and roughly simultaneous historical developments. On one hand, the 'national consciousness' that first took hold in Europe around the time of the French Revolution encouraged citizens to see themselves as the rightful authors of their own destiny. On the other hand, the voice of the public began to carry political clout thanks to the construction of the 'political public sphere'. As a result of these developments, a new democratic conception of citizenship came into being, and this was eventually enshrined in 'political' rights of political participation. The very basis for political authority was thereby transferred from the crown to the people, and the subjects of law became (in addition) the authors of laws. In this part of Chapter 3 we will examine these two historical developments in turn.

The Nation-State as the Seedbed for Democracy

According to Habermas, a crucial precondition necessary for the democratisation of the bourgeois constitutional state was the self-consciousness of the people themselves as the rightful *agents* of collective self-determination. He argues that this shift in self-consciousness was catalysed in Europe through the imaginative appeal of nationalism (PC 62–5).

Nationalism, in this context, denotes a sense of social solidarity grounded in a common ancestry, common language and common history – in short, the sense of belonging to a 'people' (*natio*).[3] Nationalism in this form is 'pre-political'. It shapes an imagination of belonging that is independent of any formally organised political association. Nonetheless, nationality becomes an organising principle of politics when it is interpreted as the basis for *citizenship* within a political community (*civitas*). This formula provides the conceptual basis for the form of state organisation we call the 'territorial nation-state'.

Nation-states first evolved from kingdoms in Europe, starting in Portugal, Spain, France, England and Sweden (BFN 493). Over time the nation-state became the most successful and enduring model of political organisation. The success of the nation-state model, according to Habermas, stems from its unrivalled ability to solve two problems of social integration that emerged in the modern era. On one hand, it provided a convincing way to *legitimate* the secular state, which could no longer ground its political authority in 'divine right': the nation-state could present itself as the representation of the will of the people and as the means to implement its will. On the other hand, it resolved difficulties of social integration caused by urbanisation and economic modernisation as populations became 'unmoored from the cooperative social ties of early modern societies' (IO 111–12). National consciousness provided a more 'abstract' form of social integration than earlier cultural forms since it no longer required a shared religious outlook or presupposed social hierarchies. But the political community based in nationality was still able to count on high levels of trust and solidarity among its members since it leveraged a 'pre-political' culture of shared identity and sense of mutual obligation (IO 113).

The nation-state provided a platform for the constitutional state and liberal rights to take root; but it also provided a platform for *democratisation*. The French case exemplifies how the process of democratisation could be catalysed by the nation-state model. First, the meaning of 'nationality' as belonging to a community of common ancestry fused with the meaning of 'nationality' as membership in 'the people of a state'. Once national consciousness had loosened its strong ties to shared traditions and common ancestry, the people could imagine themselves as participants in a future-oriented shared project of 'political self-determination'. National consciousness provided the psychological scaffolding that allowed 'republican' conviction to develop: the conviction that not the monarch nor the royal household but *the people* is sovereign (BFN 495). In France, once the consciousness of national identity came to imply partaking in democratic self-rule, then 'the intentional democratic community [took] the place of the ethnic complex' (BFN 494). Membership in the nation-state became more significant than membership in the nation *per se*, and the psychological scaffolding was, to some extent, dismantled.

From the privileged vantage point of the present, it is easy to see the ambivalent legacy of the nationalist movements of the eighteenth and nineteenth centuries. On one hand, these movements reinforced the value of popular culture and the lives of ordinary people and encouraged resistance to the predations of political rulers who are preoccupied with their own self-aggrandising agendas. To this extent, nationalist movements aligned with the cause of liberalism in pushing back against the overreach of political institutions into social life. On the other hand, the provincial, nostalgic and anti-enlightenment tenor of nationalist movements made them inhospitable to the principles of liberal constitutionalism (IO 8–9).

Indeed, the imagination of shared ethnic identity has always stood in tension with the universalising and egalitarian ideals of shared citizenship. All nation-states have had to manage this tension, but German history provides us with perhaps the most startling illustrations of the perils lurking within it. The mythology of a German people (*Volk*) who share an ancient language and a common spirit (*Volksgeist*) and who possess an essential connection to the land (*der Vatterland*) provided a convincing basis for a shared political identity in the nation-building period following the Napoleonic Wars. (Indeed, German intellectuals quite deliberatively made use of these self-conceptions to support efforts to unify the fragmented social landscape of German-speaking regions into a national whole at that time.) But, of course, the notion of a 'natural' or 'organic' unity was always a fabrication. What's more, it fed into a metaphorics of national 'health' and 'vitality' whose most notorious manifestation was the assertion in the early twentieth century of the ethnic purity of Germanic peoples and their racial supremacy as descendants of Aryan stock. By contrast, others, especially Jews, were stigmatised as parasites and vermin, a threat to the purity of the German race, with terrifying consequences (see IO 1–25). We will consider the breakdown of the nation-state model and the recent resurgence of nationalisms in Chapter 3.4. For now, we will continue the story of democratisation by looking at the other decisive historical development, the rise of the political public sphere.

THE RISE OF THE POLITICAL PUBLIC SPHERE

By the end of the eighteenth century, in France, Germany and elsewhere a novel set of social practices and institutions had emerged, in which critical discussion took place not just among scholars but also among ordinary citizens. The public of reasoning citizens first coalesced as a self-conscious collective thanks to new means of communication. Newspapers began publishing not only news but also opinion, and this made them 'a mediator and intensifier of public discussion' (PS 53). The growth in the general reading population went hand in hand with growth and diversification in publishing, and the establishment of reading rooms and libraries. New 'enlightened' societies and cultural associations sprang up. Characterised by an egalitarian and collaborative spirit, these functioned as a 'training ground for what were to become a future society's norms of political equality' (FR 424).

A 'politicisation' of these networks of communication occurred at the time of the French Revolution, when a new species of publication, the partisan journal or newspaper, began to circulate. In the period following the French Revolution, hundreds of political news journals were established (STPS 67–72). Initially the existence of such publications was illegal, and the emerging network of public communications asserted itself under threat of legal sanctions. However, in the early nineteenth century, attempts to suppress these new organs of political expression incited struggles for rights to freedom of thought and expression, a cause that became central to the liberal movements of the time. The fights against censorship set the polemical tone for writings in the emergent political public sphere, and this polemical tone persisted, long after civil rights protecting freedom of speech and publication were enshrined in many jurisdictions.

Economic factors helped to make the public sphere a politically influential social institution (STPS 14–26). In the medieval and the early modern periods, questions of policy were influenced by nobles through bargaining and negotiations with their princes on an ad hoc basis.[4] But this balance of power shifted when a newly wealthy and independent class of merchants, manufacturers and industrialists pressed for more influence vis-à-vis the princes. These independent citizens were not content merely with 'private autonomy'. Instead, they insisted upon the right to *supervise* the exercise of governments who claimed to act in the general interest. This new mentality was an essential element in the process of democratisation since it motivated struggles to attain new rights: rights to observe governmental proceedings and obtain information about governmental decision-making. The rights of citizens to participate in these spaces and modes of social interaction would be called by Habermas rights of 'public autonomy'.

To give a definition, then, the political public sphere is that collection of interactions in social life in which public opinion and shared cultures are formed. It comprises 'communicative networks amplified by a cultural complex, a press and, later, by mass media' (TCA2 319). The sphere of public communications taken as a whole is extremely diverse, and it forms around a huge variety of topics from science and technology, to entertainment, arts, sport, fashion and food. But our interest here is in what Habermas calls 'the *political* public sphere': that sphere of public communication which takes as its topic the state and its activities (STPS 51–6). The public sphere in this sense exists whenever private citizens engage in discourse about public affairs. Such interactions can be anything, from intimate conversations between friends, to publicly broadcast debates between political leaders. What makes these interactions constitutive of a public sphere is that the participants interact not merely as individuals pursuing their private interests, but as citizens concerned with the task of criticising the exercise of political power and holding it to account.

With the emergence of the political public sphere, public opinion takes on a new significance: it has the power to 'steer' the state apparatus. The very structure of political power undergoes a profound transformation as a result. The transformation does not come about by a reorganisation of the institutional structures of the state. The bourgeois model of the public sphere does not displace the position of the public authorities or disperse the responsibilities for decision-making among the citizenry. On the contrary, these functions remain concentrated in legally defined offices. Rather, the change comes about through a re-articulation of the relationship between citizens and the political authorities in the life of the society. An observing and commentating public scrutinises the exercise of political functions, and debates what the proper exercise of these functions requires. In this role, the commoners of the third estate are no longer merely *subjects* of a monarch. They are possessors of political authority in their own right, albeit not the authority to rule. Through electing, influencing and monitoring the legislative branch of government, the public possesses political authority of a new and unique kind: the authority to exercise *oversight* over the processes and procedures of government. But this, Habermas claims, is nothing other than a revolution in the nature of political power itself.

> Bourgeois individuals are private individuals. As such, they do not 'rule'. Their claims to power *vis-à-vis* public authority were thus directed not against the concentration of power, which was to be 'shared.' Instead, their ideas infiltrated the very principle on which the existing power is based. To the principle of existing power, the bourgeois public opposed the principle of supervision – that very principle which demands that proceedings be made public (*Publizität*). The principle of supervision is thus a means of transforming the nature of power, not merely one basis of legitimation exchanged for another. (PS 52)

Under the supervision of the bourgeois public sphere, European states were forced to limit themselves to a set of prescribed functions, which included upholding rights of citizens to participate in a free society of market exchange. However, Karl Marx had no difficulty demonstrating that the demands of 'the public' at this time were overwhelmingly the interests of the bourgeois class, presented as though they represented the 'general interest'. Marx mercilessly derided this self-serving conflation of the particular with the universal, and his view of the political public sphere was thoroughly cynical as a consequence. He dismissed the public sphere as a justificatory mechanism for the advancement of the capitalist class at the expense of workers (STPS 122–9). Similarly, J. S. Mill and Alexis de Tocqueville looked askance at the exaltation of public opinion as 'the voice of the people', suspicious that 'public opinion' simply reinstated a tyranny of the major in 'veiled form' (FR 441; see STPS 129–40).

Habermas sees truth in these criticisms of the early liberal notion of the public sphere. The self-conception of the bourgeois public sphere as egalitarian and inclusive was always ideological; in practice, public discussion was dominated by a narrow social demographic and many social groups were effectively excluded. And it is self-evidently the case that public sentiment can be fickle. Nonetheless, Habermas does not believe that the normative self-conception of the bourgeois public sphere can therefore be dismissed as simply self-serving propaganda (STPS 160). The ideal of the bourgeois public sphere was the carrier of norms of criticality, openness, inclusiveness, horizontality and uncensored discourse – all of which continue to be vital 'normative resources' for contemporary democracies. Without question, these ideals were contradicted by the reality of the political public sphere in the eighteenth and nineteenth centuries, which was overwhelmingly male, educated and bourgeois. However, these ideals were also a source of the self-transforming potential in modern societies. And, in fact, a process of expanding inclusivity, leveraging the norms of inclusivity and equality, has opened up public discourse to ever wider circles of previously excluded voices over the course of the nineteenth century and into the twentieth century (FR 422–9).

The public sphere in contemporary media societies

Even as the public sphere has become more inclusive, the functioning of the public sphere has been undermined by economic, social and cultural developments in recent European history. From the mid-nineteenth century, newspapers began to carry advertisements for products, and by the early twentieth century they were an important force in shaping consumer culture. The introduction of radio and television provided further opportunities for the commercialisation of mass media, and advertising soon became the primary source of revenue for publishers and private broadcasters. Today, mass media continues to be a mixed economy of news, opinion, entertainment and advertisement. Not only do profit-seeking corporations make use of mass media to shape consumer behaviour, political actors make use of mass communications to extract loyalty from the population. And the public sphere no longer functions unambiguously as a space in which 'communicative power' is generated autonomously and democratically (STPS 181–235).

> At one time the process of making proceedings public was intended to subject persons or affairs to public reason, and to make political decisions subject to appeal before the court of public opinion. But often today the process of making public simply serves the arcane policies of special

interests; in the form of 'publicity' it wins public prestige for people or affairs, thus making them worthy of acclamation in a climate of non-public opinion. The very words 'public relations work' (*Öffentlichkeitsarbeit*) betray the fact that a public sphere must first be arduously constructed case by case, a public sphere which earlier grew out of the social structure. Even the central relationship of the public, the parties and the parliament is affected by this change in function. (PS 55)

The consequence of these developments, according to the analysis in *The Structural Transformation of the Public Sphere*, is a 'refeudalisation' of the public sphere. Just as the prince and the nobility made public displays by which they represented themselves as legitimate powers before the body of citizens, so again existing powers 'promote' their products and their 'brand' to populations (STPS 193–5).

In his more recent work, Habermas continues to portray the administrative system and the economic system as generating *interference* in the public sphere and undermining the possibility of meaningful democratic discourse. The political public sphere, he maintains, is 'characterized by at least two crosscutting processes: the communicative generation of legitimate power on the one hand and the manipulative deployment of media power to procure mass loyalty, consumer demand, and "compliance" with systemic imperatives on the other' (FR 452). (We shall discuss these and related dynamics in more detail in Chapter 3.3.) What's more, over the years Habermas has become even more acutely aware of the role of the media as active participants in the communicative networks that make up the public sphere. As discussed in Chapter 1.3, the media have power to select messages and to shape their presentation, and media power is used to influence the agenda, content and presentation of public issues (FR 437; EFP 168–9). Hence, in addition to the economic power of markets and the administrative power of the state, both of which have strategic interests in influencing the flow of public communications, the power of the media as facilitators of public communication brings a third, potentially problematic, influence into the mix.

The speed with which news is produced and disseminated in the age of the internet has led to a communicative 'liquefaction' of politics:

> Political elites operate under the watchful gaze of the media and of their distrustful audiences, while at the same time anxiously tracking shifts in public opinion and in the polls in order to be able to respond to them.

The inflated volume of messages, ideas, and images in circulation creates at least the impression that contemporary politics is becoming ever more deeply entangled in processes of mass communication, indeed that it is being assimilated into and transformed by them. (EFP 153)

Under these conditions, it is an open question whether the public sphere can fulfil the role it is expected to play according to the ideal of 'publicity' advanced by Habermas. We shall return to this question in Chapter 6.

The Stabilisation of the Constitutional State Through Rights to Political Participation

The demands of a nation of citizens to supervise political institutions and to hold them accountable through public scrutiny have been recognised and institutionalised through rights of political participation. This set of political rights, the rights of 'public autonomy', stands alongside liberal rights, the rights of 'private autonomy', discussed in Chapter 3.1. Together they make up the set of basic rights that constitutes the modern liberal-democratic constitutional state. As we have seen, political rights have been won through social struggles amidst periods of considerable societal upheaval; they did not appear automatically. All the same, Habermas argues, from a sociological point of view there is a kind of logic to the process of democratisation, a logic that follows the shift from legitimation based on the aura of religious authority to legitimation based on reasons that have withstood critical (public) scrutiny.

In the eighteenth and nineteenth centuries, social integration was threatened by the dominance and success of the constitutional state on the one hand and the market economy on the other. Neither of these institutions could guarantee social cohesion at the level of the self-understanding of citizens. Yet, the legal system which regulates the economy and the administrative state itself needs to be legitimated, and to do so it had to establish its legitimacy within the lifeworld through communicative action (BFN 40). The mechanism for achieving this end is democratisation.

From this perspective, the process of democratisation represents a third wave of 'juridification': this time a juridification of the 'legitimation process' itself (TCA2 360): the constitutional state renders itself responsive to the opinion and will of the people through universal suffrage and through recognition of rights to engage in political communication and to form political parties and associations.

> Laws now come into force only when there is a democratically backed presumption that they express a general interest and that those affected could agree to them. This requirement is to be met by a procedure that binds legislation to parliamentary well-formation and public discussion. (TCA2 360)

As a result of participatory procedures, the democratic state ensures that its legally binding decision-making procedures retain a connection to the reasoning of citizens in whose eyes its decisions must appear to be justified.

But this democratic model is itself beset by difficulties in the modern context. In Habermas's estimation, 'legitimation deficits' have constantly bedevilled modern Western democracies (Chapter 3.3), and new challenges are presented by the process of globalisation (Chapter 3.4). In all of these discussion, Habermas's aim is to think through how it might be possible for a democratic politics to reassert itself in our contemporary world. (We shall discuss Habermas's proposals in Chapter 5.)

3.3 Legitimation Problems in the Welfare State

Two 'media-steered' systems have dominated in the modern era: the money-steered market economy and the power-steered administrative state. These systems were embedded within modern societies via the legal structures of the bourgeois constitutional state: the system of private law and the system of public law (3.1). Under the right conditions, the framework of liberal rights made possible a wave of democratisation (3.2). Citizens at large, armed with rights of public autonomy, are now able to participate in a variety of ways, both directly and indirectly, in the legislative procedures of the state and are able to hold politicians and governmental agencies to account when democratic expectations are violated.

Starting in the late nineteenth century, a further upheaval redrew the outlines of the nation-state and its relationship to its citizens. In particular, the efforts of an ascendant labour movement over the course of the nineteenth century and into the twentieth century achieved a number of concessions for the working class. A new 'compromise' was reached between the forces of capitalist expansion and the interests of workers upon whom capitalist expansion depends. And social welfare entitlements granted 'compensatory claims to a just share of social wealth' according to the legitimate demands of workers within the capitalist economy (BFN 78). Class conflict itself was legalised and regulated through collective bargaining law and labour law (TCA2 357). Additionally, in the post-war era, public institutions were rapidly expanded to provide education, health care, housing, aged care, as well as a suite of other social benefits funded through progressive taxation. These reforms bent the institutional architecture of the constitutional state to further serve the needs of citizens, and especially to ameliorate the worst excesses of capitalist exploitation, impoverishment and social marginalisation.

From a legal perspective, as British sociologist T. H. Marshall observed, these developments created a third category of rights alongside 'civil' rights to private property and 'political' rights of democratic participation: namely, 'social' rights to economic welfare and security (Marshall 1950). Habermas portrays this as a fourth 'wave of juridification', and it produced what we now refer to as 'the welfare state'.

From Habermas's point of view, the emergence of the welfare state has been a positive development in general. Material living conditions have improved and tangible gains in social justice have been achieved through the mechanism of state intervention in economic and social life. Class conflicts have been ameliorated, and 'market failures' have been mitigated. These welcome outcomes have led citizens to trust the welfare state system and to see it as valuable. Moreover, no alternative has yet emerged whose promise is greater than that of the welfare state model (NO 9).

However, the welfare state compromise has also brought about a series of other more ambivalent consequences within the social and political landscape. These ambivalent features of the institutional and cultural world in the era of the welfare state were a major theme of Habermas's sociological and political writings from the 1970s and 1980s. In what follows, I retrace some of the major arguments developed in these writings.

STEERING PROBLEMS AND LEGITIMATION CRISES

According to Habermas, modern welfare state democracies are especially susceptible to crises. This susceptibility stems from the challenge of balancing 'functional' needs of state and economy (system) with the needs of agents who must be convinced of the legitimacy of the social order (lifeworld). From the 'functional' side of the equation, the state's budget is dependent upon tax revenue and expectations of economic growth. Hence, economic policy is beholden to the demands of corporations and investors whose quasi-autonomous decision-making must be taken into account. At the same time, from the 'lifeworld' side of the equation, economic policy is subject to democratic demands, including demands for full employment and satisfactory levels of public services and social security. Failing to satisfy these democratic demands threatens the legitimacy of the state and diminishes its power. Conflicting and sometimes irreconcilable demands are thus made on the public power, guided not simply by the conflicting interests of the rich and the poor but more fundamentally by the competing demands of system and lifeworld. Yet, amid all of this, the nation-state has never truly had the means at its disposal to control economic conditions. Markets are affected by a variety of factors that cannot be controlled by domestic policy, and this is increasingly the case under conditions of globalisation, as we shall discuss later (NO 7–8). These complexities are grouped together by Habermas under the heading of 'steering problems' and 'legitimation problems'. 'Steering problems' faced by the state stem from the functional requirements of the crisis-prone capitalist markets, and 'legitimation problems' from cultural demands for solidarity and identity.[5]

The crisis tendencies of the welfare state paradigm provide the backdrop to the political conflicts in the second half of the twentieth century. During this period, the left largely focused on extending the programmes of the welfare state and defending it against attempts to scale back social services and to sell off publicly owned assets. 'They hope to discover once again the equilibrium point between expansion of the social welfare state and market-based modernization' (NO 10).[6] However, according to Habermas, this political project failed to take account of the negative side effects of the welfare state itself. These side effects, which we shall discuss shortly, coupled with the dislocating effects of capitalist modernisation itself, led to discontent and resistance towards the welfare state compromise.

Popular disaffection was mobilised by the right in the 1970s and 1980s to push for the dismantling of the welfare state. Indeed, Habermas observed in the mid-1980s that a 'neo-conservatism is on the rise', a movement that today (confusingly) we would describe as 'neo-liberalism' (NO 10). This new conservatism has three core policy orientations: (1) to create more favourable conditions for investment and capital accumulation; (2) to reduce expectations regarding government intervention and social programmes, leaving social problems to NGOs and businesses to a larger extent; and (3) to devalue the universalistic and critical perspectives of public intellectuals in favour of 'practical' goals of economic growth and social cohesion through patriotism and traditional values.

At the time, Habermas saw the likelihood that the neo-conservative agenda would be implemented, and in this he proved to be correct:

> Neo-conservative politics has a certain chance of being implemented if it can find a political base in the social Darwinism of the split society it is at the same time promoting. The excluded and marginalized groups have no veto power since they represent a separated minority isolated from the process of production. The pattern that has played itself out more and more in the international arena between the metropoles and the underdeveloped periphery appears to be repeating itself inside of the most developed capitalist societies: the established powers are now less and less reliant for purposes of reproduction on the labor and willingness to cooperate of the poor and the disenfranchised. (NO 12)

Nonetheless, the basic features of the social welfare state cannot easily be rolled back. The class compromise that has been achieved has set new standards for the success of the state. If a modern state were to renounce these basic functions and were to leave its population at the mercy of unrestrained market forces (inflation, unemployment, etc.), it would be perceived as a failure by its citizens and the state would have to resort to repression to protect itself from collapse. For this reason, the periodic transfer of power between left and right political parties in Western democracies scarcely challenges the basic arrangements of the modern welfare state. Neither left nor right gets at the fundamental challenge for contemporary democracies:

> One side sees the causes of crisis in the unleashing of the dynamics proper to the economy; the other side, in the bureaucratic fetters imposed on the former. The corresponding therapies are a social subduing of capitalism or a displacement of problems from administrative planning back to the market. The one side sees the source of the systemically induced disturbances of everyday life in monetarized labor power; the other, in the bureaucratic crippling of personal initiative. But both sides agree in assigning a merely passive role to the vulnerable domains of lifeworld interaction as against the motors of societal modernization: state and economy. (PDM 356)

Habermas certainly acknowledges the social pathologies caused by the commodification of labour and the bureaucratisation of modern life, as we shall discuss below. But the final remark concerning 'the vulnerable domains of lifeworld interaction' indicates the central theme of Habermas's reflections on the precarious situation faced by contemporary democracies. What is 'actually endangered' in contemporary Western societies, he argues, is the 'social solidarity preserved in legal structures' which is 'in need of continual regeneration' (BFN xlii). The fundamental challenge for contemporary democracies is to protect and nurture the basis of communicative power upon which all political power depends, and to enable communicative power to effectively steer the political system.

In the following two sections, we will look at Habermas's analysis of these deeper legitimation problems. First, we will consider his analysis of the effects of commodification and bureaucratisation. Then we will analyse the problems created by illegitimate social power and the weakness of civil society.

THE COLONISATION OF THE LIFEWORLD

Habermas agrees with Marx that the logic of capitalism has driven transformations in the organisation of labour and has fundamentally altered the character of the modern world. Traditional forms of life have been broken down by urbanisation and cultural dislocation. But, additionally, workers have had to reckon with their apparent lack of value as human beings from the standpoint of the capitalist economy, which sees them only in terms of their productive capacity and in terms of the cost of their labour. This has led to the characteristic contradictions that beset the worker under capitalism, which Marx described in his Paris manuscripts as 'alienation' (TCA2 340–1), and Georg Lukács described as 'reification' (TCA2 332–3).[7]

However, as Weber and Lukács argued, life under the bureaucratic rule of the modern administrative state produces a similar experience of alienation or reification. In this context too, individuals are reduced through a process of abstraction to their 'statistical essence'.

> The extensive discussions concerning excessive legal regulation and bureaucratization in general, concerning the counterproductive effects of government social welfare policies in particular, and concerning the overconcentration on 'trained professionals' and 'scientific approaches' in the social services have all made one thing clear: the legal and administrative means for the implementation of social welfare state programs do not represent a passive medium, devoid of its own peculiar properties. Rather, they are bound up with a practice that isolates and considers separately the legal facts of the matter, that normalizes and places under surveillance. It is this reifying and subjectivating power that Foucault has

traced into even the thinnest capillary branchings of everyday communication. The distortions within such a regulated, analyzed, controlled, and watched-over lifeworld are certainly more subtle than the obvious forms of material exploitation and impoverishment; but these conflicts, shifted into the domains of the psychological and the bodily, internalized, are no less destructive for all that. (NO 9)

Human beings are de-natured and rendered thing-like by both the capitalist economy and the administrative state.

In contrast to Lukács, however, Habermas does not believe that the instrumentalisation of human relationships *per se* results in pathological consequences. As participants in 'norm-free' social contexts, in which 'society congeals into a second nature', we *can* experience reification (TCA2 154).[8] But participation in systems interactions alone is not sufficient for pathological consequences to follow. Systems interactions involve a reduction of our vision to strategic considerations and a practical orientation that instrumentalises ourselves and others. But this does not as such lead to a loss of identity or social solidarity. Consider, for instance, playing chess with a friend. In the context of the game, our attitude is predominantly strategic; yet, we are accustomed to accepting games as a discrete social practice in which societal norms are temporarily and voluntarily suspended so that participants can enjoy a game together. The game as a practice has its own value and legitimacy from the standpoint of the lifeworld. And playing games need not undermine or erode the richness of the shared life we enjoy with friends; on the contrary, friendships can be enriched and complexified by playing games. Something similar could, in principle, be true of all institutionalised systems interactions.

What is it, then, that makes the instrumentalisation of relationships pathological? The threshold of social pathology is crossed when systems imperatives undermine the 'communicative infrastructure' of the lifeworld (TCA2 375). Habermas calls this the 'colonisation' of the lifeworld:

> [T]he imperatives of autonomous subsystems make their way into the lifeworld from the outside – like colonial masters coming into a tribal society – and force a process of assimilation upon it ... In the end, systemic mechanisms suppress forms of social integration even in those areas where a consensus-based coordination cannot be replaced, that is, where the symbolic reproduction of the lifeworld is at stake. In these areas, the *mediatization* of the lifeworld assumes the form of a *colonization*. (TCA2 355, 196)

The colonisation of the lifeworld occurs in the modern era as functional subsystems 'externalize their costs' onto the lifeworld and previously informal domains of social life are increasingly monetised and bureaucratised (PDM 363). When this occurs, the self-maintenance of the lifeworld, which can only take place in the free flow of communication, is disturbed. The very possibility of sustaining mutual understanding with others is attenuated and the communicative presuppositions of individual self-consciousness and solidarity are eroded.

The weakening and fragmentation of the shared lifeworld leads to pathological consequences because cultural reproduction, social integration and socialisation can only be sustained in the medium of communicative action:

> There is no other equivalent medium in which these functions can be fulfilled. Individuals acquire and sustain their identity through communicative interactions. They do not have the option of a long-term absence from contexts of action oriented toward reaching an understanding. (MC 102)

Simply put: 'Money and power can neither buy nor compel solidarity and meaning' (PDM 363). Hence, the colonisation of the lifeworld leads to a loss of meaning, a weakening of social norms and the loss of identity (TCA2 140–8).

The colonisation of the lifeworld has political consequences too. The weakening and fragmenting of the lifeworld causes the reservoir of 'communicative power' from which the political system derives its democratic legitimacy to dry up. Without a strong public sphere and civil society, the political system is also vulnerable to being captured or steered by other social forces, as we shall discuss presently. The 'loss of meaning' (nihilism) is thus closely followed by the 'loss of freedom' (domination) (TCA2 318–31).[9]

The structure of modern domination

The political system can find itself captured or steered by social forces other than the communicative power of the deliberating public in a number of ways and for a number of reasons.

(1) Powerful social actors can influence the political system to suit their own ends. For example, industry bodies help to draft regulation or wealthy individuals negotiate their own tax rates. Social power is converted to political power, which is then deployed in the form of

administrative power (BFN 175). In such cases, 'normatively unfiltered interest positions ... carry the day because they are stronger and use the legitimating force of legal norms to cloak their merely factual strength' (BFN 78–9).

(2) The state apparatus is prone to operate according to its own 'system-maintaining' logic. For instance, familiar routines within the halls of power generate their own momentum, and the business of politics and administration continues irrespective of any democratic mandate or steering (BFN 337). More perniciously, the administrative state – and notably, political parties – have an interest in extracting 'mass loyalty' from the population through messaging. In these ways, the activity of government can become 'self-programming' (BFN 332).[10]

> To the extent that it succeeds in *extracting* mass loyalty from the public sphere, the political system becomes independent of the democratic sources of its legitimation. Thus the flip side of a halfway successful welfare state is a mass democracy in which the process of legitimation is *managed* by the administration. At the programmatic level, this is associated with resignation: both the acceptance of the scandalous 'natural fate' imposed by the labor market and the renunciation of radical democracy. (BFN 480)

Whether by the infiltration of powerful interests or by administrative self-programming, illegitimate power can be (and often is) imposed on society. Indeed, according to Habermas, these two tendencies can be mutually reinforcing:

> The autonomy of social power vis-à-vis the democratic process fosters in turn endogenous tendencies in the administrative complex to become increasingly autonomous. Thus an increasingly independent administrative power joins forces with a social power affecting both the input and the output side. Together they form a counter-circulation that cuts across the 'official' circuit of democratic decision making steered by communicative power. (BFN 329–30)

This 'counter-circulation' of power is not equivalent to the 'colonisation of the lifeworld' but, like the latter, it is a deformation that is caused by the intrusion of money and power in society. In a vicious feedback loop, the counter-circulation of power detaches the administrative state from the 'communicative power' that should anchor the administrative system in the lifeworld, and reinforces its ties to powerful interests.

The flipside of these dynamics is the weakening of the public sphere and civil society. Habermas's analysis of these phenomena is complex. We have already noted that the media infrastructure today is inadequate for a well-functioning public sphere; political communication in today's 'media society' can be channelled according to the interests of powerful individuals or groups through the use of media power (see Chapter 3.2). In addition, Habermas argues that citizens are hampered by a tension brought about by the welfare state model itself: in our 'public' role as citizens, we are oriented by (universal) concerns of justice, but in our 'private' role as client of the welfare state, we are oriented by (particular) needs for services and benefits. As a result:

> Built into the very status of citizenship in welfare-state democracies is the tension between a formal extension of private and civic autonomy, on the one hand, and a 'normalization,' in Foucault's sense, that fosters the passive enjoyment of paternalistically dispensed rights, on the other. (BFN 79)

Finally, the dominance of functional systems and systems imperatives in contemporary societies impacts upon our language and our patterns of thinking, diminishing our capacities for creative and critically reflective deliberation.

> The special languages like money or administrative power wear down ordinary language – as the functional systems do the lifeworld – so much that neither the one nor the other presents a sounding board that would be sufficiently complex for thematizing and treating society-wide problems. Under these conditions, the political public sphere cannot provide such a sounding board, because, together with the public of citizens, it is hitched to the power code and placated with symbolic politics. (BFN 343)

For these and other reasons, the contemporary political system has a tendency to lose its connection to the democratic basis which anchors its legitimacy (and hence its stability). Combined, these threats can 'nullify' the power basis of the constitutional state.

> The independence of illegitimate power, together with the weakness of civil society and the public sphere, can deteriorate into a 'legitimation dilemma,' which in certain circumstances can combine with the steering trilemma and develop into a vicious circle. Then the political system is pulled into the whirlpool of legitimation deficits and steering deficits that reinforce one another. (BFN 386)

From Socialism to Social Democracy

Given the ongoing steering problems and legitimation problems the welfare state faces, it is not surprising that a degree of disillusionment has set in (NO 1–18). However, what is clear to Habermas (and he is by no means alone in reaching this conclusion) is that the path forward is not the path envisaged by Marx. In fact, Habermas denies several basic premises of the Marxist account of capitalist modernisation and of the anticipated overthrow of capitalism.

First, for Marx, human solidarity can only be achieved through the collapse of capitalism which is the root cause of class antagonisms. For Habermas, it is important to distinguish between the 'functional' differentiations of the economic system under capitalism, which he sees as advances from a systems perspective, and the way these developments have been institutionalised in the lifeworld in the form of class antagonisms (TCA2 340). In his view, democratic politics should aim to redress material inequalities and address the injustices of class society, but it should avoid sacrificing the advances won by the capitalist economy in terms of the organisation of labour and the processes of production. Indeed, Habermas argues that market economies are the result of a long evolutionary process of system development (of 'rationalisation' in the Weberian sense) and they perform valuable functions in modern society (TCA2 232). What's more, as the experiment of Soviet Marxism has demonstrated, 'a modern, market-regulated economic system cannot be switched as one pleases, from a monetary mechanism to one involving administrative power and democratic decision-making, without threatening its performance capacity' (FR 436). Habermas argues, similarly, that we would not want to undo the state's involvement in social problems and economic issues. The withering away of the constitutional state is not to anyone's advantage, since it represents an important institutional mechanism for establishing justice and the rule of law.[11]

Second, for Marx, the structure of economic relations holds a fundamental place in both theory and revolutionary practice. But, as we have seen, Habermas argues that the pathologies of reification are not restricted to the economic sphere. The commodification of labour can produce reifying effects for the employee, but so can the bureaucratisation and juridification experienced by clients of the state. Hence, modern societies, with their distinctive social pathologies and forms of injustices, cannot be analysed solely through the lens of a critique of capitalism (TCA2 338–43). In rejecting the singular focus on labour within the modern social structure, Habermas also rejects any suggestion that the sphere of labour might harbour within itself the means for overcoming the contradictions that beset modern societies. The logic of capitalism is and will always remain a systems logic, indifferent to the lifeworld and its normative structures. It does not tend 'dialectically' towards its own overcoming. It leaves in its wake nothing more than an ambivalent legacy of improved efficiencies and capacities in the processes of production on the one hand, and of fragmented and weakened lifeworlds unable to sustain our humanity on the other. Habermas thus rejects a particular idea of utopia based around a society of 'free labour', in which the bureaucratic state and the capitalist economy have 'withered away' (NO 3–4). Rather, in the tradition of democratic socialism (Jackson 2013), Habermas assumes the persistence of the capitalist economy and the administrative state. The aim is to 'tame' both economy and state in the service of human ends.

Third, while Marx stresses the role of emancipatory praxis, he does not provide any guidance on how to struggle to achieve the democratisation of society, the taming of the subsystems of modern life by democratic reason. But this is the central problem for politics today: the problem of re-establishing the powers of critical reflection and social solidarity against the colonising logic of media-steered subsystems. If a socialist vision is to be sustained in the contemporary world, it will have to rediscover the core 'utopian' motif of a free society of self-directing and mutually supporting individuals under the conditions of late modernity.

> The systemic spell cast by the capitalist labor market over the life histories of those able to work, by the network of responsible, regulating, and supervising public authorities over life forms of their clients, and by the now autonomous nuclear arms race over the life expectancy of peoples, cannot be broken by systems learning to function better. Rather, impulses from the lifeworld must be able to enter into the self-steering of functional systems. (PDM 364)

What must be hoped for, and strived for, is a new balance of power between systems and lifeworld: 'the socially integrating power of solidarity would have to be in a position to assert itself against the systemically integrating steering media of money and power' (PDM 364; also NO 14–7).

In place of the model of society influencing itself, we have the model of boundary conflicts – which are held in check by the lifeworld – between the lifeworld and two subsystems that are superior to it in complexity and can be influenced by it only indirectly, but on whose performances it at the same time depends. (PDM 365)

This would be a situation in which citizens achieve standing as participants in (and critics of) the political community, and exercise collective influence over the organisation of society itself. In short, the remedy to the legitimation problems in contemporary democracies, Habermas argues, is 'more democracy' (BFN xlii).

This leads to a prescription concerning the social institutions needed to respond to the challenges of modernity in the name of an enlightened humanism: (1) a well-organised and well-functioning public sphere is needed to provide the forum for democratic opinion- and will-formation; and (2) a liberal-democratic constitutional state is needed to translate democratic reason into reflective control over the subsystems of society. The public sphere must be 'shielded against the intolerable imperatives of the occupational system or against the penetrating side effects of the administrative provision of life' (PDM 364). The constitutional state must be responsive to public discourse in order to 'transpose the intersubjectively constituted self-knowledge of society organisationally into the self-determination of society' (PDM 360). We will flesh out this sketch in Chapter 5.

3.4 The Postnational Constellation

Jürgen Habermas has lived to see a remarkable series of world-historical events and political upheavals: the Holocaust, the Cold War, the fall of the Berlin Wall, the founding of the European Union, the 9/11 attacks, the Global Financial Crisis, and Brexit, to name a few. His political theory has been informed by each of these events and has evolved in response to new situations.

In the first half of Chapter 3.4, we consider Habermas's sociological analysis of the 'postnational constellation' that has emerged in recent decades. Since the 1980s, the process of globalisation has weakened the nation-state and tipped the balance of power between market forces and the administrative state in favour of the former once again. In the second half of Chapter 3.4, we shall review the 'constitutionalisation' of international law and the emergence of new political associations over the course of the twentieth century. Against the odds, Habermas will argue, this trajectory towards a 'cosmopolitan condition' must be continued if humanity is to meet the forces of global capitalism with the civilising force of law and democracy.

Globalisation

World population has quadrupled since 1929, the year Jürgen Habermas was born. Scientific and technological advances have introduced countless novelties from the jet engine, the atomic bomb, the television, and the internet, to the hula-hoop and the fidget-spinner. The contemporary world is more connected than ever before thanks to digital media and information technologies; and people and goods are able to be delivered to almost any part of the globe within a matter of hours thanks to modern transportation networks. But tensions and conflicts persist among human populations, both within nations and between them. The Global South sees the wealth gap between itself and the North growing wider decade upon decade. And within Western societies standards of living are almost as stratified and divergent today as they were in *La Belle Époque* (Piketty 2014). We have seen the creation of a new underclass of unemployed or underemployed workers who have little prospect of improving their situation (BNS 235–6). The West faces off against the threat of terrorism emerging out of Islamic fundamentalism. In some regions, cultural, ethnic and religious divisions have flared into open conflict. Flows of refugees and migrants have strained the tolerance of destination countries and provoked xenophobic reactions. The exploitation of natural resources continues at ever more rapacious speed to feed the system of production and consumption, and piles of waste are excreted at the end of the cycle and donated to the skies, the earth and the great oceans. Environmental stresses exacerbate social and political tensions (CEU 55).

In many cases, these trends are little more than by-products of the more fundamental process of economic globalisation. During the post-war era, international institutions of trade, finance and monetary exchange – the Bretton Woods system along with the World Bank and the International Monetary Fund – created a framework for global economic integration. Until the 1970s, this set of institutions 'struck a balance between national economic policies and the rules of liberalized global trade' (PC 78). But, beginning in the 1970s, a new 'free trade' agenda was pursued and the institutional architecture of the global economy was radically reformed. The result of trade liberalisation has been an intensification and expansion of commerce between nations to such an extent that it is unclear whether it is still meaningful to talk of 'national economies' that engage in foreign trade, or whether it would be more accurate to talk of a 'world economy' of which national economies are subsidiaries (BNS 236–7). Workers are more vulnerable to rapid and dramatic changes than ever before thanks to the pace of technological change and to the new possibilities of 'outsourcing' or 'offshoring' of jobs. These effects have a flipside: as barriers to relocating manufacturing and services to different locations have been gradually lowered or dismantled, multinational corporations benefit from new 'exit options' (BNS 237). As a result, a small number of multinational corporations whose annual turnover is comparable in size to the GDP of nation-states have consolidated considerable economic and political influence. The finance industry has come to rival the 'real' economy in terms of its share of GDP and in its effects on the fate of nations. The global economy, in short, increasingly transcends the regulatory frameworks of nation-states, constituting 'a very largely unregulated (and many would argue unregulatable) domain' (Cox 1997: 55; quoted in PC 67).

We can welcome some effects of globalisation. For instance, Habermas mentions approvingly trends such as the 'de-bureaucratization' of public services, the 'de-hierarchicalization' of professional organisational forms, the 'de-traditionalization' of familial and gender relations, the 'de-conventionalization' of consumer patterns and lifestyles (PC 87). All of these trends have further enhanced individuality and autonomy. But these same developments have also brought with them negative consequences:

> The 'flexibilization' of career paths hides a deregulated labor market and a heightened risk of unemployment; the 'individualization' of life projects conceals a sort of compulsory mobility that is hard to reconcile with durable personal bonds; the 'pluralization' of life forms also reflects the danger of a fragmented society and the loss of social cohesion. (PC 87)

The 'normalising' force of bureaucratic rationality (which had been the target of Habermas's critical social theory in the 1970s and 1980s) has slackened. But, in its place, we see a 'reckless monetarization of the lifeworld' (PC 87), and the effects of the colonisation of the lifeworld are felt in new ways:

> Under the constraint of economic imperatives that increasingly hold sway over private spheres of life, individuals, intimidated, withdraw more and

more into the bubble of their private interests. Willingness to engage in collective action, the awareness that citizens can at all collectively shape the social conditions of their lives through solidaristic action, fades under the perceived force of systemic imperatives. More than anything else, erosion of confidence in the power of collective action and the atrophy of normative sensibilities reinforce an already smoldering skepticism with regard to an enlightened self-understanding of modernity. (P 16)

As the world is threatened by the colonising forces of run-away capitalism, the same trends of globalisation are weakening the most robust political model the modern era has known: the democratic nation-state.

The Weakening of the Nation-State

The welfare state managed to tame capitalism to an impressive degree. It allowed markets to function, harnessing efficiencies and unleashing innovation. But it also mitigated gross inequalities of income and wealth and other social costs that are 'incompatible with the conditions of social integration in liberal democratic states' (PC 49). Taxation was used effectively to redistribute wealth, to fund infrastructure, and to provide social security for the sick, the infirmed and the unemployed. Regulation was also used with considerable success to maintain growth, stabilise market cycles and ensure low levels of unemployment.

But we have discovered that the nation-state is not well-equipped to adapt to the new situation created by the process of globalisation. In fact, the new situation has brought the familiar model of political organisation to a crisis point. The strains can be seen from at least three angles: (1) shifts in cultural and political identity; (2) the weakening of the operational capacity of the nation-state to guarantee basic rights and living standards; and – as a consequence of (1) and (2) – (3) the waning legitimacy of the nation-state.

(1) In the heyday of the nation-state, personal identity was tightly bound to citizenship, i.e. consciousness of oneself as a member of a nation. In Europe, this self-consciousness has been subjected to pressures from two directions. On one side, changing demographics within nation-states, in particular the influx of Muslims and Eastern Europeans into European cities, have provoked a 'hardening' of national identities. This feeds into ethnocentric reactions to anything foreign and to marginalised internal groups, including Jews (PC 72–3). On the other side, the influence of 'world culture' has

begun to attenuate the self-consciousness of citizens as rooted within a nation-state:

> Global markets, mass consumption, mass communication, and mass tourism disseminate the standardized products of a mass culture (overwhelmingly shaped by the United States) ... This commodified, homogenous culture doesn't just impose itself on distant lands, of course; in the West too, it levels out even the strongest national differences, and weakens even the strongest local traditions. (PC 75)

Of course, the influx of images and ideas from a globalised mass culture isn't passively received. The creative forces of culture constantly rise to meet new stimuli, producing 'a new multiplicity of hybridized forms' which is as varied and unique across social contexts as earlier 'national' cultures had been (PC 76). New differences and new modes of belonging and community are thus created against the backdrop of the dominant culture. Nonetheless, these identities are less tightly connected to a national identity than they once were. Both the tendency towards global homogeneity and the tendency towards new forms of local identity pose challenges for civil solidarity within the form of the nation-state. And, with the weakening of nationality as an integrative force, a previously vital ingredient for civil solidarity is lost.

(2) Economic globalisation has not (yet) undermined the ability of states to safeguard basic property rights or to enforce contracts. But, in a globalised world, nation-states face a growing list of challenges that have a 'transnational' character. Ecological crises, nuclear threats and organised crime (e.g. international trafficking in drugs and arms) all outpace the capacity of nation-states to effectively impose legal and administrative remedies. When they are affected by the actions (and omissions) of actors who are not subject to their laws, or they are unable to practically regulate flows across national borders, nation-states can impose effective remedies only if they act in concert with other nation-states. And, in some cases (such as the limiting of greenhouse gas emissions), no nation-state or bloc of nation-states is capable of effectively regulating the issue; the solutions must be global if they are to succeed at all (CEU 55–6).

Because of the interconnectedness of the global economy, national governments have diminishing ability to influence economic cycles through macroeconomic policy. '"Keynesianism in one country" is no longer a possibility' (PC 79). The state feeds off revenue from gross domestic product, but as national economies are forced to play a game of international competitiveness there are incentives to cut tax rates in order to stave off the threat of 'capital flight' (PC 69). It is no surprise, therefore, that total tax revenues from corporations have fallen across the OECD since the 1980s. Tax revenue has had to be supplemented by increased taxes on wage earners, for example, in the form of goods and services taxes. As nation-states suffer from lower tax revenues and the inability to stimulate economic activity through spending and monetary policy, the options left to them are few.

> In the context of a global economy, nation-states can only increase the international competitiveness of their 'position' by imposing self-restrictions on the formative powers of the state itself. And this justifies the sort of 'dismantling' policies that end up damaging social cohesion and social stability as such. (PC 51)

A 'vicious circle' of growing unemployment, overburdened social security systems and a shrinking tax base depletes the financial resources of the state and undermines its ability to deliver on social policies (PC 79). Furthermore, especially since the Global Financial Crisis, the ability of governments to increase public debt to cover social spending has diminished (CEU 4–5).

Left and right apparently agree that in the contemporary context the nation-state is faced with a 'zero sum game': economic objectives must be played off against social and political objectives. And all mainstream political parties promote themselves as 'efficient managers' of the economy through difficult times, as though they were CEOs managing a company restructure. Since the 1980s, both left and right have sought to dampen down expectations of state spending on social policies, unemployment benefits and other social security measures. Taxes have been cut and state-owned assets have been privatised. Deregulation has sought to create a more 'business friendly' environment.[12] But these are, at best, rearguard actions in the face of seemingly unstoppable global forces.

(3) Citizens of modern liberal democracies have come to expect their governments to secure basic political and social rights (see Chapter 3.3). They expect that they will have a role in the democratic self-organisation of the political community, and that they will be protected from the worst social effects of unfettered capitalism. If governments cannot fulfil these expectations, then nation-states cannot effectively ensure the conditions of democratic legitimacy and social solidarity. But, for the reasons listed above, this promissory note is becoming harder and harder for nation-states to cash.

In many 'developed' countries, public services and public infrastructure (such as transport, health care and public spaces) are underfunded and aging. National economies, given over to unrestrained market forces, are exposed again to the 'crisis tendencies' once tamed by the welfare state (PC 50). Greater wealth and income disparities, the return of the working poor in 'developed' countries, and decreased social mobility are all results of the unwinding of the welfare state compromise. Together these social trends mark a loss of social solidarity.

The nation-state is plunged into a new legitimation crisis. Growing inequalities are incompatible with the self-conception of citizens as *equals* who collectively take responsibility for shaping their society. As social solidarity wanes, so does the general commitment to a liberal-democratic political culture that has been the cultural backdrop to the political gains of the past century. Abstention from democratic participation has increased as social divisions have grown (LT 50). Furthermore, the perception that the nation-state is impotent to solve pressing problems debases the democratic rights of citizens. If the decisions which affect a citizen's life are made elsewhere, or if the forces which shape their life are out of anyone's control, then the citizen can no longer see themself as a self-determining agent but only as a passive subject of foreign powers.

> Thus the image of a postnational constellation gives rise to alarmist feelings of enlightened helplessness widely observed in the political arena today. There is a crippling sense that national politics have dwindled to more or less intelligent management of a process of forced adaptation to the pressure to shore up purely local positional advantages. It is a perception that deprives political controversies of their last bit of substance. (PC 61)

Despite these challenges, the nation-state remains the dominant institution of political organisation. And, to a certain extent, it continues to function and to adapt itself to the changing circumstances. Nonetheless, it is clear that the 'golden age' of the nation-state has come to an end. As an institutional vehicle for societal self-determination, it is proving to be inadequate in the 'postnational constellation'. It is incapable of staving off the negative social and political effects of globalisation and is incompetent to meet the pressing challenges facing humanity in the new century. As a result, the nation-state is losing its pre-eminence as a locus of decisive political decision-making and action.

The question now is whether there a way to preserve the gains of the welfare state in the 'postnational' context. We shall discuss Habermas's constructive responses to this question in Chapter 5.5. What is clear already, however, is that if anything like the regulatory and redistributive functions of the welfare state are to be maintained, this will have to be achieved by legal and political institutions operating at a more encompassing level than that of the nation-state. As we shall see, although some transnational and international legal and political institutions have begun to emerge, these structures are not yet capable of making up for the social deficits created by the weakening of the nation-state.

The Evolution of International Law and Global Politics in the Twentieth Century

The model of the constitutional state won the day in Europe as the political clout of political rulers was effectively domesticated within legal constraints (see Chapter 3.1). In the 'postnational' context, the project of juridification takes on a new meaning. There is no question of domesticating global political rulers, since there are no rulers to domesticate. The question is rather whether new legal and political structures can be erected to domesticate global capitalism.

Of course, it is not in fact true to say that there are no political structures at the global level, and still less true to say that there is a void of international law. On the contrary, frameworks of international law have existed for centuries, and these legal frameworks have undergone considerable reform over the course of the past century. According to Habermas, we are already on the path towards the 'cosmopolitan condition' envisaged by Kant (DW 147–73).

Peace conferences at The Hague in 1899 and 1907 produced a set of Conventions and Declarations aimed at establishing the conditions for a lasting peace in Europe. But these first attempts at the juridification of international relations were left in tatters with the outbreak of the First World War (DW 154–5). It was only after the war that political form was given to the aspirations for a legal community among states for the first time with the founding of the League of Nations. The Covenant on which this institution was founded represented 'a quantum leap in the evolution of law' towards the Kantian ideal of perpetual peace (DW 156). Most notably, the Covenant overturned a long-standing principle of international law by declaring a prohibition on wars of aggression. The right of sovereign states to declare war against other states (the *jus ad bellum*) would no longer be recognised (DW 118–19). However, the League of Nations lacked the institutional mechanisms to enforce the obligations that member states had accepted in the Covenant. It possessed limited judicial powers to prosecute violations of the law, and no reliable mechanisms to apply sanctions on belligerent states. The League faced a series of setbacks as it failed to effectively sanction Japan after the invasion of Manchuria in 1931, Italy after its occupation of Abyssinia in 1935, and Germany's annexation of Austria and the Sudeteland in 1938. Finally, the institution collapsed with the outbreak of war in Europe in 1939.

The atrocities of the Second World War gave renewed impetus to the pacifist cause and galvanised international determination to establish the foundations for a lasting peace. These efforts crystalised in the establishment of the United Nations in 1945, a successor body to the League of Nations. Having learned the lessons of the failed League of Nations, the UN Charter not only prohibited offensive wars but also authorised the Security Council to police breaches. The UN Declaration of Human Rights (1948) further specified the obligations placed on member states by the Charter to respect human rights. More than any other, this document has had a profound impact in shaping the moral standards and expectations of participants in international relations ever since.

Nonetheless, the United Nations has not functioned reliably as an institutional framework for global governance. For more than forty years, the United Nations was rendered impotent by the stand-off between the Soviet Union and the United States because both were permanent members of the Security Council and enjoyed the right of veto on Security Council resolutions. Indeed, the disproportionate power given to states with a seat on the Security Council has meant that the body has acted in a 'highly selective' manner with complete disregard for the principle of equal treatment (IO 180). What's more, the United Nations has had to rely on the mobilisation of forces by member states in order to enforce sanctions, and the willingness of those states to contribute resources could not be guaranteed.

After the fall of the Berlin Wall in 1989 and the collapse of the Soviet Union in 1991, the United Nations has revived its relevance as an international institution. It has mediated civil conflicts and undertaken a number of peacekeeping and peace-enforcing missions with some success. War crimes tribunals under the auspices of the United Nations were established for the former Yugoslavia and for Rwanda.

And, with the establishment of the permanent International Criminal Court in 2002, it appears that robust and resilient legal institutions for the prosecution of international crimes such as genocide, war crimes and crimes against humanity have finally take root.

However, the United Nations is still 'often little more than a paper tiger' (DW 20). It continues to depend upon cooperation from major powers, such as the United States, and military alliances, such as NATO, to enforce its resolutions. As a result, the UN Security Council cannot guarantee that its own resolutions will be complied with. When the United Nations has failed to police violations of global peace, military powers such as the United States or NATO have taken it upon themselves to step into the gap, claiming to act on behalf of international community. The United Nations experiences a legitimacy deficit as a result:

> The discrepancy between ought and can, between law and power, undermines both the credibility of the UN and the practice of intervention by unauthorized states which merely usurps a mandate – though perhaps for good reasons – and thereby debases a would-be legitimate police action into an act of war. For the would-be police action then becomes indistinguishable from a run-of-the-mill war. (DW 20)

We thus find ourselves today faced with a fledging global legal and political structure which does not yet have the ability to ensure the enforcement of international law. International affairs remain largely dominated by the interests of the stronger states, and the strongest of all in recent decades has been the United States.

The 'hegemonic unilateralism' of the United States

Since the end of the Second World War, Habermas quips, the world spirit has 'lurched forward' (IO 178). But, for most of that period, the fate of the world spirit has been in the hands of the United States. The United States was the only power to emerge from the two world wars stronger politically, economically and culturally. And since the collapse of the Soviet Union, the United States has stood as the world's only superpower. In the post-war period, US leadership was instrumental in crafting the new world order, including mustering political support for key institutions such as the United Nations and the Bretton Woods system of monetary management. But, since the end of the Cold War, the leadership of the United States has been characterised by its promotion of market liberalisation, military containment of so-called 'rogue states', and the war on terror.

In international affairs, the interests of the United States have often been pursued under the auspices of international law and through the mediation of international organisations such as the World Trade Organization. However, in other instances, where multilateralism has appeared impossible or international law presents impediments, the dominance of the United States as a trading power and a military power has enabled it act unilaterally, or in partnership with economic or military allies.

The tendency towards hegemony has been more pronounced since the events of 11 September 2001. The attacks on the World Trade Centre and the Pentagon succeeded in creating fear and alarm in the US population. At the time, Habermas hoped that the United States would channel its response to the attacks in such a way as to 'promote the transition from classical international law to a cosmopolitan order' (DW 5). But, even at the time, this seemed decidedly unlikely. The United States had recently opposed the establishment of the International Criminal Court, and it had refused to support the Biological Weapons Convention and the Anti-Ballistic Missile Treaty. The US policy was very clearly intended to prevent any new constraints upon its actions under international law.

The 2003 invasion of Iraq subsequently underscored the US's willingness to act without deference to international law. The action was not undertaken with a legal mandate and with the support of the Security Council, but instead pursued by a 'coalition of the willing'. By Habermas's lights, the war itself had mixed consequences. On one hand, it did lead to the end of a brutal regime, a 'normatively desirable' outcome (DW 26). On the other hand, it resulted in massive and horrific civilian casualties (DW 99). Most alarmingly, it signalled the willingness of the world's only superpower to assert its right to act militarily as it sees fit, without regard for the constraints imposed by the UN Charter or international law. It thus represented a major setback in the transition to a regime of effective and just international law (DW 28). Reassuringly, this renegade action by no means led to the collapse of the United Nations. Nonetheless, in Habermas's view, it set a 'disastrous precedent for future superpowers' (DW 29).

The justificatory standpoint taken by the United States in recent years is labelled by Habermas a 'hegemonic unilateralism' (DW 149). Within this approach, international law remains in effect, but only as a means for regulating relations between nation-states. The hegemonic power itself is exempt from international law but is able to utilise it as a mechanism to enforce its will on others in a quasi-juridical form. International law thus provides a medium for reinforcing *existing* power relations, rather than a means for dissolving power relations between states through juridical oversight. To the hegemonic power, its actions are justified 'by appeal to its own national values rather than in terms of established procedures' (DW 149). For instance, humanitarian interventions and military missions are legitimate if they are intended to prevent suffering and to 'spread democracy'. This, Habermas argues, is best understood as an 'imperial variant *within* international law' (DW 149).

The approach taken by the United States is not entirely novel. It continues a tradition which stretches from Hobbes and Hegel to Schmitt and Morgenthau. It is centred on the belief that the relation between world powers is a competition between sovereigns for dominance and advantage. It assumes that agreements between powers can only be the codification of their respective power positions and not the expression of shared normative principles. But such an approach is ultimately self-defeating, Habermas argues, since it lacks legitimacy and must supplement its lack of authority with surveillance and violence:

> ... even if hegemonic unilateralism could be implemented, it would generate *side effects* that are undesirable by its own normative criteria. The more political power (understood in its role as a global civilizing force) is exercised in the dimensions of the military, the intelligence services, and the police, the more it comes into conflict with its own purposes and endangers the mission of improving the world in accordance with liberal ideas. (DW 34)

Guantanamo Bay, the stripping of rights from prisoners, the expanding powers of the security agencies, all erode civil rights. What's more, even allies of the United States would have to be forced into compliance if the normative legitimacy of US actions cannot be defended by reference to principles and procedures that can be accepted by all.

For these reasons, Habermas sees an unavoidable tension between the 'ethical liberalism' of the United States and the 'cosmopolitan institutionalism' favoured by the European powers (and by Habermas himself). Habermas will argue that the only rationally consistent and democratically defensible approach in the long term is to subordinate humanitarian interventions and peacekeeping missions to the goal of making international law effective. The justificatory process of international law cannot be replaced by 'the unilateral, world-ordering politics of a self-appointed hegemon' (DW 33). This alternative, which Habermas supports, is convincing to European minds and 'binds' them together thanks to a bitter learning process during the twentieth century (DW 48).

CONCLUSION

The legitimation deficits faced by the nation-state under the pressures of globalisation require a 'constitutionalisation' of political communities at transnational and global levels. As we have seen, this process is already underway, and some institutional building blocks are in place. However, challenges remain. The hegemony of the United States – not to mention the potentially destabilising agendas of future superpowers – inhibits the necessary reforms that would continue the process of establishing a 'cosmopolitan condition' along the lines envisaged by Kant. What's more, there are distinctive challenges that will have to be faced when it comes to ensuring the democratic legitimacy of global institutions. Complex problems are posed by the need to sustain human communities of connection, meaning and identity within the postnational constellation. Nonetheless, Habermas concludes on the basis of his sociological analysis that there is no viable alternative to *more* cosmopolitanism and *more* democracy:

> The human population has long since coalesced into an unwilling community of shared risk. Under this pressure, it is thus quite plausible that the great, historically momentous dynamic of abstraction from local, to dynastic, to national to democratic consciousness would take one more step forward. (PC 56)

Notes

1. The first four 'waves' are sketched in TCA2 356–73. These are recapitulated briefly in PC 62–5 before Habermas goes on to describe the present era in which we are witnessing a fifth wave of juridification: the 'constitutionalisation' of international law.
2. The German concept of the *Rechtsstaat* connotes both the idea of a constitutional state, in which the state itself is governed by law, and the idea of the rule of law, in which society as a whole is governed by laws, not men. See the 'Translator's Introduction' in BFN xxxiv–xxxv.
3. On the changing meaning of the term 'nation' over time, see BFN 494.
4. The situation was different in England, where the evolving parliamentary system provided an institutional check on royal power with

increasing success until it finally achieved constitutional supremacy over the monarch in the late seventeenth century.
5. For a fuller analysis of these aspects of Habermas's work, see Held (2002).
6. The debates over the feasibility of a universal basic income, which were taking place at the time and have once again come to prominence today, are merely the latest variation on the theme of stabilising the welfare state in light of developments in the labour market.
7. When social relationships become 'market interactions' and labour becomes a 'commodity', then the totality of human society 'take[s] on the character of a thing' (Lukács 1971: 83).
8. This formulation echoes the language of Marx and Lukács. See Lukács (1971: 86); for a discussion, see Jütten (2011).
9. For a discussion of the twin problems of nihilism and domination in the tradition of critical theory, see Bernstein (1995: 28–34).
10. Habermas refers here, in an admittedly vague fashion, to Luhmann's late systems theory. See Baxter (2011: 83–5).
11. The target of this last criticism is not only Marx but also thinkers such as Hannah Arendt who regard the politicisation of social and economic issues as an overextension of the rightful domain of politics. See Arendt (1958: 38–49); cf. HA 13–16.
12. Despite this, even neo-liberal governments have not been averse to state spending, which is embraced where it leads to corporate profit, and military spending, which has continued apace despite the 'long peace' of the post-war era.

4
Critical Perspectives: Power and Domination in Contemporary Society

How adequate is Habermas's historical-sociological analysis for exposing the structures of power and domination in the contemporary world? In this chapter, I want to discuss and evaluate several interrelated lines of criticism. The first queries Habermas's tendency to downplay the relevance of class conflict. The second questions whether Habermas's social theory is able to make sense of the patterns of domination experienced by women in the modern world. The third line of criticism charges that Habermas's work is problematically Eurocentric and that it obfuscates the relationship between modernisation and colonial subjugation and exploitation. But before addressing these lines of criticism, I want to begin by canvassing more general criticisms that are often made of Habermas's social theory.

Criticisms of the System–Lifeworld Distinction

Questions have frequently been raised about the basic concepts of Habermas's social theory, especially his system-lifeworld distinction. Some critics have questioned whether it is plausible to distinguish 'system' and 'lifeworld' at all, let alone to conceive of these as separate domains of social action capable of 'uncoupling' from each other. The four most prominent lines of argument against Habermas's system-lifeworld distinction are the following.

First, Habermas treats the analytic distinction between system and lifeworld as though it provides a classification of social institutions and/or domains of social interaction. For instance, he treats the family as a 'lifeworld' context and the workplace as a 'systems' context. But this is not sustainable for the reasons we shall discuss presently. At most, the distinction can be used to pick out different *aspects* of contexts of social action (Honneth 1991).

Second, the social institutions of the lifeworld, such as the family, are sites of strategic action as much as they are of communicative action. As Nancy Fraser argues:

> ... few if any human action contexts are wholly devoid of strategic calculation. Gift rituals in noncapitalist societies, for example, previously taken as veritable crucibles of solidarity, are now widely understood to have a significant strategic, calculative dimension, one enacted in the medium of power, if not in that of money. And [...] the modern, restricted, nuclear family is not devoid of individual, self-interested, strategic calculations in either medium. These action contexts, then, while not officially counted as economic, have a strategic, economic dimension. (Fraser 1985: 104–5)

Third, markets and the administrative state are sites of communicative action as much as they are of strategic action (Joas 1991; McCarthy 1991). At least some basic activities of the market economy and administrative state require collective planning and communicative agreement with others. Consider, for instance, a policy initiative or a business deal. In these instances, individuals must reach agreement with colleagues and partners about action agendas and implement them cooperatively, even if these action agendas are then pursued in a 'strategic' manner in relation to other individuals or groups. In fact, government departments and businesses can be oriented towards goals and values that are collectively held by their members in much the same way as NGOs or social clubs.

Fourth, the organisations that make up the 'systems' of market economy and the administrative state must present themselves *symbolically* as legitimate components of the 'lifeworld'. This does not just happen at an abstract level, e.g. by appeal to the laws that permit their activity. Rather, businesses and public bodies represent themselves in public communications as value-oriented and responsible agents. Furthermore, the clothing, bodily comportment and titles of those who perform roles in these organisations speak of the legitimacy of these social roles (Joas 1991). Systems are thus not essentially 'norm free'; rather they possess almost all of the hallmarks of the 'lifeworld' (Honneth 1991: 278–303).

In an important reply to his critics, Habermas clarifies that for him social integration and system integration are 'two *aspects* of societal integration' (R 252). While communicative and media-steered social action are distinct mechanisms of societal integration and can be distinguished analytically (thus justifying the distinction between system and lifeworld), in fact social life is structured by both processes simultaneously. Hence, 'an approximate description can be given of *all phenomena* using *each* of the two aspects – although there is a difference in depth of field' (R 253; emphasis altered). In other words, Habermas acknowledges that markets and the administrative state are sites of communicative action, just as he acknowledges that communication is never free of coercion and power (R 254) (see Chapter 2).

Furthermore, although Habermas does insist on the 'uncoupling' of system and lifeworld as a distinctive feature of modern societies, this does not mean that systems are spheres or sites of action separate from the lifeworld (R 257). Systems always function against a lifeworld background, and agents engaged in media-steered action never entirely suppress their sense of moral responsibility and their ethical orientation. What 'uncoupling' does mean is that 'action domains have differentiated out that are *primarily* systemically integrated' (R 256). In these domains, even when other moral or ethical considerations are in play, the decisive influence over decision-making and action is exercised by legal and economic considerations. Think, for instance, of the consumer in the supermarket selecting a product. Moral and ethical considerations may be applied in decision-making, but the choices of the consumer will be determined primarily by needs and price signals: for example, I need milk, I can afford brand X's bottle of milk, and it looks to me like it offers good value. The analysis, then, is not nearly as dichotomising as it first appears. It simply aims to capture the observation that, in more and more aspects of our social life, legal rules or economic imperatives are *dominant* in structuring what decisions are made, what action is taken, and hence how society functions.

It is also important to bear in mind that, for Habermas, 'uncoupled' systems remain 'embedded' in the lifeworld. They are embedded 'informally' insofar as the individuals who participate in media-steered interactions relate to each other in morally appropriate ways (e.g. politely) and understand their activity in terms of social roles (e.g. client, manager, salesperson, labourer). These social roles have significance and (usually) legitimacy within from the standpoint of the lifeworld (TCA2 320). Systems are also embedded 'formally' through legal regulations (TCA2 309–11). And the legal system is, as we shall discuss in the next section, a social order of the lifeworld.

Criticisms of the 'Systems' Conception of the Administrative State

A potentially more damaging objection to Habermas's system-lifeworld distinction relates to his characterisation of the administrative state as a 'system' whose medium is 'power' (Baxter 2011: 41–5; Scheuerman 2013: 578–80). The parallel between power and money is initially intuitive: just as price signals allow a simplified decision-making procedure that bypasses the need for 'consensus formation in language', so a requirement coupled with a threat of sanctions influences individual action in a way that need not suppose principled agreement with the requirement (TCA2 263). For example, the police officer's instruction to 'step out of the vehicle' gives a reason to comply without by any means implying that the reasons for the instruction are intelligible and judged acceptable by the addressee. But does it make sense to describe the administrative state as a system 'steered' through the medium of power in the way that the capitalist economy constitutes a system 'steered' though the medium of money?

Habermas takes over the idea that power serves as an abstract medium of social coordination from Parsons. However, sociologists have long questioned whether power can be regarded as a medium in the same way as money, as Parsons proposed (Coleman 1963; Giddens 1968). Displays of power can be used, like money, to convey signals or information between actors. But unlike money, power is not easily quantifiable, and it cannot be stored or transferred between parties.[1] What's more, as Habermas himself admits, social action that is regulated by the use of power cannot easily be 'uncoupled' from the lifeworld, since power derives from perceived authority and the perception of authority rests on *normative* judgements (TCA2 269–71). Because power relationships by definition render some parties 'structurally disadvantaged' in relation to others, any system of power 'requires an advance of trust that signifies not only "compliance" – a de facto obedience to laws – but "obligation" – a duty based on the recognition of normative validity claims' (TCA2 271). Therefore, Habermas concludes, the medium of power is 'dependent upon processes of consensus formation in language' in a way that the medium of money is not (TCA2 272). Curiously, despite acknowledging these significant dis-analogies between power and money, Habermas goes on to consider power and money as comparable 'steering media' that can bypass the need for consensus in ordinary language (TCA2 280).

But, even if Habermas insists that the administrative system can be viewed as a system steered in the medium of power, a number of questions are left unanswered. For instance, systems are supposedly steered through a 'code' in which they are 'programmed'. But if the administrative system is steered in the code of 'power', then how can it be directed by democratic consensus in the code of ordinary language? It becomes hard to conceptualise how the communicative agreement among citizens could influence the administrative system in any way. For this reason, Hugh Baxter claims that the system-lifeworld model developed in TCA renders genuine democracy 'literally inconceivable' (Baxter 2011: 87).

However, according to Baxter, Habermas overcomes this problem in BFN by conceiving of the 'power code' in terms of the medium of law. Legal rules are the code that programmes the system of power. The legal structure of the political system determines who may issue binding decisions or commands, and those decisions and commands then determine what behaviours will be deemed 'legal' or 'illegal' (BFN 143–4). With this clarification, it can now be explained how ordinary language can be translated into the power code: namely, 'communicative power' is converted into 'administrative power' via the medium of law:

> The language of law brings ordinary communication from the public and private spheres and puts it into a form in which these messages can also be received by the special codes of autopoietic systems – and vice versa. Without this transformer, ordinary language could not circulate throughout our society. (BFN 354)

This is a considerable theoretical improvement, Baxter argues. But, in making these revisions, Habermas 'reworks the notions of system and lifeworld so substantially that Habermas's official conceptions no longer apply' (Baxter 2011: 149).

Perhaps this overstates the discontinuities between TCA and BFN (Flynn 2014b). But even it if does, it brings to light an ambiguity in Habermas's theory of the administrative state. In Habermas's theory, both law and power are referred to as the 'code' or 'steering medium' of the administrative system.[2] Which is it? Habermas's metaphor of the law as a 'transformer' implies that law operates as a third thing between ordinary language and the administrative system; it is something in addition to the 'power code' through which the administrative state is steered (BFN 150). But his historical reconstruction (see Chapter 3.1) presents the process of 'juridification' as transforming the very nature of political power such that political power is *subsumed* under the medium of law. The 'secondary rules' of the legal system, those which authorise binding decision-making, *generate* and *organise* political power (BFN 144). Thus, it is not merely that the medium of law 'communicates' with administrative power, but that the law *constitutes* the power code in the sense that law is the *form* or *medium* in which (administrative) power is organised (BFN 56, 169). But, if so, is there any sense in speaking of both *power* and *law* as 'codes' or 'media' (BFN 143–50, 168–9)? Why not just treat the legal code as the code in which the administrative system is 'programmed'?

But if this is the best resolution of the ambiguity, then it is not clear that it makes sense any more to conceive of the state as a 'self-organising' (autopoietic) dynamic like a market. Instead, the administrative state looks rather more like a highly organised social institution. If there is a 'system'-like character to the behaviour of individuals under law, it is not because there is a 'system of power' that operates according to its own logic, but because a predictable pattern of behaviour has been secured through the construction of legal rules backed by sanctions.

This reading is consistent with what Habermas says about the 'janus-faced' character of law in BFN. Laws can be obeyed in a performative attitude (out of recognition of their legitimacy) or they can be obeyed in a strategic attitude (out of a motivation to maximise outcomes or avoid penalties) (BFN 28–34). Habermas appeals to this 'janus-faced' character of laws to argue that only 'cynical' sociologists take the political system to be reducible to a play of forces. These sociologists have '[lost] sight of what political power owes specifically to its formal constitution in legal terms' (BFN 330): namely, that the system of legal rules provides a normative anchor for the political system as a whole, helping to secure its legitimacy. Overall, the best way to understand the thrust of the argument in BFN, then, is to see it portraying the administrative state as a highly regulated social institution which can, nonetheless, take on a life of its own under unfavourable conditions and come to *approximate* the picture of an 'autopoietic' system (BFN 329–30). (We will return to this question in Chapter 5.3.)

If this interpretation is correct, then Baxter is right that the 'systems' conception of the administrative state is 'incompatible' with Habermas's normative theory of democracy, even though Habermas continues to officially endorse the systems conception of the administrative state in BFN (Baxter 2011: 87–8). The most generous reading of these confusions is to say that Habermas's social theory has undergone some revisions, but that he has failed to arrive at a new position that is theoretically stable and consistent.[3] The important question is whether these confusions weaken Habermas's diagnosis of the contemporary political situation and his prescriptions for reform. Marxist readers of Habermas are inclined to think so.

Marxist Criticisms

Marxist readers of Habermas's TCA were alarmed that, despite being billed as an updated critical theory of modern capitalist society, it downplayed the reifying tendencies of the capitalist economy and focused instead on the problem of bureaucratisation. Of course, Habermas acknowledges in TCA that the process of capitalist modernisation has been painful and that it has provoked considerable resistance.

> The path to capitalist modernization is strewn with resistance to the uprooting of the plebian rural population and the urban proletariat, with revolts against the establishment of the absolutist state; against taxes, price decrees, and trade regulations; against the recruitment of mercenaries, and the like. (TCA2 321).

However, he claims that the social institutions that have resulted – the capitalist economy and the bureaucratic state – are now seen as legitimate by a majority of people because of the 'greater efficiency and superior level of integration' that they afford (TCA2 321). Furthermore, while Habermas notes the reifying tendencies that individuals continue to experience as a result of being commodified by the labour market, he argues that by the mid-twentieth century 'the burdens resulting from heteronomously determined work are made at least subjectively bearable – if not through "humanizing" the work place, through providing monetary rewards and legally guaranteed securities' (TCA2 349). Thus, Marx was wrong to think that capitalism was incompatible with human flourishing, even though he was fully justified in criticising the merciless exploitation of workers during the Industrial Revolution. The evolution of systems mechanisms, especially markets, has brought social advances, even as it has generated new problems. The question today is not how to dismantle market-mediated economic activity but how to achieve a meaningful *democratic counter-steering* of markets (and of the administrative state), such that they are institutionally constrained and their negative side effects are counteracted (R 261).

Critics have seen in Habermas's accommodation of contemporary capitalism the symptoms of deep-seated theoretical problems. In particular, critical attention has been directed towards his treatment of the capitalist economy as an 'autopoietic' social system. If economic activity is conceptualised as a 'self-organising' system, then the commodification of labour is the result of impersonal and autonomous social forces, not something that is imposed upon workers in the interests of the capitalist class. The responsibility of human agents for the design and implementation of practices and modes of economic activity is rendered invisible. Likewise, if the evolution of social systems is part of the 'progressive' history of modernisation, then the indignities and suffering of modern workers is nothing more than an unfortunate but inevitable side effect of necessary historical developments (Sitton 1998; Breen 2007).

By contrast, if we understand capitalism as the consequence of institutional and organisational design, then we begin to see why economic arrangements have been the focus of class conflict. The interests of those who gain from corporate profits (i.e. business owners) are opposed to those who gain from wages (i.e. workers), and this struggle plays out politically as interest groups vie to influence the rules of the game (e.g. corporate law, employment law, tax law, and other relevant regulatory regimes). This is where Marx's analysis contains an insight that is arguably lost in Habermas's systems-theoretic analysis of capitalist markets:

> ... unlike Habermas's theory, Marx's emphasis on class relations expressed through property forms focuses our attention on the social structures that embody capitalism, and arguably, govern its historical trajectory. Any political project that seeks to influence that trajectory so as to actually bring the benefits of market arrangements to the global majority, as Habermas's evidently does, must analyze how these class relations steer the fruits of the vaunted efficiencies of capitalism into the pockets of the few. (Sitton 1998: 81)

A related criticism follows from reflecting upon Habermas's classification of markets as 'norm-free' media-steered interactions (i.e. social systems). This classification, it is claimed, licenses a view that sees market participants as strategic actors who enter into transactions (or not) in accordance with their own free choice. But Marx showed that a whole category of transactions basic to the capitalist system – namely, those in which someone sells their own labour – is never free and un-coerced. Rather, the capitalist system creates a class of people (the proletariat) who do not have the independent means to sustain their lives and thus must sell their labour in order to survive. This renders them systematically vulnerable to exploitation (Jütten 2011: 714).

During the heyday of the welfare state, it was perhaps understandable for Habermas to focus his critical attention on the negative side effects of bureaucratic interventions in social life and to focus less on the effects of rampant capitalism.[4] But since that time, class divisions and social inequalities have re-emerged with a vengeance.[5] And, as Habermas himself has stressed, the assumption that the state has at its disposal the means necessary to neutralise the negative social consequences of capitalist accumulation has become ever more incredible under the conditions of a globalised economy. Even more so today than in earlier periods, the imperatives of capitalism transform the very fabric of social life, creating conflict and antagonisms between classes, between workers (who are competitors for jobs), and even within workers (who must suppress their own values and inclinations in order to enter the world of work). The value and purpose of economic activity for society is subordinated to the quasi-autonomous logic of the accumulation of capital.

Does this indicate that Habermas ought to shift the focus of his critical theory back towards the traditional concerns of Marxist theory, i.e. the critique of capitalism, as some commentators have suggested?

On the one hand, because Habermas views markets as 'norm-free', self-organising systems, he argues that it is a political question to determine the 'ends' that markets should serve and how best to regulate markets such that they serve those ends. Legal regulation is the most effective and appropriate means to impose moral expectations on markets, he claims (BFN 118). There is no sense in moralising about markets *per se*.[6] So, for instance, after the financial crisis of 2008 he could state that the failure lay with politicians not with bankers, since 'Politics, and not capitalism, is responsible for promoting the common good' (EFP 184). From this point of view, it makes sense that Habermas has concerned himself primarily with sketching avenues for overcoming the social pathologies caused by capitalism and not with analysing the dynamics of capitalism itself.

On the other hand, Habermas leaves himself open to criticism for not asking reflective questions about the capitalist economy itself and for too readily assuming that its basic internal organisation is essentially settled. A mainstay of socialist theory at its best has been the exploration of alternative models of economic organisation. But Habermas shows little interest in considering new or different ways of organising labour (Noonan 2005). Furthermore, Habermas has little to say about the mechanisms by which capitalism generates and exacerbates social and material inequalities. He also pays surprisingly little attention to the commodification of culture, a dynamic so thoroughly examined (and lamented) by the leading figures of the Frankfurt School with whom Habermas is often associated. These are real deficits.

Feminist Criticisms

As soon as it was published, Habermas's TCA was subjected to searing criticism by feminist theorists. The most prominent of these critics was Nancy Fraser, who took Habermas to task in an influential essay for his patriarchal assumptions and for his romantic and unrealistic view of the domestic sphere (Fraser 1985). In her essay, Fraser voices concerns that Habermas's characterisation of the domestic sphere as a sphere of 'symbolic reproduction' obscures the fact that nuclear families can be 'sites of egocentric, strategic and instrumental calculation as well as sites of usually exploitative exchanges of services, labor, cash and sex, not to mention sites, frequently, of coercion and violence' (Fraser 1985: 107). In particular, she notes that Habermas's failure to recognise that the domestic sphere is a site of labour ('albeit of unremunerated and often unrecognized labor') could reinforce the perception that 'women's work' is rightfully *unpaid* since it falls outside the bounds of the 'real economy' (Fraser 1985: 109–11).

However, the fundamental criticism that Fraser raises is that the new critical lens developed by Habermas, his idea of the 'colonisation of the lifeworld', is of little use to feminists. The crisis for women is *not* the colonisation of the lifeworld. The crisis stems from the lifeworld itself, which sustains 'the familiar "normatively-secured consensus" concerning male dominance and female subordination' (Fraser 1985: 125). The struggle, therefore, is not to 'decolonise' the lifeworld; it is to overturn the gender biases and patterns of subordination internal to the lifeworld, and to ensure patriarchal patterns of social organisation are not replicated in workplaces and in public life. In this regard, Habermas's focus on the critique of 'juridification' in the welfare state is potentially problematic because it forecloses the possibility that legal remedies might present the most potent mechanism for dismantling the patriarchal structure of modern society.

Jean L. Cohen defends Habermas's system-lifeworld distinction against Fraser's criticisms (Cohen 1995: 64–7), but she agrees with Fraser that Habermas's social theory is seriously deficient in its analysis of gender. Habermas's upbeat presentation of the transition to 'post-conventional morality' overlooks the stubborn and pervasive persistence of gendered norms in modern societies. Gender role divisions still serve in many arenas as the implicit principle by which social action is coordinated, and these role divisions go unquestioned. But gender roles are deeply problematic since they are both the product of power relations and serve to perpetuate power relations (Cohen 1995: 68–71). For example, the feminine role of housewife and the masculine role of breadwinner, which are accepted features of 'social order', ensure that males enjoy greater opportunities for self-development and self-determination than females. Furthermore, while the welfare state does have the potential to reconfigure these domestic roles, the welfare state has made women dependent in a new way, namely as 'clients' of the welfare state who rely upon its services and benefits (Cohen 1995: 72–3; see also Fraser 1985: 122–3). Carol Brown (1981) describes this as a shift 'from private patriarchy to public patriarchy'. At best, then, 'the rationalization of society' has been a partial and selective process, and a critical social theory has to account for this selectivity (Cohen 1995: 67–8).

This analysis of gendered norms has a flipside. If women have a primarily 'client' relationship to the welfare state, men have a primarily 'active' relationship to it as participants in public discourse. As Carole Pateman (1988) and Nancy Fraser (1992) have shown, the exclusion of women was 'constitutive' of the bourgeois political public sphere. The public-private distinction is practically sustained by a gender division between citizens who contribute to the public sphere (coded 'male') and homemakers who administer life in the domestic private sphere (coded 'female'). However, this does not mean that women have in fact been absent from public discourse or that they have had no influence on political developments. On the contrary, even though Habermas's early work on the public sphere virtually ignores their political activism and contributions to political discourse, women played a crucial role in the process of democratisation as several studies have shown (Eley 1992; Fraser 1992; Landes 1995).

There have been points of learning for Habermas in the work of Pateman, Fraser and others. For instance, after reflecting on the historical evidence regarding the role of women's movements in the process of democratisation, Habermas reformulates his account of the sociological drivers of democratisation. He argues that the mechanism of exclusion intrinsic to the capitalist economy and the bourgeois public sphere had fortuitous but unintentional 'counter-effects': the exclusion of women and workers from public life catalysed the formation of 'competing public spheres'; and these, in turn, shaped the democratising and liberalising trends of the past two centuries (FR 425). Also, at least since BFN, Habermas has fully embraced the assumption that legal remedies will often present the most potent mechanism for dismantling social patterns of domination, including patriarchy. In general, Habermas has come to consider the critical perspectives of feminists as an important resource for his own work, and he has also sought to demonstrate the relevance of his work for the feminist struggle (BFN 409–27; IO 208–10, 262–4).

The Problem of Eurocentrism

Habermas is famously a philosopher of European civilisation and a defender of the achievements of the Enlightenment. But is he therefore a Eurocentric philosopher?

To give a definition, Eurocentrism is the assumption that Europe is the social and cultural pacesetter for humanity. Within this view, it is European civilisation that has brought humanity to its highest realisation: European civilisation is the most culturally advanced, the most 'enlightened', the most civilised. Not only that, Eurocentrists assume that the intellectual products of European civilisation – its moral values, its knowledges and its social and political institutions – are valid and beneficial *for all*. Naturally, therefore, Western values, knowledges and institutions should be adopted throughout the world. This will bring other 'less developed' societies up to speed with the achievements of European 'modernity', bestowing on them the gifts of liberal culture, material affluence and good governance.

Eurocentric thinking has come under attack, most notably in recent work by postcolonial theorists.[7] First and foremost, postcolonial theorists have sought to pop the bubble of the Eurocentrist's self-congratulation by highlighting the dark side of European civilisation and its history. The subjugation of foreign lands and peoples has been integral to the construction of the West's affluence and its sense of cultural superiority. Western imperialism and capitalist expansion have brought in their wake suffering, exploitation and dehumanisation on a global scale. The 'gifts' it has bestowed on the people of the world have included the 'gift' of being recruited as slaves to European masters, of being dispossessed of traditional lands and of having cultural treasures ransacked. Furthermore, it has been suggested that the achievement of democratic inclusion in the 'centre' of the world order (i.e. in the West) requires subordination and exploitation in the 'periphery' (Amin 2009: 259–79).

Crucially, postcolonial theorists have sought to show how Eurocentric and progressivist frameworks of thought have provided ideological cover for imperialism. Specifically, the idea of empire, it is claimed, has been 'nourished' by 'a philosophical and cultural imaginary that justifies the political subjugation of distant territories and their native populations through claims that such peoples are less advanced, cognitively inferior, and therefore naturally subordinate' (Allen 2016: 1). To give just one historical example, Kant explicitly claimed that European races, unlike Native Americans, Africans and Asians, are especially *capable* and *predisposed* towards culture and civilisation (McCarthy 2009: 42–68). A defence of the 'universalism' of reason in Kant thus sits alongside – and indeed justifies – an *exclusionary* division between 'the cultivated' and 'the crude' (McCarthy 2009: 46). What's more, according to Thomas McCarthy, Kant had some indirect influence on the development of racial thinking in the nineteenth century, the thinking that spawned the idea that it is the 'White Man's Burden' to civilise the primitive peoples of the world (McCarthy 2009: 48, cf. 70, 81).

So, is Habermas's social theory Eurocentric and imperialist in the same problematic fashion? Does his theory of modernity uncritically gloss over history of colonisation and, inadvertently or not, provide ideological cover for the projection of European power over non-European societies?

European intellectuals have been self-conscious about the biases of Eurocentrism for more than a century, and Habermas is no exception. Nonetheless, it is true that his work is Eurocentric in a number of ways. To begin with, it is Eurocentric in the trivial sense that his historical reconstruction of societal transformations is overwhelmingly centred on developments within Europe, and, even more narrowly, on developments within the 'major' European powers of England, France and Germany. This feature alone, however, does not warrant criticism; we are all entitled to a parochialism of interests. But there are at least four other ways in which Habermas is arguably Eurocentric, and these are potentially more problematic.

First, the social suffering and violence caused by the onward march of 'modernity' in the guise of imperialism and colonial expansion is rarely discussed by Habermas.[8] This is surprising given the critical ambitions of his political theory. There is no excuse for ignorance.

The truth about the devastating impacts of colonialism in distant lands was already well known by the early nineteenth century. Marx, for instance, had no trouble compiling evidence of atrocities when writing *Capital* (Marx 1990: 914–26). There is little recognition that the economic and cultural achievements of the West have come through colonial exploitation of non-Western peoples and with enormous impact upon their economic well-being and cultural life (Bhambra 2016).

Second, Habermas's historical reconstruction of modern lifeworlds makes the progressivist assumption that cultural and social developments in the West have *in fact* delivered increased levels of freedom and justice, knowledge and rationality. Of course, he acknowledges that Western societies have by no means reached perfection in the attainment of these goals. Nonetheless, he assumes that failures to realise these goals are apt to be remedied through use of the resource that European modernity has bestowed upon us, the most important of which is the resource of Enlightenment reason mobilised through public discourse.

Third, Habermas's historical reconstruction takes Occidental (i.e. Western) rationality to have a superior status to other non-Western and pre-modern forms of rationality, and he explains the superiority of Occidental rationality by reference to a process of 'social learning' within Western civilisation (TCA1 43–74). This learning process has occurred at three levels:

1. At the level of social institutions and social systems. At this level, system and lifeworld are differentiated. Subsystems grow in complexity, resulting in the institutions of the administrative state and the capitalist market economy.
2. At the level of cultural beliefs and norms. At this level, the lifeworld is 'rationalised'. A theoretical learning process yields the fruits of modern science. A moral-practical learning process gives rise to the values of equality, freedom, democracy and the idea of universal human rights.
3. At the level of the structures and practices of reasoning itself. At this level, a learning process gives rise to a fallibilist, post-metaphysical understanding of rationality that severs its ties to religious dogma.

Fourth, Habermas explicitly argues for the claim that moral and social developments within the European societies have a *universal* validity. The Western tradition has arrived at a number of fundamental normative insights, notably concerning the moral legitimacy of human rights and the indispensability of democratic participation as the basis for political legitimacy. These insights are embodied (imperfectly) in the legal and political institutions of the contemporary West. As such, these institutions should serve as the starting point for thinking about models of international law and global politics (PC 113–29).

Given these features of Habermas's thought, it is not surprising that postcolonial theorists and critical theorists informed by postcolonial perspectives have taken Habermas as a prime target for criticism (Dussel 1993; Tully 2009; Bhambra 2016).[9] Amy Allen's recent extended critique is the most detailed and formidable contribution to this genre, and I will focus on it here (Allen 2016: chapters 1 and 2).

Criticisms of Habermas's 'Neo-Hegelianism'

There is no question for Allen that Habermas's theory of modernity asserts 'the developmental superiority of European modernity over pre-modern or traditional cultures' and hence evidences 'a particular form of self-congratulatory bias that is deeply bound up with the legacies of colonialism and imperialism' (Allen 2017: 685). The question is why Habermas is so especially wedded to Eurocentric patterns of thought. Her hypothesis is as follows:

> The problem of Eurocentrism continually plagues Habermas not merely because he just so happens to be a staunch defender of the ideals forged in the European Enlightenment, but also because the theory of social evolution – along with the theory of modernity to which it gives rise – plays a crucial role in validating the critical standards of Habermasian critical theory. (Allen 2016: 39)

Specifically, she argues, Habermas represents a 'neo-Hegelian strand of contemporary critical theory' that 'has drawn on the notion of progress to justify and bolster its normative claims in order to avoid the twin evils of *foundationalism* and *relativism*' (Allen 2017: 682; emphasis added). To avoid foundationalism, critical theory must ground its normative claims 'immanently', i.e. within the existing social world; but to avoid relativism, critical theory must justify its normative claims in a way that does not rely upon values that merely happen to be endorsed by contemporary societies. Habermas's strategy avoids the Scylla of foundationalism and the Charybdis of relativism by showing that the social institutions and normative principles of contemporary society are the product of 'a process of progressive social evolution or sociocultural learning' (Allen 2016: 14–15). Thus, in Habermas, the normative social orders of the modern lifeworld are presented as rational insofar as they demonstrably overcome problems within earlier configurations of social organisation.

Allen detects a problem of circularity in Habermas's attempt to provide a normative foundation for critical theory through reconstructing historical learning processes: namely, the belief in historical progress rests on normative commitment to the 'development superiority' of the modern West, and this perspective structures in advance a reading of the historical record (Allen 2016: 61). In other words, the evidential basis presented by Habermas is subject to a confirmation bias. But if so, then the detour through historical reconstruction can do no independent justificatory work; it is rigged from the start to confirm what it is supposed to confirm. What reason do we have, then, for believing that Habermas's conception of rationality and of the normative principles of law and democracy are 'universally valid' and not merely an expression of modern consciousness (TCA1 137–8)?

It is true that the rhetorical force of Habermas's social and political theory relies strongly on the historical narrative that he offers to demonstrate why our political norms and institutions are (and must be) the way they are today. This is precisely why I have dedicated a whole part of this book to presenting this historical narrative. If this narrative is false or misleading, then at the very least it will undermine the rhetorical force of his case, and it should motivate us to look elsewhere (as well) for moral and political resources from which to construct a political theory. The work of postcolonial theorists does in fact give ample reason to think that Habermas's historical account is indeed blinkered and that it requires significant reworking to take account of the social and political transformations that have taken place during the 'modern' period. (In his recent writings, Habermas has had more to say about the barbaric underside of the Enlightenment and European colonialism (RR 130; DW 145–6; PT2 69). But Allen is right to note that he has not seen any reason to alter the main lines of his philosophy and social theory (Allen 2016: 72–3).)

However, it should be noted that, despite some equivocations, Habermas ultimately rejects the idea that historical developments by themselves can be taken as the sign and guarantor of truth or moral validity: 'An act of *insight* that arises from working through good reasons and is not contradicted by better arguments for the time being does not need *additional* genetic justification' (PT2 93–4). Hence, for instance, he wants us to view his justification of the system of basic rights and of constitutional democracy as being ultimately based in the discourse principle and not in genealogy. If we read it this way, there is no circularity in Habermas's argument.

But this is not the end of the matter. It raises a further question: if moral and political justification rests on the discourse principle, on what does the discourse principle rest for its justification? Why should discourse be trusted as a guarantor of truth or moral-practical insight? According to Allen, here too the historical reconstruction turns out to be essential to Habermas's argument. His discourse theory, and his discourse ethics in particular, ultimately rests on his modernisation theory (Allen 2016: 50–67). This is because the discourse principle (which states that norms are valid only if they could be accepted by all in a practical discourse) is acceptable only on the 'postmetaphysical' assumption that metaphysical or religious reasons are inadmissible as justifications for moral norms. This means that the discourse principle presupposes and makes sense only from 'the point of view that members of post-traditional societies themselves intuitively adopt' (IO 7). But if the justification for the discourse principle rests on Habermas's theory of modernisation, then his 'discourse ethics quite obviously can't serve as the normative foundation for that theory' (Allen 2016: 63). He seems to have found himself once again in a circle of self-confirmation.

However, it seems to me that there is a confusion here. Habermas pursues a number of strategies to justify his theory of discourse and his discourse principle, all of which are mutually reinforcing but none of which offers an irrefutable deduction: he reconstructs the implicit know-how of rational speakers; he refers to psychological studies of cognitive development; he offers philosophical arguments to demonstrate the 'unavoidability' of the pragmatic presuppositions of discourse; and he also presents a social-historical reconstruction, a story about the social evolution of rationality itself. But Habermas's discourse theory does not 'rest' on his theory of modernity as Allen claims.

First, the assumption of universal validity by no means arises for the first time in the post-traditional context. Habermas takes it for granted that all human beings endowed with language have always taken their beliefs and norms to be valid (e.g. true, right or good). Second, just as claims to universal validity are not peculiar to modern societies, so conflicts over validity are not peculiarly modern. Discursive practices of conflict resolution are as old as human civilisation itself. Hence, the discourse principle is entirely compatible with pre-modern lifeworlds and their practices of argumentation and conflict resolution, even if the role of discourse is not thematised or fully exploited in those contexts and even if the reasons that would be appealed to in those contexts would be unacceptable to us.

Habermas's point about the transition to post-traditional morality is that when widespread consensus on moral norms fails, as it does to a greater extent in pluralistic and intellectually conflictual societies, the cognitive and social pressures that result *compel us* to 'reassure ourselves in a reflexive manner of a residual normative substance' (IO 45). We do this, he argues, by developing practices of reasoning to make up for the failing consensus. But noting the peculiar relevance of discourse for resolving conflicts over norms in the modern period does not essentially *tie* discourse theory or discourse ethics to modernity. What changes in the post-traditional context is merely that we are thrown back on the resources of reason in a more emphatic fashion, since we can no longer assume a moral consensus and we must generate consensus on universal validity. The discourse principle, therefore, does articulate a distinctively 'modern' consciousness insofar as we moderns simply take it for granted that argumentation is the appropriate court of appeal for disputes over validity rather than, say, consulting the sages. But it does not, for all that, tie the discourse principle *as such* to modern conditions.[10]

At the same time, Habermas does claim that the beliefs and norms of the modern West have benefited from a long history of contestation and critical scrutiny. This process of 'rationalisation', which has ancient origins, was catalysed in the West by the process of secularisation which marks the beginning of the modern period. Furthermore, according to Habermas, not only beliefs and norms but also practices of justification themselves have evolved over time.[11] We have revised our understanding of what will count as *good* reasons in light of what we have learned as attempts to offer reasons have been subjected to critical scrutiny. And, just as importantly, we have learned to clearly distinguish between claims about what is the case (truth claims) from claims about what should be the case (normative claims). It is for this reason, in particular, that Habermas regards the *modern* worldview to be superior to *mythical* worldviews (see Russell 2017: 179–87). But this is not to deny that learning processes of a similar kind (or other kinds) have occurred in non-Western societies, albeit differently. Nor is it to claim that in the West the learning process has reached completion. After all, as Habermas says: 'The whole thrust of postmetaphysical thinking [is] to deconstruct the divine standpoint which by definition has the last word. Its place is taken by the impartiality of the practice of argumentation among participants to which there is no alternative' (PT2 96).

It seems to me plausible that Habermas is prevented by his assumptions about 'the developmental superiority and unavoidability of certain features of European modernity' from engaging in genuine dialogue across cultural divides, as Allen (2016: 73) claims (see also Chakrabarty 2002: 33–6). Certainly, Habermas's own attempts to engage in cross-cultural dialogue on questions of political theory have been minimal. And it may well be that Habermas and his ilk have considerable 'unlearning' to do in order to correct for their Eurocentric biases (Bhambra 2016). However, from a theoretical point of view, if genuine dialogue is the ideal, then this line of criticism is ultimately not a repudiation of the Habermasian conception of discourse but rather an attempt to more adequately realise its ideal. On this point, Habermas's critics are Habermasians after all. They merely think that for genuine dialogue to be possible it must be accompanied by an intellectual humility that is not exhibited by Eurocentric thinkers like Habermas. That is undoubtedly true. But, if we take Habermas at his word, he agrees completely with these exhortations in principle. As he stated recently:

> ... intercultural discourses about the foundations of a more just international order can no longer be conducted one-sidedly, from the perspective of 'first movers'. These discourses must become habitual under the symmetrical conditions of mutual perspective-taking if the global players are to finally bring their social-Darwinist power games under control. The West is one participant among others, and all participants must be willing to be enlightened by others about their respective blind spots. (PT2 60)

A Note on the Question of Progress, Modernisation and Social Learning

This leaves the question of what to do with the very notions of 'modernity' and 'progress'. Are these notions irredeemably compromised by imperialistic assumptions? Or are they, on the contrary, indispensable categories of thought? For her part, Allen takes the view that the way forward for critical theory is to abandon talk of 'historical progress' altogether, at least as macro-level descriptions

(Allen 2016: 225–30). She acknowledges that we can judge specific historical developments to be 'progressive' or 'regressive' by applying normative standards. But we cannot meaningfully judge history as a whole to be either 'progressive' or 'regressive'. Nor can we use alleged facts about 'historical progress' to justify the normative standards that we employ (Allen 2016: 32–3). Likewise, Allen argues that the very idea of 'modernity' is problematic. The most succinct justification for this claim is given by Dipesh Chakrabarty, whom Allen (2016: 23) cites: 'Can the designation of something or some group as *non-* or *premodern* ever be anything but a gesture of the powerful?' (Chakrabarty 2002: xix).

Nonetheless, there is still considerable disagreement in the literature over the category of modernity and over the question of how the full diversity of social histories across different global contexts should be described once we abandon the ideological biases of the 'Occidental understanding of the world' (see Delanty 2006). Many theorists maintain that the category of 'modernity' retains meaning and relevance even once we correct for Eurocentric biases. Nicos Mouzelis (1999), for instance, has argued that, far from being a sign of 'the uniqueness of the West', the dynamic of modernity can be seen at work in all human societies, even though for historically contingent reasons the process of modernisation took off in Western Europe. Similarly, Shmuel Eisenstadt has sought to describe a set of 'multiple and divergent modernities' which were seeded by Axial Civilisation, became widespread in Europe, and were then appropriated by non-European societies each in their own way (Eisenstadt 2001: 333). (Eisenstadt's concept of 'multiple modernities' has been adopted by Habermas himself in recent years; see PT2 59–60.) Influenced by Habermas's own articulation of 'modern consciousness' (PDM 1–22), other theorists understand 'modernity' not so much as a historical epoch as a mentality of self-reflective transformation or creative self-overcoming (Delanty 2006: 275). All we can say at this juncture is that the debates over the uses and significance of concepts of progress, modernity and social development remain very much open.

Conclusion

The great strength of Habermas's intellect has always been his remarkable ability to bring modern life into view as a complex whole, capturing nuances as well as large-scale trends. However, feminist,

Marxist and postcolonial critics have exposed serious limitations in Habermas's social theory, especially with regard to its ability to account for well-documented structures of power and domination in the contemporary world. To some extent, Habermas has sought to modify his framework in light of these criticisms. But his theoretical framework remains inadequate in a number of respects. It could be said that his great strength – his breadth of scope – has proved to be his greatest weakness, as Habermas has found himself lacking sufficiently detailed analyses of social phenomena at both the interpersonal and societal levels. While his historical and sociological analyses are not without merit, in retrospect it appears that the most robust contributions in Habermas's corpus are to be found in his work on the pragmatics of communication and the theory of discourse. In the final chapters of the book, we shall consider whether these are sufficient to found a compelling theory of law and democracy.

Notes

1. These are features of the medium of money which make it useful as a medium of exchange according to Habermas. See TCA2 264–5.
2. Descriptions of law (and not just power) as a 'medium' are found in both TCA2 365, and BFN 302, 320. These confusions are apparently a hangover from Parsons's theory of political power, which Habermas follows with some modifications.
3. For an attempt to resolve these theoretical problems, see Baxter (2011: 177–91).
4. Although, even during the 1970s Habermas's diagnosis that juridification was the primary cause of reification could only be plausibly applied to a small number of highly developed welfare states (see Scheuerman 2013: 580–81).
5. For an authoritative analysis of the economic data, see Piketty (2014).
6. For a discussion of the equivocations in Habermas's views on markets and morals, see Jütten (2013: 587–8, 594–5).
7. Theorists who have developed the critique of colonialism discussed here, following the pioneering work of Frantz Fanon and Edward Said, include Gurminder Bhambra, Dipesh Chakrabarty, Enrique Dussel, Walter Mignolo, Aníbal Quijano and Gayatri Chakravorty Spivak.
8. In an interview given in 1984, Habermas even denies that he has anything to learn from anti-imperialist and anti-capitalist struggles in the Third World as a critical theorist, and he also denies that his critical theory has any lessons of relevance for those engaged in such struggles. See Dews (1986: 187).

9. Dishonorable mentions are also found in Said (1994: 278) and Spivak (1987: 173, 275).
10. This reading places Habermas in closer proximity to Kant than Hegel (or, in the recent literature, closer to Forst than Honneth), without denying that worldviews and the practice of argumentation are themselves subject to development over time. Cf. Allen (2016: 77–8).
11. Here we need to distinguish between the norms justified *by* the practice of argumentation and the norms *of* the practice of argumentation. Allen's critique is hampered by a failure to consistently make this distinction.

5
Deliberative Democracy

We have traced the historical formation of the political organisation of society and shown why, from a sociological point of view, legal and political institutions have come to take on a constitutional and democratic form. But Habermas is aware that a historical reconstruction tells us why we have arrived at the situation we are in, but not whether the situation we are in is where we ought to be. In this chapter, therefore, we consider his answer to the question of the *legitimacy* of constitutional democracy. What makes constitutional democracy a just form of political association? How must democracy be institutionalised and practised in order to fulfil its promise of securing a context of freedom and equality for all? How must our existing legal and political institutions be reformed if they are to fulfil their promise and thereby enable us to realise our desire for freedom and equality, the dismantling of relations of domination?

Habermas takes on the challenge of explaining why an association of free and equal citizens must be conceptualised as a system of rights and instituted as a democratic form of life in *Between Facts and Norms* (1992, trans. 1996), his major contribution to legal and political philosophy. In Chapter 5.1, we situate Habermas's position within the history of Western political thought and, in particular, we present his work as an attempt to construct a coherent and compelling reformulation of the Locke-Rousseau-Kant tradition. We then survey Habermas's conceptual analysis of the system of rights in Chapter 5.2 and his analysis of the principles of the constitutional state in Chapter 5.3. In these discussions, we shall see that, for Habermas, it is essential that a well-organised political community also possesses a healthy democratic culture – and, in particular, a functioning public sphere. The freedom-guaranteeing potential of constitutional democracy atrophies without democratic participation. In Chapter 5.4, we situate Habermas's approach in relation to the well-known political philosophy of John Rawls and consider the sensitive question of the place of religion in the public sphere.

In more recent political writings, Habermas has expanded on a number of further topics in political theory. Most notably, he has dedicated a great deal of effort to considering the question of political legitimacy at the transnational and global level. The final part of this Chapter, 5.5, surveys Habermas's constructive contributions to the debates over the European Union and the future of the United Nations.

5.1 The Sovereign State and Consent of the People

Jürgen Habermas's constructive political philosophy can be understood as an attempt to resolve a tension that has characterised Western political thought since the time of Hobbes at least. The tension is that between the principle of sovereignty and the principle of consent: between the right of the state to overrule the will of citizens and the right of the people to overrule the state.

Already in the medieval period, legal theorists were aware of this tension. In an effort to explain why monarchs, unlike ordinary people, enjoyed the right to levy taxes and proclaim laws, legal theorists in the twelfth and thirteenth centuries developed the principle of *ratio publicae utilitatis* ('by reason of the utility of what is public'). According to this principle, the 'superior right' of the 'kingly estate' is justified because it is equally in the interests of all that the kingly estate be endowed with such privileges. As Miguel Vatter explains, 'the reason (*ratio*) that gives a superior right (*jus*) to an office or estate (*status*) [. . .] grows out of the judgment that the kingly estate exists for the good of the public, or of the entire society (*status regni*)' (Vatter 2008: 245).

Yet the same legal principle implies that the sovereign's 'superior right' is legitimate only insofar as it in fact serves the good ('utility') of the society as a whole. Who then is to judge what serves the good of society as a whole? In answer to this question, medieval jurists converged on the principle that 'whatever touches all, must be consented by all' (*quod omnes tangit, ab omnibus approbetur*). In practice, this legal principle obliged the sovereign to legislate with 'the counsel and consent of his council', a body within which full powers of representation (*plena potestas*) had to be extended to all affected (Post 1964: 113). The test that verifies the 'public utility' of the kingly estate and affirms its 'superior right' is the fact that all affected parties are willing to give their un-coerced consent to new laws.

The medieval principle thus established both: (1) the superiority of the decision-making and coercive power of the state over private individuals – including the right of the state to interpret and decide what the good of the community requires; and (2) the superiority of the political community as a whole over the sovereign in its right to consent to policies affecting its interests.

The tension between the principle of sovereignty and the principle of consent in the medieval legal doctrine has persisted as a theme in modern Western political theory to the present day. It was source of debate in the early modern period, most notably in the work of Hobbes, Locke, Rousseau and Kant, and the same basic tension underlies the dispute between Schmitt and Habermas in the twentieth century, as we shall see in Chapter 6. Habermas's own position broadly speaking opposes the Hobbesian tradition and endorses the Locke-Rousseau-Kant tradition. And so, by way of introduction, we will first rehearse the disagreements over sovereignty and consent in the early modern period and consider Habermas's critical reception of these arguments (5.1) before considering Habermas's own position in detail (5.2–5.5).

Sovereignty and consent in Hobbes

In the context of the English Civil War, Thomas Hobbes provided an innovative justification for the absolute power of the state via the idea of a 'civil' contract. Free and equal persons have reason to enter into a 'civil state' and to install a sovereign with irresistible power over them: although this entails giving up unfettered freedom of choice and entering into a relationship of mutual obligations and legal rights, such a state is preferable to the state of nature since it aids survival and preserves individual freedom to the greatest extent possible.

Hobbes's argument proceeds from a conventional starting point: the authority of the sovereign must be consented to by the people. But his novel reasoning, which locates the act of consent in a hypothetical act of entering into a civil contract, leads to a radical conclusion: citizens who already live under the rule of a sovereign do not have the right to withhold consent from the sovereign and the sovereign's judgements. Why? Hobbes reasoned as follows. The goal of leaving 'the state of nature' and entering into a 'civil state' is to overcome the threat of internal division and warfare. But this goal cannot be fulfilled if there is any doubt about who has final authority to make law and to judge in matters of law; there can be no question of who and what must be obeyed. 'Obedience' to the sovereign is a condition of 'protection' by the sovereign (Hobbes 1994: 219). Hence, when the people consent to be ruled by a sovereign, the people must be taken to *alienate* any claim they might have to exercise a role as a final court of appeal in questions of what is right (i.e. lawful). In fact, they must cede to the sovereign the authority to decide what is in the common interest of all (see Ivison 1997: 130–36; Chambers 2009: 252–4).

Hobbes's argument for the necessary supremacy of the sovereign's decision-making power in matters of law rests on the fact of pluralism. Roughly, the argument runs as follows. The opinions of the public are diverse and inconsistent. To assume that 'the public' can and should decide matters of law is a recipe for incoherence and can only lead to the dissolution of legality itself. A sovereign power with the ability to make singular and coherent decisions must therefore be established to tame the clamour of conflicting opinion and to establish the unitary voice of the law. This voice of the law will inevitably contradict the opinion of at least some; but this outcome is necessary in order for the higher good of public law and order to be realised. An argument of this kind is meant to give reasons – reasons that are acceptable to all – for the legitimacy of coercive rule by the sovereign, even when its decisions contradict public opinion (or some segment of public opinion).

Habermas's political theory belongs broadly to the social contract tradition initiated by Hobbes. It offers a reflection upon how a group of people can rationally construct a constitutional framework to govern their life together as a political community. What's more, Habermas agrees with Hobbes that there can be no legal order without a set of political institutions empowered to make law and to decide how legal norms are to be applied. He calls this the 'internal relation between law and politics' (BFN 133–51).

Nonetheless, Habermas rejects Hobbes's reasoning about the civil contract and his endorsement of the absolutist state. According to Hobbes, the absolutist state can be justified purely on the basis of individuals' 'enlightened self-interest' (BFN 90). However, implicit in Hobbes's argument, Habermas contends, is a view of what is morally justified and not just what is pragmatically preferable. Specifically, the argument trades on the intuition that liberty – specifically, the private autonomy of participants in a market economy – is a 'good' for individuals and for society at large. The absolutist state is then justified insofar as it secures this 'good' through enforcing the system of property rights (BFN 91). In other words, while Hobbes hoped to demonstrate the rational acceptability of the absolutist state purely on the basis of individuals' 'enlightened self-interest', in truth he implicitly offers a *normative* justification for the constitutional state.

The upshot of this insight, for Habermas, is that a social contract theory cannot proceed on the model of rational choice theory; if it is to justify a model of political organisation it must proceed by way of normative reasoning. Specifically, we must suppose that parties to a social contract are able to think from the standpoint of the 'we', not just the 'I', i.e. are able to judge what is in *the equal interest of all*. In other words, we cannot understand how a system of rights would be endorsed by a set of individuals unless we assume from the outset that these individuals are communicative agents, and not merely strategically acting, success-oriented agents. But that is to say we must assume that the individuals entering into a political association already possess powers of moral, ethical and pragmatic reasoning, and that they understand what the practice of discourse requires of them (BFN 110). On this basis, Habermas will go on to offer a quite different reconstruction of the social contract, one that includes rights of democratic participation from the outset.

Sovereignty and consent in Locke, Rousseau and Kant

The theory that Habermas defends is a descendant of the Locke-Rousseau-Kant tradition. In opposition to Hobbes, John Locke asserts that the public must retain its standing as a final court of appeal in questions of 'public utility' as an inalienable right. This is because the people are the source of the 'deputised' authority of the prince or legislative power. The people, therefore, always hold a legitimate claim to decide whether that authority has breached its trust. What's more, the role of the public as judge of the prince or legislative authority cannot itself be expropriated or deputised to a higher court or guardian set over the prince or legislative authority, since this would simply institute a new deputised authority whose acts may be placed in question by the people. Therefore, the people alone can be and must be the final judge of the legitimacy of the sovereign's actions (the only higher court being God himself). The role of the people as a final court of appeal is thus inalienable (Locke 1980: 123; see Ivison 1997: 136–40; Chambers 2009: 254–9).

Jean-Jacques Rousseau champions the sovereignty of the people and gives this concept force in a way that decisively goes beyond earlier theories. He denies, for instance, that any transfer of sovereignty from the people to the ruler ever takes place. Hence, no ruler can ever be said to have been given the authority to overrule the will of the people. The will of the people must determine the content of law if that law is to be legitimate. What then counts as the will of the people? In Book II, Chapter 3, of the *Social Contract*, Rousseau articulates the view that the will of the people should be identified with the 'general will', that is, the demand for what is equally in the interests of all. This 'general will' is to be distinguished from the 'will of all' (the aggregate of all individual wills), which can err (Rousseau 1968: 72). (For instance, the people may be misled into demanding something that is not in the interests of all.) How then is the content of the general will to be determined? The general will, which is 'always rightful', is what emerges from 'the deliberations of a people properly informed' (Rousseau 1968: 73).

Like Locke and Rousseau, Immanuel Kant rejects Hobbes's conception of the sovereign as a supreme individual to whom the people must submit themselves – but for different reasons. Influenced by the thought of Rousseau, Kant's 'republican' conviction is that the purpose of political association is freedom, and that freedom exists when the people are only subject to laws that they give themselves (see Pettit 2013). For Kant, as for Rousseau, the general or united will of the people is sovereign; and legislative authority resides with the people (BFN 496). For laws to be legitimate, then, they must be understood to be co-authored and consented to by citizens who freely unite in a 'public will' (Kant 1996a: 295).

And yet, Kant sides with Hobbes against Locke when he argues that resistance towards the state is always unlawful (Kant 1996a: 462–4). Why is resistance towards the state always unlawful? On one hand, Kant reasons that the state of law is always to be preferred to a state of nature since without a state of law it is impossible to be free in our relations with each other (see Flikschuh 2008). On the other hand, Kant argues that the *actual* consent of the people is not required in order for laws to be legitimate. In fact, the legislator has the right to make laws that are contrary to the will of the people and to require that those laws be obeyed. How is this consistent with the principle of popular sovereignty? Extending Rousseau's distinction between the 'general will' and the 'will of all', Kant gives the principle of popular consent a 'counterfactual' or 'hypothetical' reading. As Kant interprets it, this principle amounts to nothing more than the idea of a hypothetical 'original contract' which binds the legislator to

... give his laws in such a way that they *could* have arisen from the united will of a whole people and to regard each subject, insofar as he wants to be a citizen, as if he has joined in voting for such a will. For this is the touchstone of any public law's conformity with right. In other words, if a public law is so constituted that a whole people *could not possibly* give its consent to it [. . .], it is unjust. (Kant 1996a: 296–7)

The principle of consent so conceived enables the *legislator* to determine a law's 'conformity with right' without having to test its acceptability in the eyes of the people. All that is required is to show that it would not be contradictory for the people to consent to the law. Thanks to this interpretation of the principle of consent, Kant's model of state sovereignty does not ultimately diverge significantly in practice from Hobbes's, despite Kant's republican convictions.

Where Kant's model does differ from Hobbes's model is in the role it gives to 'the public use of reason'. In an age of criticism, Kant argues, both church and state must submit to free and public examination ('the public use of reason') lest they attract the 'just suspicion' that comes upon those who seek to exempt themselves and their doctrines from critical scrutiny (Kant 1998: 100–1). Hence, a wise and prudent government will accept the existence of 'an opposition party' consisting, in the first instance, of 'the philosophy faculty's bench', and it will listen to what its servants present to it regarding questions of truth and reason (Kant 1996b: 261).

As we shall see, both the liberal ideal of private autonomy (as per Locke) and the democratic ideal of popular sovereignty (as per Rousseau) are fundamental to Habermas's conception of political legitimacy (Chapter 5.2). What's more, Kant's idea of public criticism provides inspiration for Habermas's 'two-track model' of deliberative politics (Chapter 5.3). However, it is also important to note that Habermas identifies some problems with the contributions of Locke, Rousseau and Kant, and that his political theory is by no means simply a rehash of their ideas.

The liberal tradition represented by Locke is seen by Habermas as one-sided. It does not perceive that 'the claim to legitimacy on the part of a legal order built on rights can be redeemed only through the socially integrative force of the "concurring and united will of all" free and equal citizens' (BFN 32). Habermas argues that liberal rights must be complemented by democratic rights in order to establish a legitimate system of laws (Chapter 5.2). On the other hand, for reasons we shall discuss below, Habermas finds Rousseau's conception of popular sovereignty untenable. Instead, he argues for a new model of democratic politics and a new conception of popular sovereignty, one that dissolves the idea of the 'general will' or 'public will' into the 'subjectless' flow of communications that take place via democratic procedures and 'the communicative network of public spheres' (BFN 299). At the same stroke, he replaces Kant's austere and rationalist interpretation of popular consent with a more democratic and empirically grounded interpretation of consent (Chapter 5.3).

5.2 The Democratic Principle and the System of Rights

Habermas repeatedly sounds a fundamental note in his mature political writings: democracy and the rule of law are not incompatible but are actually 'co-original'; the rule of law must go hand in hand with democracy. Habermas's discourse theory of law and democracy is supposed to justify and amplify this central thought. In this part of Chapter 5, we shall examine his argument for this claim in stages.

THE DEMOCRATIC PRINCIPLE

Habermas is convinced that the legal system plays a vital role in complex and pluralistic modern societies. Legal rules provide a means to secure social cohesion when moral consensus cannot be assumed and when social subsystems have taken on a life of their own (see Chapter 3.1). But for a system of laws to serve such ends, it needs to be legitimate – or, at least, be seen to be legitimate from the perspective of those who are subject to the laws. Otherwise, the legal rules will be experienced as unjust and oppressive, and they will be the cause of social conflict rather than of social cohesion. How then can laws be generated and applied in contemporary societies in such a way as to ensure the legitimacy of the legal system?

Habermas contrasts his own answer to these questions with two dominant traditional approaches. *Legal positivism* hold that the legitimacy of laws can be guaranteed by a process of lawmaking that is itself 'legal' in the sense of taking place in accordance with accepted legal procedures. There are no further questions to be answered about the legitimacy of laws beyond whether they are legally enacted. The legitimacy of law therefore ultimately rests on customary practices of lawmaking, customary practices that are already accepted and that cannot be further justified. By contrast, *natural law theory* holds that the legitimacy of laws derives from a rational (i.e. philosophical or theological) justification that can be given for those laws independently of how they are enacted. That is, the validity of laws derives from their relationship to non-legal norms or principles that stand above the law, e.g. norms of 'natural justice'.

Habermas endorses elements of both approaches, but he also argues that both approaches are flawed. The procedure of lawmaking is a vital component that underwrites the legitimacy of laws. But legal positivists are wrong to think that legitimacy can be guaranteed simply by a process of lawmaking that is itself legal. To produce legitimate law, something more demanding is required: the procedure of lawmaking must itself be *legitimate*. The question of legitimacy thus reappears, and it must be answered by an appeal to reasons. On this point, Habermas sides with the tradition of rational natural law. However, in pluralistic modern societies, a lawmaking process cannot be deemed legitimate by virtue of the fact that it accords with basic norms or principles derived from philosophical or religious worldviews. Whatever the reasons are that make a lawmaking process legitimate, they must be independent of metaphysical or religious commitments (BFN 135, 448; LT 47).

Habermas offers a third way, an alternative to both legal positivism and natural law theory, which he calls a discourse theory of law. According to this view, laws acquire legitimacy neither from their 'legal form' nor from their 'moral content', but through the '*procedure* of lawmaking' (BFN 135): more specifically, laws are legitimate if they are found to be acceptable to all citizens in 'a consensual procedure of deliberation and decision-making' (LT 48). It is the democratic procedure that 'provides the statute with its justice' (BFN 189). This view requires some justification and some explanation.

Why should we think that a democratic procedure of deliberation and decision-making will secure the validity of laws? The justification for this procedural view of legitimacy rests upon Habermas's discourse theory (see Chapter 1.1). In particular, it rests on Habermas's 'discourse principle', which articulates the standard for the validity of any practical norm. The discourse principle states that 'Just those action norms are valid to which all possibly affected persons could agree as participants in rational discourses' (BFN 107). In other words, the discourse principle says that an inclusive process of reasoning is the sole forum in which the validity of normative claims can be demonstrated. For instance, the obligating force of moral norms is demonstrated through a discourse including all people in which the validity of the norm is tested. Likewise, legal rules must prove their validity through a process of discursive testing.

However, legal discourse is a variety of practical discourse that is distinct from moral, ethical and pragmatic discourse (see Chapter 1.2). It is distinct for at least three reasons (BFN 107–11).

The first reason is that the lawmaking process produces norms that are addressed to a determinate set of *citizens* and that are binding within a determinate *territorial area*. If the validity of norms must be acknowledged by 'all affected', then in the case of legal norms the 'all' refers to the set of citizens subject to the laws, an abstract community 'first produced by legal norms themselves' (BFN 112). The scope of the 'all' for legal-political discourse is thus more circumscribed than for moral discourse, which in principle includes all human beings.[1]

The second distinctive feature of legal discourse is that it is a 'mixed' form of discourse. Legal rules need to be rationally acceptable in a number of different ways. They need to be practically feasible (pragmatic reason). They need to be morally impartial (moral reason). They need to be culturally appropriate (ethical reasoning). Legal discourse is distinct from moral, ethical and pragmatic discourse not because it involves a distinct fourth kind of reasoning, but because it draws on all forms of practical reasoning at the same time (BFN 108; IO 215–18).

The third distinctive feature of legal discourse derives from the fact that the authority to enact laws rests with a legislative body. Unlike moral and ethical norms, which are negotiated through an informal and open-ended dialogue among a community of people, legal rules can be 'enacted' through a formal process of lawmaking. Not all citizens are empowered to make binding decisions about proposed laws, and it is not expected that all citizens will personally evaluate proposed laws and debate their merits, despite the fact that they will be bound by these laws.[2]

When the lawmaking process is delegated to a legislative body, the citizenry's conviction that laws are legitimate must be sustained by their trust in the 'reasonable quality' of the delegated procedure of lawmaking (BFN 304). Specifically, citizens must be confident that the outcomes of the legislative process *would have been* acceptable to them (and, indeed, to *all* citizens) had they been able to participate personally in the deliberations and decision-making. Hence, for example, as an ordinary citizen Paula might have reservations about a bill before parliament, but she can (according to Habermas) view the resulting legislation as acceptable if she believes that her concerns will have been considered in the lawmaking process and judged to be outweighed by other considerations (about which she is perhaps not well informed). This level of confidence is warranted only if citizens have reason to believe that all relevant information and the opinions of all citizens will have been properly considered in the deliberative process. This is why the legitimacy of the procedure of lawmaking rests on its being sufficiently *inclusive* and *discursive*, since only under these conditions will citizens have reason to believe the laws are rationally justifiable to all. (The same will be true when it comes to the application of law by the courts.)

When it is applied to the question of the legitimacy of lawmaking in this way, the discourse principle assumes the shape of a 'principle of democracy': the principle that lawmaking must be institutionalised as a democratic procedure. Habermas formalises his democratic principle of legitimacy as follows: 'only those statutes may claim legitimacy that can meet with the assent of all citizens in a discursive process of legislation that in turn has been legally constituted' (BFN 110).

On this conception, the 'assent of all citizens' is taken seriously as the touchstone of democracy (BFN 496). However, this principle of universal assent is not interpreted in a plebiscitary fashion. (Indeed, Habermas regards this as an incoherent interpretation.) Rather, it is interpreted as a demand that all citizens be able to endorse the legislative process as having a 'reasonable quality'. Habermas thus endorses a 'counterfactual' interpretation of popular consent insofar as his standard of legitimacy does not require that all citizens concur with the results of the lawmaking process. On the other hand, his democratic principle of legitimacy does require that all citizens be able to judge that the lawmaking process itself is rationally acceptable. In this way, Habermas sees himself as correcting the democratic deficit in Kant's principle of legitimacy (see Chapter 5.1).

From the Democratic Principle to the System of Rights

The principle of democracy does not tell us how the discursive process of legislation must be organised ('legally constituted') within a political community in order to satisfy the standard of democratic legitimacy. It simply says that laws can only be regarded as legitimate if they are the product of a legally constituted deliberative process of lawmaking that all citizens can see as appropriately inclusive and discursive. Nonetheless, according to Habermas, there are features that any such political process must possess if it is to be legitimate. (These features are necessary but not sufficient for satisfying the standard of democratic legitimacy.) In particular, Habermas argues that a system of basic rights can be derived from the democratic principle of legitimacy. How so?

Habermas claims that a system of rights can be derived by reflecting on the presuppositions of 'the performative meaning of the practice of self-determination on the part of legal consociates who recognize one another as free and equal members of an association they have joined voluntarily' (BFN 110). In other words, the system of basic rights which Habermas articulates is an expression of the rights that citizens must grant to one another if they are to operate as an association of free and equal members of a political community that governs itself through democratic lawmaking. His system of rights is not derived from natural law, nor is it presented as a set of inferences about what participants in some ideal constitution-making situation would agree to (à la Rawls). Rather it is presented as nothing more than an explication of what is presupposed by 'the intersubjective practice of self-legislation in the medium of positive law' (BFN 129).

How then does Habermas's derivation proceed? The basic strategy is to clarify in the abstract what types of 'subjective freedoms of action [citizens] must confer on each other before they can legitimately regulate any given matter by means of modern law' (LT 49). To this end, Habermas applies the discourse principle to the legal form in a stepwise fashion. His presentation follows the following path (BFN 121–31):

1. The discourse principle is applied to the general right to equal liberties. (This yields three basic rights of 'private autonomy'.)
2. The discourse principle is then applied to specify the legal rights necessary for the discursive exercise of political autonomy. (This yields the basic rights of 'public autonomy'.)
3. The discursive exercise of political autonomy in turn leads to an elaboration of the legal shape of private autonomy. This yields a further set of rights ('social rights').

The next section traces the three steps of Habermas's presentation in more detail.

The system of rights

(a) Rights of private autonomy

Habermas's presentation begins with Kant's 'universal principle of right'. The universal principle of right represents laws as rules aimed at resolving conflicts that arise from *social action*, specifically, conflicts that arise when the behaviour of one affects the options available to others. In such matters, a particular form of practical reason is required to determine the legitimacy of behaviour, a form of reasoning about norms of 'rightfulness'. Kant's principle states that individuals act 'rightfully' if their action 'can coexist with everyone's freedom [of choice] in accordance with a universal law' (Kant 1996a: 387). On the one hand, the test of 'rightfulness' means that laws are to be *freedom-preserving*. On the other hand, because rights articulated in the form of laws or legal statutes are addressed to all subjects and afford *the same* liberties to all legal persons, they institute a form of *equality*. The system of rights is thus supposed to 'protect the autonomy' or 'secure the freedom' of 'all persons equally' (IO 257). Following this principle, Habermas asserts that 'a legal code should be set up in the form of *legitimately distributed* rights that guarantee the protection of the private autonomy of legal subjects' (BFN 124). The first and most basic category of rights, therefore, is:

1. Basic rights that result from the politically autonomous elaboration of the *right to the greatest possible measure of equal individual liberties*.

The next two categories of rights are presented as 'necessary correlates' of the first.[3] Because legal rules are elaborated by members of the legal community and apply to members of the legal community, rules of membership are essential. The legal community must self-define, and the rights of citizens must be distinguished from those of aliens.[4] Hence, the second category of rights is:

2. Basic rights that result from the politically autonomous elaboration of the *status of a member* in a voluntary association of consociates under law.

Furthermore, the idea of rights implies 'actionability': the legal community must ensure that the rights of members are recognised and that members of the legal community are able to make appeals on the basis of their rights. Habermas thus suggests that basic rights of due process – such as equal legal protection, equal claim to a legal hearing and claims to equal treatment before the law – can be justified 'in light of the discourse principle' (BFN 125). (He does not attempt to lay out that justification itself.) The third category of rights, therefore, is:

3. Basic rights that result immediately from the *actionability* of rights and from the politically autonomous elaboration of individual *legal protection*.

(b) Rights of public autonomy

The fourth category of rights provides citizens with the standing to be *authors* of laws and not merely their *addressees*. Rights of public autonomy provide the liberties necessary for citizens to exercise their political autonomy, i.e. to participate in the collective practices of self-governance through the public use of reason.

4. Basic rights to equal opportunities to participate in processes of opinion- and will-formation in which citizens exercise their *political autonomy* and through which they generate legitimate law. (BFN 123)

Unlike the set of rights to private autonomy (1, 2 and 3 above), the rights of public autonomy are easily derived from the principle of democracy. As Habermas succinctly puts it:

> The conditions under which citizens can judge whether the law they make is legitimate (in light of the discourse principle) must in turn be legally guaranteed. This end is served by the basic political rights to participate in processes that form the legislator's opinion and will. (BFN 127)

Like all rights, however, rights of public autonomy are legitimate only to the extent that they accord with the universal principle of right: the liberties they afford are rightful only to the extent that they are compatible with the same liberty for all. This implies that the rights of public autonomy must provide *equal opportunities* for the public use of reason and must provide for democratic procedures in which all have an *equal opportunity* to participate (BFN 127).

(c) Social rights

In every society, it will be the case that material and social conditions affect the ability of citizens to take up their rights of private autonomy and public autonomy. It is possible for citizens to possess rights in law but to have no resources or real opportunities to exercise those rights. If a political community is to enact its intention to found a political association of free and equal citizens under law, then it must collectively accept responsibility for ensuring that all members of the association have at least the minimum social conditions of existence necessary to enable them to exercise their rights of private and public autonomy and to participate in the political association as free and equal members. The integrity of the political association itself is undermined if social conditions preclude participation by all members of the association in the manner required by the principle of democracy. Civil rights must therefore be 'supplemented' by social rights (CEU 79):

5. Basic rights to the provision of living conditions that are socially, technologically and ecologically safeguarded, insofar as the current circumstances make this necessary if citizens are to have equal opportunities to utilise the civil rights listed in (1) through (4).

This fifth and final category of rights is 'relative' to the four categories listed above in the sense that it merely aims at ensuring that citizens are genuinely able to possess and make use of those rights.

We cannot say in the abstract what this standard will require in any particular social context. This is a matter that needs to be considered and resolved by the members of the political association themselves. This will involve a learning process and even a re-learning process as social conditions change. Nonetheless, some lessons have been learned over the course of Western political history. For instance, it is not enough that the law ensures equal opportunities for all private citizens to secure their means of living through participation in the market economy (as per the liberal or neo-liberal paradigm). Enjoying equal rights of private autonomy is not equivalent to being a free and equal member of a political association. What is required, in addition to equal enjoyment of liberal rights, are equal opportunities for participation in the *political* life of the society.

Furthermore, the principle of democratic legitimacy provides a compelling reason why a political community must effectively counteract social disadvantage, poverty, marginalisation, discrimination and social relationships of domination. Not simply because inequalities *per se* offend against a principle of justice (e.g. a fair distribution of material wealth). Nor because the equal worth of moral persons should be reflected by an egalitarian social order. But rather because material and social inequalities, if sufficiently egregious, can materially affect the ability of certain individuals and social groups to participate as peers in the political life of the society, and hence can undermine the legitimacy of the legal order itself (BFN 388–427). What is needed, Habermas argues, is a set of social policies that facilitates what Nancy Fraser (2003: 36) calls 'parity of participation' for all citizens, i.e. social arrangements that 'permit all (adult) members of society to interact with one another as peers'.

Resolving the paradox of constitutional democracy

By laying out a set of basic rights and saying that these are required for any collective that is intent on democratic self-organisation, it might appear that Habermas paternalistically imposes a series of constraints on the democratic process. But he insists that this is not the case.

The first point to note is that the rights that Habermas enumerates are presented as 'unsaturated placeholders' (BFN 125). There must be a 'politically autonomous elaboration' of these abstract rights by those who aim to establish a political association. That is to say, these rights need to be interpreted and codified by a constitution-making process. The need for a 'politically autonomous elaboration' of rights is stressed by Habermas because rights need to be given by citizens to themselves if they are to be instituted in a democratic manner. For the same reason, as we shall discuss in Chapter 6, Habermas argues that we must view even constitutional law as an ongoing 'project', not as a fixed inheritance, since only under this interpretation can democracy continue to be an exercise of self-determination (BFN 384; CD 766–76).

Still, Habermas maintains that the rights the people confer on themselves and elaborate for themselves must reflect the abstract categories enumerated by the discourse theory of democracy (BFN 125–6). Is this not a paternalistic imposition and a limitation of the sovereignty of the people?

In response, Habermas argues that his system of rights is not in any way a challenge to the 'sovereignty' of the people. It is merely a specification of what will count as a democratic association of free and equal consociates under law (BFN 126). In other words, the system of rights merely articulates what the framers of a constitution and what democratic citizens are already constrained by insofar as they aim to express and preserve their political autonomy using the legal medium.

... as soon as the legal medium is used to institutionalize the exercise of political autonomy, these rights become necessary enabling conditions; as such, they cannot *restrict* the legislator's sovereignty, even though they are not at her disposition. Enabling conditions do not impose any limitation on what they constitute. (BFN 128)

In short, both the system of rights and the idea of democracy are implied by the singular intention to 'establish a voluntary association of free and equal legal consociates' and to formulate this association 'in the language of modern law' (LT 49). On one hand, persons can be 'free' and 'equal' only insofar as they enjoy the same rights. On the other hand, they are only 'free' and 'equal' if they are also the authors of those very rights. Hence, there is no antagonism between ('liberal') rights of private autonomy and ('republican') rights of public autonomy; they belong together as a freedom-conferring package and this is what justifies the basic model of constitutional democracy.

We can now see why Habermas presents his discourse theory of law and democracy as a resolution to the ongoing conflict between the 'liberal' and 'republican' traditions in political theory. Liberals argue that the subjective freedoms of citizens in market-based societies should be treated as the foundation of any political association. According to liberals, laws (including constitutions) are legitimate 'only if they are consistent with human rights stipulated in advance by morality, in which case the democratic legislator cannot make legitimate decisions in a sovereign way, but only within imposed constraints' (LT 48; also CD 770). However, according to Habermas, this assertion of the priority of liberal rights sets itself at odds with the ideal of democracy, and unnecessarily so. Provided that liberal rights are interpreted strictly as articulating the requirements of self-organisation *under the form of law*, and not as imposing a set of *moral* demands, then they are perfectly consistent with the project of democracy.

By contrast, republicans argue that rights of political participation should be treated as foundational. According to republicans, laws (including constitutions) are always legitimate provided they emanate from the will of the people, from the people's 'ethical-political self-understanding' (CD 771). However, on this conception, the sovereign people can legitimately give itself 'any arbitrary constitution and enact any arbitrary norms', such that 'breaches of the norms of the rule of law cannot be ruled out' (LT 48–9). The error in the republican conception is that it fails to see that a democratic practice which violates the system of rights undermines the conditions of its very existence as a voluntary association of free and equal consociates under law. The system of rights is the only medium in which democracy can be practised self-consistently as a form of political association.

By integrating the rights of private and public autonomy within his discourse theory of law and democracy, Habermas sees himself as articulating a superior conceptual framework for political theory, one that preserves the insights of the liberal and republican traditions while at the same time overcoming their one-sidedness. But can such a system of rights be consistently institutionalised in a constitutional arrangement and in a form of democratic practice in complex modern societies?

5.3 *The Constitutional State and Deliberative Politics*

Habermas is at pains to point out that even if we possess a coherent and well-founded theory of the rights required by an association of free and equal consociates under law, the establishment of a set of such rights remains a 'metaphorical event' unless it is legally institutionalised in connection with the institutions of political power (BFN 132). In Chapter 3, we traced the historical development of the 'political' system. But now we turn to the normative question: under what conditions can we call 'just' or 'legitimate' not only laws but also the legal and political institutions to which they are tied?

In Habermas's model, the legitimacy of a political order rests on two basic principles: (1) *the principle of the rule of law*: the principle that every use of state power must be publicly authorised and legitimated in terms of legitimately enacted law; and (2) *the principle of popular sovereignty*: the principle that the legal system should convert the 'communicative power' of democratic opinion and will into legal form. Correspondingly, the two key questions, from an institutional point of view, are: (1) how can public institutions be organised so that they are 'programmed' by (and only by) legitimately enacted laws? And (2) how can the legislative process be organised so that it is steered by (and only by) democratic opinion and will? Habermas sketches an answer to these two questions in his account of the constitutional state and in his 'two-track model' of deliberative politics. We shall discuss these two components of his theory in turn.

The constitutional state

From his sociological analysis, Habermas concludes that the mechanism of law is the appropriate means available by which coercive power – both the administrative power of the state over its citizens and the social power of actors over each other – can be 'rationalised' and 'domesticated' (see Chapter 3.1). Hence, from a normative point of view, the state ought to be organised according to the rule of law in such a way as to neutralise its domination over us:

> ... the constitutional state has a twofold task: it must not only evenly divide and distribute political power but also strip such power of its violent substance by rationalizing it. The legal rationalization of force must not be conceived as taming a quasi-natural domination whose violent core is and always remains uncontrollably contingent. Rather, law is supposed to dissolve this irrational substance, converting it into a 'rule of law' in which alone the politically autonomous self-organization of the legal community expresses itself. (BFN 188–9)

The question that must be resolved at the level of institutional design, therefore, is how to ensure that the law rules, and in such a way that the state is non-dominating. What institutional structures will guard against the self-empowering and self-programming state? How can we ensure that the state performs all and only those tasks for which it is expressly authorised by democratically legitimate law? In short, how can a state be organised as a 'republic of laws'?

The model of the constitutional state that Habermas offers in response to these questions is not new. It articulates a familiar governmental structure with three distinct branches: legislative, judicial and executive. It defends the idea of the separation of powers and emphasises the need for the branches of government to monitor each other in order to ensure conformity with law. However, there are some distinctive features of Habermas's model that flow from his discourse-theoretic approach to political philosophy.

(1) *The legislative power*. For Habermas, as we have seen, legitimacy ultimately derives from procedures of deliberation and decision-making that can be viewed from the standpoint of citizens as guaranteeing 'a rational treatment of political questions' (BFN 170). A legally institutionalised system of democracy is well organised to the extent that it can sustain the presumption that decisions are made in a sufficiently deliberative fashion to warrant acceptance as valid. What shape must the legislative process take in order to

satisfy this criterion? The first difficulty that must be faced, as noted above, is that it is impossible for all citizens to participate in a process of debate and decision-making. Habermas nonetheless insists that a democratic system must involve a (sufficiently) egalitarian and inclusive procedure of face-to-face deliberation and decision (Chapter 5.2). This impasse is overcome by 'the parliamentary principle' which states that in order to be legitimate laws must be passed by representative assemblies (BFN 170). Although the argument is not spelled out in much detail, presumably the reason for the parliamentary principle is that a representative assembly, even though it contains only a relatively small number of citizens, can be *sufficiently* inclusive and egalitarian (and can satisfy the other procedural requirements) to justify a presumption of validity provided that it is sufficiently *representative*.

Habermas acknowledges that the parliamentary principle raises further questions. For instance, what is the proper composition of the representative body? How should members be elected? What procedures should be followed in organising parliamentary business and what rules should be followed in making binding decisions? Apart from brief remarks on the issue of representation (BFN 181–5) and the principle of majority rule (BFN 171, 179–80, 291–5), Habermas leaves these complex questions largely undiscussed. He simply asserts that such questions should be regulated 'in light of the discourse principle' (BFN 171).

(2) *The judicial power.* Citizens must enjoy basic liberties in relation to each other as well as 'rights against the state' to protect their private autonomy (BFN 174). The legal system must ensure that all such rights are 'actionable' (BFN 125, 455). Habermas calls this the principle of 'comprehensive legal protection for individuals'; that is, the principle that all citizens must be able to make claims based on rights they enjoy under law and have access to legal remedies in case of breaches (BFN 172). Practical requirements follow from this for the organisation and administration of the judicial system.

The principle of judicial independence has a different justification. The need to separate legislative and judicial powers follows from the distinction between 'discourses of justification' and 'discourses of application'. The standards of acceptability in adjudication, such as consistency and fairness, are quite unlike the standards of acceptability in lawmaking. The role of courts is to take the reasons that are packaged in statutes and to apply them consistently over time

(BFN 192). Furthermore, because the judiciary has at its disposal the ability to compel obedience, Habermas argues that it must be careful to 'treat existing law as law' and not make law itself (BFN 186). However, for this same reason, the judicial branch has a special responsibility to oversee the activities of the government (including its legislative activity) in order to ensure that they do not infringe upon the basic rights and constitutional rules that have been democratically instituted.

(3) *The administrative power*. Like the judiciary, the executive branch of government has to be bound by law in order to ensure that it is 'programmed' solely by the democratic decision-making of the legislative branch and that it does not become autonomous or 'self-programming' (BFN 188). The state apparatus must be legally empowered to implement all and only legally mandated programmes and to facilitate the activity of the legislative and judicial branches. Any executive decision or executive action that does not have statutory authorisation must be deemed illegal and invalid. For the same reason, the activity of the executive branch of government must remain 'subject to parliamentary oversight and judicial review' (BFN 188). Conversely, the administration must not be allowed to interfere in the legislative process (BFN 173–4, 192).

Over the course of time, the administrative state has taken on more and greater responsibilities, e.g. for ensuring public safety, public health, environmental protection and town planning. New administrative agencies have been set up to implement each of these new programmes and regulatory functions. In connection with each of these new domains of state activity, the same logic of the separation of powers should be applied. New modes of democratic accountability are called for as well as a range of new judicial bodies (e.g. administrative tribunals) to adjudicate disputes and hear complaints (BFN 190–3, 440–1).

THE TWO-TRACK MODEL OF DELIBERATIVE POLITICS

The principle of popular sovereignty is not satisfied by the mere existence of a legislature of elected representatives. To truly exercise popular sovereignty, the people must not only elect representatives to parliament but must also have an active role as scrutinisers of political decision-making and as supervisors of the activity of public institutions. The principle of popular sovereignty thus requires that citizens enjoy not only opportunities for political participation in elections and referenda, but also the opportunity and ability to participate in political parties and to contribute to debate in the public sphere.[5]

This view of the principle of popular sovereignty is practically worked out in what Habermas calls his 'two-track' model of deliberative politics. The two 'tracks' refer respectively to the deliberations that occur in *institutionalised deliberative bodies* and to the deliberations that occur in *informal communication in the public sphere*. Habermas's two-track model of deliberative politics is built upon a distinction drawn by Nancy Fraser between 'strong' and 'weak' public spheres (Fraser 1992; BFN 302–8). 'Strong' public spheres have the authority to make binding decisions and the authority to implement those decisions, including applying sanctions if they are disobeyed. These contexts are regulated by formal procedures of deliberation and decision-making, and they are shaped by the requirement to reach a conclusion. By contrast, 'weak' public spheres arise spontaneously through communication between citizens. In these contexts, an open-ended discourse takes place that is unregulated or 'wild' and that is not constrained by the need to reach a decision (BFN 307).

Habermas sees a division of cognitive labour occurring between 'strong' and 'weak' public spheres (BFN 307; EFP 147). Because 'strong' public spheres bear the responsibility for making binding decisions, deliberations in these contexts are oriented towards decision-making. They function as 'contexts of justification'. By contrast, 'weak' public spheres specialise in working up issues that need to be dealt with by the political system. They function as 'contexts of discovery'. What does Habermas mean by a describing the weak public sphere as a 'context of discovery'? Habermas employs a variety of metaphors to describe the important cognitive functions performed by the 'weak' public sphere: it serves as a 'sounding board', as a 'warning system', as a network of 'sensors' that registers politically relevant problems, and as a 'filter-bed' that sifts and sorts relevant contributions to topics of general interest (BFN 359–62; EFP 141). The anarchic character of the 'weak' public sphere also allows for the emergence of new social movements and subcultural 'counterpublics' whose presence contributes to the vitality and epistemic quality of the deliberative system as a whole (BFN 312).

In more recent work, Habermas has revised this picture slightly, arguing that we should analyse political communication as circulating between three levels:

- the level of 'institutionalized discourse' at the centre of the political system, where the binding decisions concerning political programmes and their implementation are prepared;
- the level of 'media-based mass communication' with a more or less passive public of readers, listeners and viewers, where public opinions take shape;
- the level of 'everyday communication in civil society' among face-to-face interlocutors (or virtual addressees) in 'arranged' or informal publics, in which the latent attitudes of potential voters take shape over long periods of time. (All quotations from EFP 159.)

To talk about a 'public sphere' is specifically to speak about the second of these levels. It is at the level of media-based communication that public opinions are registered and articulated, broadcast back to citizens, and put on the formal agendas of the responsible bodies:

> The elites which take part in public communication are expected on the one hand to absorb impulses from civil society and to send them back, in a reworked form, to the public of voters, and on the other hand to place relevant issues and suitable inputs onto the agendas of the political bodies and to observe and comment upon the institutionalized deliberation and decision-making processes themselves. *Reflected public opinions* – as products of the public sphere itself – are supposed to result from this communicative circuit running between the centre and the periphery. (EFP 162)

The 'communicative circuit' that flows through the public sphere between the 'centre' and the 'periphery' – between the strong and weak public sphere, the state and citizens – underwrites the assumption of democratic legitimacy. The 'weak' media-based public sphere contributes to democratic legitimacy in the political system by 'producing political communication', and by 'keeping it active, by steering – and filtering – it' (EFP 159). By contrast, the 'strong' public spheres at the 'centre' of the political system (the parliamentary system and the courts) contribute to democratic legitimacy by receiving communication flows that start at the 'periphery' and by 'translating' them into the medium of law (BFN 356). The parliamentary system and the courts are supposed to function as a 'sluice' that channels public will and opinion in such a way as to ensure that legally binding decisions are consistent with democratic and constitutional norms (BFN 356).

Although it might sound paradoxical, according to Habermas

the legal regulation of decision-making to ensure that it is consistent with the system of rights does not blunt the democratic legitimacy of the laws that are generated but rather *guarantees* their democratic legitimacy. This is because, for the reasons discussed at the end of Chapter 5.2, the system of rights must be respected in order for a democratic form of life to be enacted and sustained. Hence, political decision-making must be made to conform with the system of rights lest it undermine the very democratic nature of the polity. Thus, even popular opinion must be constrained by democratic and constitutional norms if the political community is to remain faithful to the intention to organise itself as an association of free and equal citizens under law.

Provided that (1) the constitutional state is steered by communicative power, and (2) communicative power is channelled through 'the sluices of democratic and constitutional procedures', the democratic legitimacy of laws can be guaranteed. By the same token, these same arrangements are supposed to ensure (1) that the political system is not co-opted by powerful social actors who are able to exercise undue influence over it, and (2) that the administrative system is not able to set its own agenda (BFN 341; see Chapter 3.3). Periodic elections are important in this regard, as is the oversight that governmental bodies exercise over each other (BFN 487). But just as important in holding the political apparatus to its legal and democratic mandate is the supervision exercised by citizens who are active in the public sphere itself. The transparency of government ('publicity') before a watchful public is an essential check on governmental power.

How then is a democratic culture and a vibrant supervisory public sphere to be generated? Legal freedoms such as the freedom of the press and the freedom of information are essential, and these freedoms must be protected by the state. But an inclusive civil society cannot be generated by such provisions. Habermas recognises that a healthy democracy is contingent upon social practices and cultural convictions that can only be sustained by citizens themselves. Nonetheless, laws can establish a favourable environment for a vibrant civil society and public sphere to emerge. For instance, laws can foster a free and independent media system that is protected from colonisation by system imperatives (EFP 173). Indeed, Habermas's deliberative model of democracy provides a robust rationale for protecting diversity in the mass media through legislative means and for regulating media ownership to prevent monopolisation of arenas of public communication by powerful interests (EFP 141). Similarly, it provides a strong justification for policies that support the participation of typically marginalised social groups in public discourse. (Here we see an implementation of the 'social rights' that are designed to redress the social inequalities that prevent the exercise of rights of public autonomy; see Chapter 5.2.)

Reinterpreting the Idea of Popular Sovereignty

Habermas's interpretation of the principle of popular sovereignty departs from the classical conception of popular sovereignty devised by Rousseau. Contrary to Rousseau's view, Habermas denies that the body of citizens can be understood as a *group agent* able to express a unified opinion or will. There cannot be a 'popular' or 'general' will as such because the people do not and cannot have a unified opinion or will (BFN 469). 'Public opinion' is no unified thing. It is a fiction, therefore, to suppose that there could be a 'popular will' that expresses 'the current general interest'; and it is a fiction to suppose that 'under the conditions of democratic self-determination, this will largely converges with the empirical popular will' (BFN 184).

For Habermas, the legitimate role that public opinion has in democratically anchoring the political system is to feed 'inputs' into the more strictly regulated formal processes of democratic decision-making. Public opinion must be 'worked up via democratic procedures into communicative power' in order to have rational coherence and it must flow through the 'sluices' of democratic and constitutional procedures in order to enjoy democratic legitimacy (BFN 300, 356). The basis of democratic legitimacy thus resides in something more abstract than a 'popular will': namely, the opinions that emerge through a complex network of communication and argumentation. The voice of 'the people' to which we should attribute democratic weight is to be located in 'the, as it were, "subjectless" forms of communication circulating through forums and legislative bodies' (BFN 136, 186).

In a sense, then, it would be accurate to say that there is no sovereign in Habermas's procedural model of democracy, popular or otherwise:

> The sovereign power of the king has been dissolved, disembodied, and dispersed in the communication flows of civil society, and it has at the same time assumed the shape of procedures, be it for general elections or the numerous deliberations and decisions of various political bodies.

> Claude Lefort is right in maintaining that sovereignty left behind an 'empty place.' (P 27)

And yet, Habermas cautions against a wholesale rejection of the notion of popular sovereignty (as had been encouraged, for instance, by Arendt (1977: 163)). The notion remains meaningful – even indispensable – since it expresses the self-understanding of a political association in which the members see themselves as collectively responsible for the governance of their polity. This is the 'radical-democratic content' of the idea of popular sovereignty which must not be lost (BFN 136).

THREE NORMATIVE MODELS OF DEMOCRACY

By way of concluding our review of the main components of Habermas's normative political philosophy, it will be helpful to return to the contrast between his own position and the standard liberal and republican positions, this time with a view not to their differing understandings of the system of rights but to their differing conceptions of democratic citizenship and democratic politics (see BFN 267–86, 296–302 and IO 239–52).

According to the liberal model, the citizen is primarily conceived as a possessor of negative rights vis-à-vis the state and other citizens. The first duty of the constitutional state is to protect private autonomy and to enable the free and independent functioning of civil society. Democracy is understood as a means by which the private interests of individuals can be aggregated and brought to bear on the political system so that it acts in ways that maximally fulfil the preferences of individuals.

According to the republican model, the citizen is primarily conceived as a possessor of rights of political participation. The legal and political institutions of the society are to reflect the self-understanding of the polity. Freedom is achieved not through protecting society from the state, but through participation in the activity of self-government. Democracy therefore is understood as a medium for the creation and expression of social solidarity; it is the reflective form of the 'ethical self-understanding' of the society (see Chapter 1.2).

For Habermas, the liberal model overlooks the fact that individuals are not merely oriented toward success, the maximisation of their self-interest; they are also oriented towards validity, the rational justifiability of policies by standards of truth, justice and goodness.

Even if it is true that politics consists, in part, of a competition between interest groups, this dynamic takes place within a broader social context that is communicatively saturated.

The republican model has advantages over the liberal model insofar as it recognises the 'binding and bonding' powers of communication. However, the republican model – especially in its more 'communitarian' interpretations – moves towards a problematic 'ethical foreshortening of political discourse' (IO 244). Politics cannot be reduced to a 'hermeneutic' process of negotiating a political community's 'ethical self-understanding'. In a modern society that is culturally and socially pluralistic, citizens will always come up against conflicts of interests and of value-orientations that cannot be resolved through a shared 'ethical' discourse. Such conflicts can only be resolved through 'fair' or 'just' compromises or bargaining procedures (IO 245; also BFN 165–86). Moreover, the republican model errs by placing expectations on political participation that are too demanding. Our conception of democracy, and our ideals of political participation, should not become overly burdensome or negate the 'good' of private autonomy.

Habermas's 'procedural' or 'deliberative' model thus seeks to respect both private autonomy and public autonomy, and to incorporate into its conception of political freedom the good of freedom *from* politics as well as the good of freedom *for* politics. But it is not merely a synthesis of the liberal and republican models. It differs from both in its emphasis on the connection between democratic legitimacy and rational acceptability:

> For the republican model, the democratic process has the expressive status of an articulation of will; and for the liberal model it performs the function of binding the policies of the government to the rational self-interest of private citizens. For the deliberative model, by contrast, embedding the will of the electorate and the formal procedures of deliberation and decision-making in the vibrant and maximally unregulated circulation of public opinions exerts a rationalizing pressure towards improving the *quality* of decisions. (EFP 143)

We have seen how the need for rational acceptability in lawmaking leads to the 'principle of democratic legitimacy' which ties the legitimacy of laws to the ability of those laws to 'meet with the assent of all citizens in a discursive process of legislation' (Chapter 5.2). In this part of Chapter 5, we have seen how Habermas's model of constitutional democracy 'operationalises' this democratic principle in the institutional design of the constitutional state and in the two-track model of deliberative politics. The two-track model of deliberative politics describes the system of communication that is required for public opinions to be 'freely' formed and for these opinions to serve as inputs into a formal process of deliberation and decision-making. The constitutional state provides the means to translate communicative power into law and to implement those laws. The constitutional state secures the rule of law; the two-track model of deliberative politics ensures that the laws that rule are democratically grounded. Together, these institutions and practices are expected to nullify illegitimate power and to establish the political conditions necessary for citizens to live together as free and equal consociates under law.

5.4 Rawls, Habermas and Religion in the Public Sphere

Modern pluralistic societies face the problem of how to reconcile a diversity of worldviews at the political level so that the state's institutions and actions are equally justifiable to all. We have already sketched in outline how Habermas approaches this problem. However, after writing *Between Facts and Norms*, Habermas recognised that he would need to further clarify how his discourse theory of law and democracy can resolve these questions. Around the same time, John Rawls was also engaged in a process of rethinking his monumental contributions to political philosophy with such questions in mind, and their differing theoretical strategies were a focus of the debate between Rawls and Habermas in the 1990s. It should be said that Rawls and Habermas hold similar positions within the field of political philosophy. Nonetheless, as we shall see, they differ on some key points, and a consideration of the debate between them will help us elucidate Habermas's mature position on the question of pluralism and, in particular, on the question of the role of religion in the public sphere.

RAWLS AND HABERMAS: DISPUTING 'THE POLITICAL'

Rawls accepts that there will be disagreement on philosophical and moral doctrines in any modern pluralistic society. Still, he argues that this need not imply a disagreement on basic principles of justice. In fact, Rawls claims that, despite substantive disagreements, support for basic liberal principles can be found within a variety of 'reasonable' philosophical and religious worldviews. He refers to the set of liberal principles common to these comprehensive doctrines as a 'political conception of justice'. This set of principles, which he tries to articulate in his *Political Liberalism* (1993), constitute a 'political' not 'metaphysical' conception of justice in that they are not tied to any specific conception of the good or to any specific philosophical doctrines. In this sense, they represent a 'freestanding' theory of justice (Rawls 1995: 133). But their content is derived from fundamental ideas found in the public political culture, and so they can be taken to represent a really existing 'political' consensus around the basics of liberal democracy (Rawls 2005: 10–15). This analysis shows how modern liberal democracies, despite their pluralistic character, can still be founded on a democratic basis of support. Hence, the ideal of 'consent by all' is not merely a hypothetical construct; it has social reality in contemporary liberal societies.

To this point, Rawls's argument presents a kind of 'public justification' for the consensus on liberal democracy. But that still leaves open the question of how contentious questions of policy and law should be handled in pluralistic societies. In Rawls's mature work, the task of resolving this problem falls to what he calls 'the idea of public reason'. In Rawls, the idea of public reason refers to the *constraints* or *limitations* on political discourse and decision-making that are implied by liberal principles of justice. Specifically, the idea of public reason stipulates that political reasoning and decision-making must be limited or disciplined such that it remains justifiable in terms of ideas and values that we sincerely believe others as free and equal might reasonably be expected to endorse and that are 'consistent with the recognition of other citizens as free and equal' (Rawls 2005: 430).

However, these 'constraints' of public reason do not apply in all contexts or to all topics. For instance, the constraints of public reason do not apply to personal deliberations or reasoning in associations such as churches and universities (Rawls 2005: 220–2). In the 'background culture of civil society' all proposals are open to debate and 'comprehensive doctrines' are brought into play. Citizens only bear a burden of public justification when it comes to 'political' actions, i.e. those actions that involve the use of coercive force over others. This applies to the decisions and actions of legislators, judges and agents of the executive (Rawls 2005: 216, 252). But it can also apply to ordinary citizens insofar as they exercise some measure of coercive power over other citizens (for instance, in their voting behaviours at election time or when they serve on juries) (Rawls 2005: 217–18).

The criterion of reciprocity and the duty of public justification are thus only incumbent upon us in an attenuated and non-demanding way; we need not furnish ourselves with public justifications 'all the way down'. In this way, Rawls's principle of legitimacy is supposed to remain a *liberal* principle of legitimacy (Rawls 2005: 137, cf. 217).

Habermas and Rawls are in agreement on many points. Both affirm the priority of the principle of popular sovereignty: political authority is the possession of the association of free and equal citizens, and it is theirs to exercise. Both accept that the political system must conform to constraints of public justifiability with regard to its reasoning and decision-making. And both affirm the importance of unconstrained discourse in the public sphere as a complement to the processes of governmental decision-making. However, Habermas articulates a number of criticisms of Rawls (see IO 49–73 and 75–101) and Rawls of Habermas (Rawls 1995, reprinted in Rawls 2005).[6]

Habermas's first criticism concerns the device of the 'original position' which Rawls uses in *A Theory of Justice* (1971) to model the ideal of impartial deliberation. In the original position, rational and reasonable representatives of ourselves deliberate and agree on the principles of justice and basic structure of society behind a 'veil of ignorance', not knowing which social positions each would occupy in society. According to Habermas, Rawls's devices of representation smuggle in substantive moral commitments, and hence cannot be thought to generate conclusions that will be acceptable to all. As an alternative, Habermas argues that the ideal of impartiality should be modelled in terms of the procedure of democratic discourse itself, without making assumptions or inferences about what participants in such a discourse would conclude (see Chapter 5.2). This approach, claims Habermas, is better able to serve as a basis for political theory in modern pluralistic societies than is Rawls's political liberalism since it articulates a *purely procedural* theory of justice that is not wedded to any metaphysical worldview.

Rawls is not convinced by this line of argument. It supposes, he claims, that substance and procedure in politics can be separated. But this is not so. The procedures of argumentation must be judged by reference to values and norms of fairness, and these are substantive matters. What's more, fair procedures alone are not sufficient to ensure just outcomes. Hence, principles of justice must say something about the fairness of outcomes as well as the fairness of procedures (Rawls 1995: 170–9). Indeed, Rawls turns the tables on Habermas and criticises his proceduralism for being tied to a comprehensive philosophical doctrine, in particular a theory of moral argumentation (Rawls 1995: 135–6). That is to say, from Rawls's perspective, Habermas presents a 'metaphysical' (in Rawls's sense) and not a 'political' conception of justice. But, as such, his theory of justice cannot hope to be acceptable to a diverse group of liberal citizens; it can only be acceptable to those who are convinced by its philosophical claims.

Rawls's political liberalism is supposed to avoid reliance on substantive metaphysical claims. But this does not mean that it is unprincipled or unreasoned. On the contrary, Rawls claims that the political consensus on the fundamentals of liberalism must be stable 'for the right reasons', and it will be stable for the right reasons when all reasonable citizens can find the political conception of justice *morally acceptable* from the standpoint of their own comprehensive doctrines (Rawls 2005: 142–4). Rawls calls this an 'overlapping consensus'. It is a 'consensus' not a 'compromise' because it is acceptable to all for moral, not self-interested, reasons; but it is merely an 'overlapping' consensus because the moral reasons each has for accepting it are not necessarily the same as those of others (Rawls 2005: 147–9). Public justification can never be a matter of *jointly* agreeing on principles of justice *for the same reasons*. But that does not prevent a public justification serving as a genuine source of social solidarity, since a plurality of citizens each see it as valid by their own lights. Rawls's political liberalism, therefore, claims for itself 'reasonableness' from the perspective of any set of reasonable people, but not to have demonstrated its 'moral truth'.

For his part, Habermas questions whether the idea of an 'overlapping consensus' is adequate to ground the strong claims to validity that a theory of justice must make if it is to claim legitimacy (IO 89). It is not enough that all accept the principles of justice for their own reasons, since this would represent nothing more than a 'lucky convergence' on a set of principles, not a demonstration of their reasonableness (IO 83). A conception of justice can claim to be properly 'neutral' or 'impartial' only if the rational justification for its principles of justice *transcends* particular worldviews. To meet this standard, a stronger form of justification is required than Rawls allows: namely, a conception of justice must be grounded in *reasons that all can accept*.

From Rawls's point of view, this is once again to aim at a deeper 'metaphysical' justification for a conception of justice and, hence, once again to ignore the challenges of public justification under conditions of cultural pluralism. However, Habermas does not agree that this is the case. The discourse principle is a principle of 'postmetaphysical' not 'metaphysical' reason, he claims. It is derived not from moral principles or ethical convictions but from the basic structures of discourse itself (see Chapter 1.1). And, similarly, the principle of democratic legitimacy is not a moral norm nor an ethical principle; it is derived from the discourse principle. It merely articulates the communicative presuppositions required to achieve a 'shared perspective' through argumentation in a political context (see Chapter 5.2). Hence, Habermas feels entitled to claim that his discourse theory of democracy and law is 'morally freestanding' (BNR 80) in the sense that Rawls demands. He even calls his view a 'political liberalism', implying that he sees it as a 'freestanding' module of reasoning akin to Rawls's own 'political liberalism' albeit one that is inspired more directly by Kant's republicanism (IO 101).

Of course, Habermas recognises that the actual decisions that are made by constitutional conventions and governing bodies within pluralistic societies will appeal to 'moral' as well as 'ethical' and 'pragmatic' reasons (BFN 99–110, 151–68). Any law will have to be plausible in light of empirical realities (pragmatic reasoning), and it will have to take account of cultural norms and customs (ethical reasons).[7] It is to be expected, therefore, that the religious and metaphysical worldviews of actual societies – and the values and ideals of the good they hold – will shape how the basic principles of justice are interpreted and applied. But this is as it should be since political institutions and political decision-making need to be acceptable in the eyes of citizens themselves. Abstract principles, even if they are philosophically valid, need to be interpreted in a way that is going to be motivating for citizens, which means not only that they must be interpreted in light of cultural resources but also that a common political culture must develop which interweaves with cultures that exist within a nation-state (BNR 104–6). But the principles that are being interpreted in this way are themselves derived at a higher level of generality and enjoy a strict universal validity (see Chapter 5.2).

Religion in the public sphere

How do these abstract philosophical debates impact upon practical questions of public debate? At this point, we return to the central question of this sub-chapter: how the plurality of social groups and cultures can be accommodated by a legal and political framework that is equally justifiable to all. Can Habermas's theoretical approach plot a plausible path for solving the problem of the 'inclusion of the other' within modern pluralistic society? Habermas has explored this problem from a number of angles, including in relation to feminism (BFN 409–27; IO 208–10, 262–4) and multiculturalism (IO 215–36; BNR 251–311). In what follows, we will focus on an especially controversial test case: the inclusion of religious groups within the democratic life of modern pluralistic societies.

From a sociological point of view, it is undeniable that religious belief and practice continues to be widespread in contemporary societies and also that, in some contexts, religious differences are a source of considerable social conflict (BNR 114–19). In the contemporary West, the most widely accepted basic formula for handling religious differences is furnished by liberal constitutionalism. (Indeed, liberal principles, such as freedom of expression and religious toleration were themselves forged under the pressure of religious conflict; see Chapter 3.1.) The liberal paradigm has three main components. First, it aims to maximise freedom for religious belief and practice through the system of civil rights (rights of 'private autonomy'). Second, it aims to preserve the religious neutrality and impartiality of the state by prohibiting religious justifications for laws and public policies and by prohibiting state support for particular religious communities (the so-called separation of church and state). Third, it allows private religious views to influence politics indirectly through voting behaviour (BNR 120–1).

Is the liberal paradigm a sufficient basis for guaranteeing equal freedom for all – for both religious and nonreligious citizens? Some religious critics argue that it is not. The prohibition on religious justification in public matters, these critics argue, privileges the viewpoint of nonreligious citizens over religious citizens. This is because the 'secularity' of the state effectively institutionalises the assumption that nonreligious citizens are reasonable and that religious citizens are not.

Habermas has genuine sympathy with this critique, and he cautions against a model of secularism that amounts to 'the political generalization of a secularized [i.e. nonreligious] worldview' (BNR 113). Furthermore, he acknowledges that abstract liberal constitutional principles alone – rights to private autonomy and the doctrine of the separation of church and state (both of which he defends) – are insufficient to guarantee equal freedom for both religious and nonreligious citizens. Instead, to establish genuinely fair legal arrangements, e.g.

concerning the limits on religious (and nonreligious) freedoms, these arrangements must be negotiated through a democratic process in which all citizens are equal participants.

> It is not enough to rely on the condescending indulgence of a secularized authority that comes to tolerate minorities who previously suffered discrimination. The parties *themselves* must come to an agreement on the precarious demarcations between the positive liberty to practice a religion of one's own and the negative liberty to remain unencumbered by the religious practices of others. If the principle of tolerance is to be above the suspicion of defining the *limits* of tolerance in an oppressive manner, then compelling reasons must be found for the definition of what can still be tolerated and what cannot, reasons equally acceptable to all sides. (BNR 120)

Only such a process, Habermas argues, can ensure that arrangements are based in 'reasons equally acceptable to all sides' and that 'the addressees of the laws can also understand themselves to be the authors of those laws' (BNR 120–1) (see Chapter 5.2). In short, it is not the rights of private autonomy but the rights of public autonomy that provide the key to correcting the deficits of liberalism.

Where does this leave Habermas on the question of religious discourse in the public sphere? On one hand, Habermas accepts that religious communities and their discourse shape politics and he recognises this as entirely legitimate. Within society at large, we should expect that the interaction between religious and nonreligious people will shape its collective identity over time. In the political sphere, similarly, public policy and lawmaking will be influenced by arguments made by religious people. Indeed, this is rightfully the case because all citizens should be able to participate as equals in democratic processes, notwithstanding their religious or irreligious views. Even the 'frictions' between religious and nonreligious communities should be welcomed since these frictions 'stimulate an awareness of [the] relevance' of normative issues and inspire critical reflection (P 25).

What then of the separation of church and state? On this issue, Habermas seeks to chart a course between the 'laicist' and the 'revisionist' interpretation of the principle. The 'laicist' interpretation strictly prohibits the state from taking any policy positions that would either support or constrain religious communities. But Habermas rejects this strict interpretation. At least since Marx it has been understood that a formal equality of rights is inadequate to establish equality among citizens. In some cases, it may be necessary for public policy to recognise or accommodate religious practices in order for believing citizens to enjoy equality with other citizens.

On the other hand, the 'revisionist' interpretation seeks to reinterpret the idea of the 'secular' state as compatible with, for example, the state accepting religious justifications for legislation.[8] However, Habermas rejects this interpretation as a violation of the fundamental and well-founded normative insight that motivates the principle of separation of church and state in the first place. Habermas insists that the state must be 'strictly impartial vis-à-vis religious communities' (BNR 124). The reason is that the legitimacy of public institutions rests on their being acceptable to all citizens equally (see Chapter 5.1). If the decision-making of public institutions is to be seen as legitimate by all citizens equally, then official decision-making by political institutions cannot be couched in religious language. All legally enforceable decisions have to be formulated and justified 'in a language that is equally accessible to all citizens' (BNR 122; drawing on Forst 2002: 126–33). A corollary of this requirement is that all citizens, including religious citizens, need to accept that, if they are to influence governmental institutions, whatever reasons they offer will have to be translated into a 'generally accessible language'. Habermas calls this a 'translation proviso' (P 26).

On this point, Habermas's position can be compared to that of Rawls, who argues that:

> Reasonable comprehensive doctrines, religious or non-religious, may be introduced in public political discourse at any time, provided that in due course proper political reasons – and not reasons given solely by comprehensive doctrines – are presented that are sufficient to support whatever the comprehensive doctrines introduced are said to support. (Rawls 2005: 462)

Habermas worries that Rawls's 'proviso' inadvertently imposes additional burdens on religious citizens over nonreligious citizens, and thus undermines their equality as contributors of reasons to public discourse (BNR 124–30). In order to avoid this asymmetry, Habermas proposes a model in which both religious and nonreligious citizens have civic duties to seek to understand and render intelligible each other's views. His proposal differs from that of Rawls's on four points.

First, for Habermas, there should not be any restrictions at all on the use of religious language in the public sphere. To do so would be exclusionary since it would place a special burden on some citizens that is not placed on others. A democratic process should accept the contributions of all citizens as important and worthy of consideration. Second, just as religious citizens are expected to take seriously the views of nonreligious citizens, so nonreligious citizens are obliged 'not to dismiss religious contributions to political opinion- and will-formation as mere noise, or even nonsense, from the start' (P 26). Third, if there is a duty to 'filter' religious language and reasoning, this duty does not fall one-sidedly on religious citizens. Not only religious citizens but also nonreligious citizens should expect to 'take part in the efforts to translate relevant contributions from religious language into a publicly intelligible language' (BNR 113). Fourth, not only religious citizens but also nonreligious citizens must reflect on the limits of their own (secular) reasons in order to discover the ways in which their disagreements with religious compatriots might be considered 'reasonable' disagreements (BNR 112). In this spirit, it is incumbent upon all parties to generate justifications that can be accepted by all.

> In spite of their ongoing dissent over questions concerning worldviews and religious doctrines, citizens should respect one another as free and equal members of their political community. And, based on this civic solidarity, they should seek a rationally motivated agreement when it comes to contentious political issues – they owe one another good reasons. (BNR 121)

In summary, Habermas envisages the properly democratic form of relation between religious and nonreligious citizens as a '*complementary* learning process' (BNR 111). When we hear descriptions of the present age as a 'post-secular society', this can be taken as a sign perhaps that both religious and nonreligious people are beginning to recognise that they must take each other's contributions to public controversies seriously.

There is an autobiographical dimension to this last point. Habermas's own attitudes towards religious belief have changed considerably over the course of his career. He has come to embrace the role that religious communities have played and can continue to play in the public deliberations of contemporary democracies. He admits, for instance, that he is deeply impressed by the 'beneficial political influence that churches and religious movements have actually had on the realization or defence of democracy and human rights' (BNR 124). He refers, in particular, to the role that Martin Luther King

Jr and the civil rights movement played in the struggle for political rights in the mid-century in the United States. He has also increasingly acknowledged the role that religious traditions have played in establishing the normative foundations of modern consciousness. For instance, he credits the idea of equal respect for persons to religious sources (BNR 109–10; P 27). What's more, it seems that Habermas has lost confidence that Western culture can simply kick away the ladder of religious tradition and go on purely by appealing to the resources of secular reason alone. Postmetaphysical thinking, he argues, still has more to learn from religious traditions and continues to rely on the impetus of religious sources for some of its central convictions. While the insights of religious traditions have been appropriated by secular culture, it is not clear to Habermas that secular reason is able to generate these insights out of itself (BNR 110).

Nonetheless, Habermas's qualified endorsement of 'post-secularity' language should not be misunderstood. He still holds that the demands of democratic reason in fact require religious communities to learn to accommodate themselves to a new postmetaphysical age. In much the same way that religious communities have had to learn to renounce the exclusive authority to teach what is true in the wake of organised scientific enquiry, so they must also learn to situate themselves as contributors among others in the process of democratic deliberation and decision-making. To do so, religious communities must find the resources to embed a democratic and liberal consciousness within their own culture. A 'module' of secular justice, Habermas writes, 'should fit into each orthodox context of justification even though it was constructed with the help of reasons that are neutral toward different worldviews' (BNR 112).

Conclusion

For Habermas, the system of rights provides the framework in which the terms of political association must be negotiated. This is true in the case of relationships between religious and nonreligious communities, just as it is in the case of relationships between women and men, and minority and majority cultures. The question in each case is how the rights of inclusion as equals within the political community should be explicated and interpreted; cultural and social differences 'must be interpreted in increasingly context sensitive ways if the system of rights is to be actualized democratically' (IO 210). What is required in each case is a complementary learning process and, at the level of legal norms, a '*dialectic* of *de jure* and *de facto* equality' (IO 208). That learning process can only take place (fallibly) through the ongoing work of public discourse, which is itself facilitated by the system of rights (Chapter 5.2) and the institutions of a constitutional democracy (Chapter 5.3).

Through the work of public discourse, however, it is possible to establish a common political culture – a culture constructed by the polity itself – which interprets constitutional principles 'from the perspective of the nation's historical experience' (IO 225). This common culture does not constitute a fully formed 'ethical' form of life; it cannot displace or replace the cultural identity of subgroups within society. But it can function as a more abstract dimension of political integration within the society across a diversity of subcultures. Habermas calls this abstract form of common commitment to procedural democracy 'constitutional patriotism' (IO 226). (The terminology is somewhat ill-chosen. The term 'constitutional patriotism' refers to a commitment that is not patriotic in any nationalistic sense, nor is its object the constitution *per se*. See Baxter 2011: 222–7.)

Even if Habermas's approach to the politics of inclusion is successful at the level of the nation-state, it is another question whether it has the resources to solve problems of political integration at higher levels of abstraction: across national borders and, ultimately, encompassing all human communities. It is to this question that we turn in the final part of Chapter 5.

5.5 *Transnational Democracy, Cosmopolitanism and Human Rights*

While the nation-state remains the primary level of political integration in the early twenty-first century, economic and cultural forces unleashed by globalisation have put it under unprecedented pressure (see Chapter 3.4). The challenges to the nation-state posed by globalisation have provoked a range of political reactions, from fierce nationalist protectionism – a determination to police borders and stem the tide of information, capital, immigrants and refugees in an effort to defend 'our' way of life – to an eager embrace of free markets and open borders as a liberation from the oppression of the bureaucratic state. From Habermas's vantage point, protectionism seems a hopeless cause in the face of insistent trends towards ever more connectedness between national economies. No more plausible is the pragmatic 'third way', the path of adaptation to the globalising trends, which is now embraced by most mainstream political parties on both the left and the right. This too is a dead end, Habermas argues, since it offers no hope for a future in which the existing social functions of the nation-state can be sustained. The looming collapse of the welfare state is a genuine crisis and potentially portends a regression into a new form of barbarism.

In recent years, Habermas has tentatively voiced a hope that we may be standing on the brink of a 'great transformation' akin to the emergence of the new global order after the Second World War. But nothing is certain. Dangers also lurk in any time of transition, as is evidenced by the 'regressions' that occurred in the first half of the twentieth century following the expansion of free trade at the end of the nineteenth century. The present moment is one in which humanity is forced to think forward and to reorganise itself once again.

It is not enough to be nostalgic about the welfare state of the post-war years. The 'functional integration' achieved by networks of market interactions must be rebalanced by new forms of 'social integration'. Only this must now be achieved at an even more abstract level. New legal institutions are required to construct a global rule of law, and new political institutions are required to reassert popular sovereignty at a global scale. (This belief makes Habermas a 'political' cosmopolitan, an advocate of global political society and not just a 'moral' cosmopolitan, an advocate of fulfilling moral duties to all human beings.) The challenge is to conceive how political integration at higher levels of abstraction can be achieved without sacrificing the beneficial forms of political integration that already exist at the level of the nation-state, and to conceive how the more encompassing forms of political integration can be furnished with a sufficiently democratic basis. Habermas addresses these questions in two parallel lines of argumentation. The first relates to the political integration of populations through 'transnational' political associations at the regional level, such as the European Union. The second concerns the reform of legal and political institutions at the global level, in particular the United Nations and associated entities responsible for human rights and coordinating action among states. In what follows, we shall provide a précis of Habermas's writings on the European Union and global institutions in turn.

The Future of the European Union

The European Union is viewed by Habermas as a test case for the possibility of political integration beyond the nation-state. The faltering experiment of European integration illustrates the difficulties such a project faces. But, for Habermas, who has been a close observer of European politics for more than forty years and has also played an active role in events, the European case is also a stimulus for reflection on the conceptual foundations for the transnationalisation of democracy.

The first steps taken to integrate Europe by the Treaty of Rome (1957) were driven by economic goals: a desire to break down barriers to trade and to the free movement of labour and capital. An administrative layer of bureaucracy was created to facilitate these economic developments. The Economic and Monetary Union, which was phased in from 1990, was intended to promote economic integration further by introducing a common currency and general rules binding on all states. The Maastricht Treaty of 1992 realised an intention to integrate Europe at a political level, and the European Union was constituted in 1993. But moves to introduce a constitution for the European Union in 2004–5 exposed an existing democratic deficit. Elites had forged the European Union with only 'passive consent' from 'more or less indifferent populations' (LT 3). Citizens within the European Union had accepted the developments predominantly on the basis of promised economic benefits, not because of a desire for political unification. When citizens were required to consent to 'more Europe', they were hesitant. The flimsy economic basis for popular acceptance of the European Union unravelled during the financial crisis of 2008. On the one hand, a number of innovations were adopted to try to resolve the financial crisis (the Fiscal Compact, the European Stability Mechanism and the so-called Six Pack). These mechanisms led to an expansion of power in the executive bodies of the European Union (LT 33). On the other hand, when the European Council sought to solve crises through imposing austerity on less financially stable member states, placing heavy burdens on wages, social benefits and public infrastructure, the angry response was both predictable and warranted.

In recent years, divergent agendas have been pursued by those who want to see political integration in Europe and those who want to see merely economic integration. Proponents of economic integration alone (in particular, Britain and the Scandinavian countries) have wanted to preserve the sovereignty of states yet reap the benefits of economic liberalisation. Proponents of political integration (France, Germany, Italy and the Benelux countries) have hoped to create a European bloc capable of absorbing the cultural and ethnic antagonisms that once drove the European powers to war (LT 4). Habermas is strongly in favour of political integration. This is because the only way Europe can rebalance the relationship between markets and politics, and maintain its social welfare model of society and the diversity of its cultures is through 'concerted action'; and effective and democratically legitimate collective action is only possible on the basis of political integration (LT 17, 31). Political integration at higher levels of abstraction is the price that must be paid if the 'democratic substance' of the nation-state is to survive (LT 39). Hence, citizens of Europe should desire a Union that operates democratically and has the necessary resources to secure economic and social goals in the interests of European citizens. They should also desire a system that preserves and enhances the member states as democracies and as 'guarantors of the already achieved level of justice and freedom' (LT 40; see CEU 20–8, 40–2).

But political integration must be accompanied by more democracy in order to avoid the legitimation deficits of technocracy. The European Union has been quick to expand its governance structures but slow to adopt democratic mechanisms. Its decision-making has played out more like a set of trade negotiations between member states than like a procedure of collective decision-making in which the interests of all are given equal consideration. Ad hoc technocratic solutions to systemic problems have reinforced nationalist resistance and have made political integration harder to achieve, to the detriment of the people of Europe. What's more, without democratic accountability, centralised governing bodies will not have sufficient incentives to conform to standards of justice and to track the needs of the people (LT 11–12). For these reasons, Habermas argues that the European Union needs to be 'converted from an elite project into one that includes citizens' (LT 9). The European Union does need greater 'steering capacity', e.g. in order to resolve fiscal, budgetary and economic issues in a concerted fashion; but Europeans cannot have confidence that these powers will be exercised justly and in the interests of Europeans (and the member states) unless the democratic credentials of the European system are 'irreproachable' (CEU 3). Hence, Habermas sides with the 'Euro-democrats' who want to strengthen the democratic credentials of the European Union against the 'Euro-technocrats' who promote what Habermas calls 'executive federalism' according to which the European Union merely performs bureaucratic functions and need not see itself as a state-like entity (CEU 6; LT 13).

How then is political integration to be achieved with the required level of democratic legitimacy? Can a regional political association such as the European Union satisfy the standards of democratic legitimacy that we are familiar with in nation-states?

The problem of transnationalising democracy

Democracy means the self-empowerment of the collective of free and equal citizens to act as decision-makers over their own affairs (the principle of self-legislation). To be democratic, an alliance of states such as the European Union needs to be not only an agreement between sovereign states but also a pooling of the sovereign peoples themselves to create a newly imagined people whose sovereignty is constitutionally enshrine and embodied in the political institutions of the federation (CEU 19–22). The primary difficulty for transnationalising democracy, however, is how to accommodate the fact that citizens are already members of democratic states. If these states are not to be dissolved (and Habermas is adamant that they should not be), then what should it look like to be a citizen of Europe?

Habermas argues that we ought to conceptualise the regional political community in terms of a 'shared' or 'divided' popular sovereignty (CEU 35–8). The framework for European political integration should assume that there are two constituting (i.e. 'sovereign') powers: namely, the citizens of Europe and the European states. With this conception, citizens are not first members of a state and then represented by their state within the transnational forum. Rather, the sovereignty of the people of Europe is expressed simultaneously by the people directly *and* by the states which the people have already constituted (CEU 18; LT 58–9).

What political institutions are recommended by this principle of 'shared' or 'divided' popular sovereignty? To answer this question, Habermas employs a thought experiment which he calls a 'higher level constitutional process' (CEU 34–53, LT 40–5). In the thought experiment, a constitution is negotiated between the two 'sovereigns', the citizens of Europe and the states of Europe (LT 40). The two sovereigns participate on an equal footing in the constitutional deliberations to constitute the new political association. They negotiate with each other to reach a balance between their corresponding interests. The result of such a procedure, Habermas suggests (with remarkably little argumentation it must be said), would be a convergence on the need for a *multilevel* system such as that seen in the United States. In the US federal system, legislation must be approved by both the House of Representatives, which institutionalises the equal status of all citizens, and the Senate, which institutionalises the equal status of the member states. Similarly, in the European case, Habermas infers that the two hypothetical assemblies would require that all decision-making at the European level be agreed to by two legislative bodies with equal rights. In practice, these roles would be played by (some version of) the European Parliament, representing all citizens as equals, and the European Council, representing the member states equally.

What then does Habermas propose for the European Union at a constitutional level? Habermas's model accepts that European law must prevail over state law in the matters in which the European Union has competence (LT 29). However, he strongly asserts that the European Union should not take on a state-like character, and that the integrity of the member states within the Union must be preserved. There should not be a 'supreme constitutional authority at the European level' (CEU 39). For this reason, he defends some features of the existing institutional arrangement: (1) no centralisation of police powers; (2) no central administrative capacity to implement EU law; (3) amendments to EU constitution require unanimous assent by member states; (4) states retain a right to exit (LT 9–10). For the reasons laid out above, Habermas argues that the Council and the European Parliament must make 'joint decisions' on federal guidelines for fiscal, economic and social policies (LT 15–16). If this is to be the model, then the legislative procedure, not executive decision by the Council, must be enshrined as the normal mode of rule-making, and the European Parliament's powers must match its democratic mandate, which means they must increase and the power of the Council must decrease.

Even if these reforms yield a democratic and just constitutional arrangement, Habermas recognises that this alone is not sufficient for the embedding of transnational democracy in Europe. In addition, a political-cultural background is required (PC 73–6). Citizens must see themselves as members of the political association and must be able to participate in the democratic process in meaningful ways. This political-cultural background cannot be created through law; at most, it can be promoted through political measures. Thankfully, Europeans already share a largely overlapping political culture. However, Habermas singles out two especially crucial aspects of this political-cultural background, both of which are lacking in Europe today.

First, a European-wide public sphere is lacking (CEU 48–9). Existing national media must open themselves up to each other. They must learn to report on discussions occurring in other countries and to facilitate participation in these debates across borders (EFP 181–3). This is vital for the development of mutual trust across national borders, which is the second crucial aspect.

Second, citizens must possess a sense of 'civic solidarity', a sense of trust that citizens of other member states will act not only in the national interest but also in the interest of the Union. Without the willingness to adopt a 'common perspective' in this fashion, it is not possible for any citizen to presume that parliamentary decisions will take their interests into account. Although European unification has stalled for a variety of reasons, according to Habermas the main reason is 'the lack of mutual trust that the citizens of different nations would have to show each other as a precondition for their willingness to adopt a common perspective' (LT 37).

This failure of mutual trust should not be attributed to cultural and political divisions within Europe. There is no reason in principle why civic solidarity cannot exist in Europe despite cultural differences. If an artificial identity such as a national consciousness could be successfully constructed in the nineteenth century, then a new artificial identity could be constructed again at the level of Europe (DW 67–82). Multiple identities and loyalties can coexist, provided they do not conflict (CEU 47). Neither cultural differences nor existing political loyalties are the principle barrier to the cultivation of civic solidarity in Europe. The principle barrier, Habermas argues, is the extent of social inequalities within and between member states. So long as one member state can gain an advantage from the suffering of another, social solidarity cannot be fostered. For this reason, political integration must go hand in hand with the redistribution of wealth between member states, the communalisation of debt among member states and the provision of social welfare (CEU 52–3).

From Regional to Global Political Integration

Even if the project of European integration were entirely successful, efforts to tame global markets that have run amok and to revive flagging nation-states cannot stop with the formation of regional alliances such as the European Union. The challenges posed by globalisation require new structures of political integration and cooperation at a global level. Because we are enmeshed in a globally interconnected web of actions and relationships, it is desirable that we should institute a form of political association that is global in extent in order to collectively govern aspects of our shared life. We all share an interest in the good governance of our global interactions and of the finite resources of our planet. For these reasons, Habermas is inclined to view the European experiment as at best an 'important stage along the route to a politically constituted world society' (CEU 2).

However, once again, thorny theoretical and practical questions arise. How can the essential components of a democratically organised political community be given expression at a higher level of abstraction? Can international law be 'constitutionalised' and brought into line with demands of democratic legitimacy? Can globally effective capacities for joint action be established? And can global political institutions be constituted in such a way that they preserve and strengthen more local forms of political community?

Habermas's cosmopolitanism

Habermas recognises that the step towards global political integration brings with it a specific set of dangers. The spectre of 'world government' has long haunted the consciousness of modern humanity and caused it to shudder. Habermas acknowledges the fear that a world government would stand as an irresistible alien power over us, impervious to democratisation, and indifferent to the interests and concerns of ordinary human beings. For this reason, he agrees that a 'world government' is 'neither desirable nor feasible' (CEU 94n34). Nonetheless, he maintains that a 'constitutional world society' is both desirable and feasible. What does this distinction amount to?

Habermas is committed to the ideal of a community of *world citizens* integrated under a single legal system of rights (CEU 58). That is to say, he argues (with Kant) for a conceptual shift beyond 'international law' – regulating interactions between states – to 'cosmopolitan law' – a set of legal norms applicable to individuals, a political community of world citizens (BNR 314). However, the establishment of a political community of world citizens does not preclude us from holding citizenship within nation-states or within other additional levels of political association for that matter (such as the European Union). As the various federal systems around the world – including the European Union – demonstrate, there is no contradiction in holding citizenship simultaneously within smaller and larger political communities. Contra Kant, the 'cosmopolitan condition' need not imply an ultimate annihilation or subsumption of states within a 'world republic' (BNR 315).

Global citizens have good reasons to want their interests as citizens of the world and the interests of their nation-states represented in the global political arena, since it is within nation-states that citizens already enjoy a political association that ensures justice and solidarity. Although, admittedly, the interests of world citizens can be at odds with the interests of nation-states (LT 56). For instance, as world citizens we would plausibly insist on 'equal opportunity and equal distribution' while as national citizens we would insist on maintaining the freedoms and welfare we already enjoy through our membership of nation-states (CEU 59). According to Habermas, both of these perspectives will have to be institutionalised in the constitution of a global political community in order for the interests of all human beings to be properly taken into account. Specifically, and analogously to the European situation, the global political community will require a representational system that includes the representation of citizens and of member states.

Conceptually, Habermas thus proposes that the global level of political integration be understood as a 'supranational association of citizens and peoples' in which states retain monopoly over the use of force (CEU 58). The case of the European Union shows that it is possible for binding law to be in force while the responsibility for enforcement remains with member states (LT 53). And Habermas now argues that this is the way we should conceptualise the status of laws passed by a world organisation: they should be seen as both legitimate and enforceable, but not coercively enforced by a world government. Thus, for instance, the norm should be that states use their monopoly over the use of legitimate force to enforce cosmopolitan law. There should be no centralised policing power to coerce participation in the political association, and the military power of the United Nations should be maintained through free contributions of military resources by member states, not through the establishment of an autonomous standing army. Such precautions provide a useful check on the power of the global political institutions (CEU 58).

The upshot of these considerations is what Habermas describes as 'the political constitution of a decentred world society as a multilevel system' (DW 135). With this model, nation-states remain the fundamental components of the global political order. However, the 'state of nature' that has traditionally obtained at the level of international relations, in which sovereign states assume that every other is engaged in a battle for strategic advantage, is overcome by the rule of law. The mark of success for the cosmopolitan project of global political integration is therefore that nation-states come to see themselves not as 'sovereign powers' but as 'members of the international community united by bonds of solidarity' (CEU 61).

Human rights and global domestic policy

If the global political community and its legal rules are to exist alongside other regional and national political communities and their legal rules, there arises the question of coordinating competences – that is, of determining what each level of governance should have responsibility for and how their legally binding decisions should relate to each other.

The first question to be resolved is whether there are normatively binding rules that could, in principle, be endorsed by all people regardless of cultural differences. Is there anything at all that could legitimately be passed down by a world parliament as binding law? We can imagine a set of moral concerns that are genuinely shared by all global citizens, e.g. concerns of justice. But can we also imagine a set of *legal* and *political norms* that can be universally accepted? We can, Habermas argues, since there is a set of legal rights that can be 'justified exclusively in moral terms', namely 'human rights' (see CEU 71–100). Not only are human rights acceptable according to canons of moral reasoning, they are already reflected in and supported by a wide diversity of world cultures. There exists, in Rawls's terms, an overlapping consensus on the legitimacy of human rights.

> The relevant principles of distributive justice as well as the negative duties to refrain from justiciable human rights violations and wars of aggression are rooted in the core moral contents of all of the major world religions and in the cultures they have shaped. (CEU 65)

It is the set of human rights that define precisely the areas to which the United Nations should confine itself as a legislative body. So long as it restricts itself to decisions that concern issues of fundamental human rights, the United Nations can avoid making culturally imperialistic decisions whose legitimacy could (rightly) be questioned. Hence, according to Habermas, the legislative body of the United Nations should be principally responsible for defining binding minimum standards for human rights and for determining rules concerning the prohibition of violence (CEU 60). These legally binding rules would in turn be the basis for human rights policy, for the regulation of the peacekeeping activities overseen by the Security Council and for the global administration of justice.

However, questions of 'global domestic policy' remain. Falling into this category are issues of global concern such as environmental crises, the regulation of risky technologies and weapons, regulation of financial market-driven capitalism, and 'the distributional problems that arise in the trade, labour, health and transportation regimes of a highly stratified world society' (CEU 57). Here we are faced with substantive matters of policy that must be decided at a global level but which cannot be decided simply through the application of human rights law. Such matters therefore cannot be subject to binding legislation by a 'world parliament'. Instead, they must be addressed through a system of negotiation involving all affected parties.

By and large, such global issues are already dealt with through international negotiations and governed by treaties. However, these negotiations are rarely subject to democratic legal oversight and in many cases the large imbalances of power lead to unjust outcomes. To generate a legitimate legal order at the international level, a fair and impartially regulated system of negotiations is required and the influence of powerful agents (such as multinational corporations and wealthy states) must be neutralised. For Habermas, this implies that the negotiation system must be 'embedded in the context of the constituted world society' (CEU 68). That is to say, the United Nations must be responsible for establishing the frameworks for negotiations and for overseeing their implementation. (Habermas evidently has in mind institutions such as the World Trade Organization and initiatives such as the United Nations Framework Convention on Climate Change, although no doubt he would regard these as very imperfect instantiations of the model; see BNR 349–50.)

In summary, at the international level the policy questions split into two different fields, each of which has a different standard of legitimation. On the one hand, questions of global security and human rights stand on a secure and universalistic normative footing. They are to be handled by the United Nations and can be administered with juridical force. On the other hand, questions of 'global domestic policy' must be agreed on a case-by-case basis by all parties. They are to be handled through international negotiations administered by the United Nations and legally binding decisions are to be enforced by member states in accordance with mutually agreed contractual terms. In both cases, Habermas refers to a 'constitutionalisation' of international law, a process by which an impartial framework is set up to pacify conflicts, adjudicate disputes, and broker fair and just agreements. The framework consists of a set of offices, rules and procedures, but must also wield sufficient power to make its processes effective and to enforce its decisions.

The reform agenda

A political association of all nation-states already exists in the form of the United Nations, and the 'constitutionalisation' of international law has already begun (see Chapter 3.4). The question today is not how to begin such a process but how it should be continued.

Habermas's blueprint for the reform of the United Nations, as we have seen, is aimed at embodying a form of 'cosmopolitan community', i.e. a 'politically constituted community of states *and* citizens' (CEU 57). He initially proposed that the General Assembly should embrace the role of a 'world parliament' and that it should undergo a process of democratisation in which a second chamber of directly elected representatives was added to the current assembly that is an assembly of government delegations (IO 187). However, Habermas has downgraded his expectations concerning democratisation at that global level. He still maintains that the decision-making processes at the international level should be more open to public scrutiny and to input from civil society in order to harness the epistemic and legitimation benefits of inclusive deliberation (PC 110–11), and he still calls for the General Assembly to be transformed into a world parliament of some kind (EFP 120). But he now gives more weight to the objection that the global community cannot operate as a singular self-determining community because it lacks a shared political culture (PC 107).

What remains to be carried through at the level of the United Nations, then, is less a project of 'democratisation' and more a project of 'constitutionalisation' – that is, of bringing the international order under the rule of law and of ensuring all human beings are treated as bearers of rights (DW 138).

In addition to reforms of the representative system, reforms are required in the executive arm of the United Nations. In general, the United Nations requires an *effective* and *impartial* executive or administrative apparatus to (1) defend international peace through global, even-handed and effective enforcement of the prohibition of violence; (2) take constructive measures to protect internal order within failing states; and (3) monitor the domestic enforcement of human rights and protect populations against criminal governments (CEU 60–1). The United Nations Humans Rights Council is to monitor and report violations of human rights, and the International Criminal Court is to function as a permanent judicial body to prosecute those violations. As mentioned above, Habermas argues that the resources required for these tasks should, for the most part, be sourced through the contributions of member states. But there is much work to be done to ensure that the system of international law is universal and effective in its reach and impartial in its content and procedures. In particular, democratising reforms of the Security Council are vital so that the Council can effectively represent the interests of all nations and citizens and not just the interests of a powerful few. The veto power of nuclear powers must be abolished and unanimous decisions must be replaced with some form of majority rule (IO 187). The executive actions of the Security Council must be constrained by the laws concerning global justice endorsed by the General Assembly (or its successor) and must be subject to judicial review by competent courts of international law (CEU 65). These reforms are essential in order to ensure that the functioning of the global political association is impartial and democratically anchored.

Notes

1. Of course, laws can also affect non-citizens. Laws of citizenship and rights of immigration are obvious cases. Environmental laws, e.g. regulation of greenhouse gas emissions, are another. We shall discuss how Habermas handles some of these issues in Chapter 5.5.
2. This does not mean that Habermas relegates ordinary citizens to the role of mere spectators in the lawmaking process. All citizens have standing as participants and an important role to play in his 'two-track model' of deliberative democracy, and not just as electors, as we shall discuss in Chapter 5.3.
3. The English translations calls them 'corollaries' (BFN 122), but this is a mistranslation. The second and third categories of rights cannot be derived from the first. The thought is rather that the first three basic

categories of rights are interrelated and that all three are necessary for any package of liberal rights.
4. On this point, Habermas claims that the discourse principle implies a right to emigrate and a protection from 'unilateral deprivation of membership rights'. He also claims that an application of the discourse principle implies that immigration must be 'regulated in the equal interest of members and applicants' (BFN 124–5).
5. The competition between political parties for access to power motivates responsiveness to the interests and value-orientations of voters. As such, it is an important component of the institutional design of the democratic state in its own right (BFN 298).
6. For more detailed discussions of the Rawls-Habermas dispute, see Finlayson and Freyenhagen (2011).
7. To complicate matters, it must also be noted that Habermas insists that any law will have to be consistent with 'basic moral principles' (BFN 106). This seems to indicate that, while his principle of democratic legitimacy does not rest on moral foundations, it nonetheless implies a constraint by moral principles. For a discussion of these points, see Finlayson and Freyenhagen (2011: 8–12).
8. Habermas considers the work of Paul Weithmann and Nicholas Wolterstorff to be 'revisionist' in this sense.

6

Critical Perspectives: Power, Conflict and Deliberative Politics

Throughout his career, Habermas has opposed the legacy of the German jurist and political theorist Carl Schmitt (1888–1985). In fact, it would be no exaggeration to describe Habermas as the anti-Schmitt of twentieth-century political theory. As William Scheuerman (2011: 248) remarks, 'opposition to Schmitt runs like a red thread throughout his political and legal theorizing: Schmitt is a key target not only in Habermas's early political writings but also in his latest discussions of globalization and the postnational democratization'. In this chapter, the conflict between Schmitt and Habermas will be used as a touchstone to introduce some critical questions that have been raised in the contemporary literature concerning Habermas's discourse theory of law and democracy.

The Schmittian Challenge

There are few more prominent critics of the liberal-democratic paradigm in the twentieth century than Carl Schmitt. Admittedly, he presents his political theory as a democratic theory. For Schmitt, sovereignty ultimately lies with the people. Indeed, he asserts that the democratic will of the people ('constituent power') is necessarily superior to any constitutional arrangement ('constituted power') (Schmitt 2008: 125–46). However, this strong affirmation of popular sovereignty is interpreted by Schmitt in a paradoxical fashion. For Schmitt, democracy can mean nothing more nor less than the expression of 'acclamation', the voicing of the people's approval (or disapproval) of a leader and of the decisions they make (Schmitt 2008: 258–72). In other words, the people's 'constituent power' must be exercised on their behalf by the dictator who is the representative of the people and who acts in their name. Schmitt's affirmation of the people's 'constituent power' thus serves to justify the dictator's authority to overturn the 'constitutional' component of political organisation at will.

In the 1920s and 1930s, Schmitt developed a set of powerful arguments concerning the 'metaphysical kernel' of politics, which he calls 'the political': the moment of 'pure decision not based on reason and discussion and not justifying itself' (Schmitt 2005: 66). First, Schmitt argues that the sovereign must have the right to suspend laws in a state of emergency. By definition decisions regarding 'the state of exception' (or 'the state of emergency') cannot be subject to legal constraints. If they were, this would lead to a regress: the legal constraints would themselves constitute a set of laws subject to suspension by the sovereign. It follows that there can be no legal order without a sovereign authority who decides whether and how legal norms are to be applied (Schmitt 2005: 5–35). Second, in order to fulfil its duty as protector of the people, the sovereign must decide who belongs to the political community and must judge when an existential threat to the political community exists that has to be met with force (Schmitt 2007). In decisions regarding who is friend and who is foe, decision-making cannot be prescribed in advance by laws. As in the matter of suspending law, it is necessary for the sovereign to exercise a decision-making power that stands above the law – even above the constitution. The sovereign in Schmitt, following Hobbes, is thus a quasi-divine, transcendent figure – a figure who has the authority over life and death – whose decisions cannot be domesticated by legal oversight or public debate. For Schmitt, as for Hobbes, the quasi-divine transcendence of the sovereign is necessitated by the idea of public reason itself, since it is in the interest of all equally that there exists a sovereign authority who exercises irresistible power and is not subject to legal constraint in all matters (see Chapter 5.1 and Vatter (2008: 247–52)).

Schmitt regards the kind of deliberative theory that Habermas will endorse as a pitiful attempt to neutralise 'the political'. Liberals, he says, want 'to dissolve metaphysical truth in a discussion' and avoid 'the definitive dispute, the decisive bloody battle' (Schmitt 2005: 63). Likewise, Schmitt is deeply suspicious of the kind of cosmopolitanism that Habermas will promote. Liberal cosmopolitans assume that we can treat all people (humanity) as equals under a universal rule of law. But Schmitt denies that this is possible. Citizens enjoy equal rights under their constitution, but they do so as the result of the decision of the politically self-determining nation. Political self-determination means the self-assertion of a people (*Volk*) in distinction to all other peoples. For Schmitt, consequently, there can be no 'political' meaning to the whole of humanity: 'Humanity as such cannot wage war because it has no enemy, at least not on this planet. The concept of humanity excludes the concept of the enemy' (Schmitt 2007: 54; cited in IO 198). In international relations, therefore, the language of humanism ought to be regarded with deep suspicion. If the 'moral universalism' of humanist thinking becomes the legitimating ground for regulating international conflict, then the inevitable result will be inhumanity:

> When a state fights its political enemy in the name of humanity, it is not a war for the sake of humanity, but a war wherein a particular state seeks to usurp a universal concept against its military opponent. At the expense of its opponent, it tries to identify itself with humanity in the same way as one can misuse peace, justice, progress, and civilization in order to claim these as one's own and to deny the same to the enemy. The concept of humanity is an especially useful ideological instrument of imperialist expansion, and in its ethical-humanitarian form it is a specific vehicle of economic imperialism. (Schmitt 2007: 54; cited in IO 188)

Habermas's Critique of Schmitt

Despite his prominent affiliation with the National Socialist party in Germany, Schmitt's ideas have enjoyed considerable influence in the post-war era. Schmittian themes have been taken up, for instance, in the work of Claude Lefort, Jacques Derrida, Ernesto Laclau, Giorgio Agamben, Jean-Luc Nancy and Chantal Mouffe. What's more, Schmitt's suspicion of human rights, international law and cosmopolitanism is widely shared among contemporary critical theorists and postcolonial theorists. Why then has Habermas so tenaciously opposed Schmitt's political theory?

Habermas agrees with Schmitt that there can be no legal order without a set of political institutions empowered to make law and decide how legal norms are to be applied. The political community must authorise political institutions and entrust them with the authority and functional capacity to make binding decisions. Discussion alone is not enough to constitute a political community. What's more Habermas acknowledges that forming and protecting a community of citizens against 'external enemies and internal disorder' is among the essential functions of these institutions (BFN 133; see Chapter 5.1).

But Habermas rejects what he calls Schmitt's 'clericofascist conception of "the political"' (P 23). He argues that, in portraying the sovereign dictator as standing above the reciprocal relationships of rational accountability that bind ordinary citizens, Schmitt's constitutional theory subverts the principle of the rule of law and cynically dismisses the goal of domesticating the irrational power of the state. In fact, his theory brazenly presents the state as necessarily and inevitably a source of violence and domination, untameable by democracy and reason, and thus 'preserves the authoritarian kernel of a sovereign power with its legitimizing relation to sacred history' (P 22). At the same time, despite Schmitt's claims to be a defender of democracy, his conception of political authority represents a denial – not an affirmation – of the principle of popular sovereignty. Schmitt's political theory is 'tailored to a homogeneous population and led by a charismatic leader' (P 22). It clings to a nostalgic but dangerous image of the heroic leader who asserts him-/herself against internal and external enemies, including minorities within the body of citizens. In short, Schmitt's conception of political authority is regressive and fascistic; it stands 'for revelation and against enlightenment, for authority and against anarchism, for obedience to God and against human self-empowerment and progressivism' (P 23).

History is not on Schmitt's side. Modern constitutional democracies have rejected the notion of 'internal *enemies*' as illegitimate, since such a notion pictures the maintenance of civil order as an ongoing civil war against certain classes of citizens and provides rhetorical cover for the suppression of political opponents. They have also relinquished the assumption that the political self-maintenance of the nation-state necessarily implies the assertion of a homogeneous national culture to the exclusion of other cultures (IO 139–42). Moreover, in modern constitutional democracies, the figure of the 'sovereign' has been deflated; it has been democratised and proceduralised. The state no longer has the mythical aura of quasi-divinity, and neither are 'the people' viewed as the quasi-divine source of the force of law. 'The political' now finds an impersonal embodiment in the constitutional framework of the state and in the democratic opinion- and will-formation of citizens within civil society. In short, 'everything feared by Carl Schmitt in fact happened' (P 27).

Habermas offers a theoretical framework to make sense of these historical developments and to justify them. The key, for Habermas, is to understand political association not in terms of belonging to an ethnically homogenous 'nation' but in terms of belonging to a voluntary association of free and equal citizens who participate in a practice of democratic self-determination. If we make this conceptual shift, then the need for the self-assertion of one people *against* others – both internal and external – dissolves. The coherence of the political community no longer seems to depend on maintaining its 'unique' character as a nation (IO 147), and hence it no longer seems to require the repression of minority cultures or forced assimilation in order to preserve itself.[1] The mark of a legitimate political order is not that it reflects the 'national identity' of its citizens but that it gives reality to civil rights.

According to Habermas, Schmitt's fundamental error is his failure to see how 'the political' and the 'constitutional' elements of political society can be reconciled (P 31n13). In fact, there is no need to attribute to the people a quasi-divine authority to overthrow the constitution at will. And there is no reason to think that a legal order is impossible without a sovereign who stands above the law. Neither the procedure of constitution-making nor life under the rule of law requires any decision-making authority that stands above the procedures of democratic self-determination; and the procedures of democratic self-determination are themselves governed by norms of rational accountability. Indeed, a properly organised system of rights is what makes it possible for the people to act as a political association in the first place; and, even in revolutionary moments when a new constitution is written, the process of constitution-making must follow norms of deliberation in order to satisfy the demand for legitimacy (see Chapter 5.2).

As for Schmitt's defence of 'belligerent' relations between states (moderated only by the minimal safeguards of classical international law), Habermas is equally unconvinced. He questions two basic assumptions that undergird Schmitt's suspicion of human rights discourse. First, Habermas denies that an international politics of human rights rests on a 'universalistic morality':

> The concept of human rights does not have its origins in morality, but rather bears the imprint of the modern concept of individual liberties, hence of a specifically juridical concept. Human rights are juridical by their very nature. What lends them the appearance of moral rights is not their content, and most especially not their structure, but rather their mode of validity, which points beyond the legal order of nation-states. (IO 190)

Habermas's claim appears to be that human rights are actionable legal rights like all others, and they can be suspended or changed; yet human rights can be justified 'exclusively from the moral point of view', which is to say they can be justified solely on the basis of universalistic (i.e. 'moral') reasons relating to what is 'in the equal interest of all persons qua persons' (IO 191). Human rights enjoy universality in the sense that they must be respected wherever social interactions are to be governed by valid law. In this way, human rights are 'constitutive for the legal order as a whole' (IO 190). Thus, human rights are unusual among legal norms in that they do not appeal to anything peculiar to a given culture. But they are not moral judgements concerning the actions or omissions of individuals or groups. The importance of this point is that it preserves the gap between legal and moral norms, the gap that is the essential mark of liberalism. According to the liberal view, laws are not to coercively enforce morality; they must establish justifiable spheres of 'negative liberty' to act as seems best to oneself despite moral disagreement with others (see Chapter 3.1). The logic of rights thus rests on a different basis than the logic of morality, even though both suppose universal rational justifiability. So long as this distinction is sound, then in principle we need not equate human rights with 'moral universalism' as Schmitt does.

Second, Habermas denies that human rights discourse illegitimately overrides legal restrictions on military conflicts and leads to inhumanity. Of course, human rights discourse can be misused in this way; human rights 'fundamentalism' is possible (see Chapter 3.4). But the way to avoid human rights fundamentalism is to insist on the separation of the moral and the legal (as above), so that coercive authority is not used as a tool to impose one culture's moral norms but only in the service of actionable rights. Indeed, far from being a barrier to justice, the language of human rights, with its norms of equality and freedom, is indispensable as it provides the very critical resources needed to unmask unjust and self-serving interpretations and applications of moral and legal norms (IO 193–6; PC 119–20). Hence, Habermas concludes that 'Human rights fundamentalism is avoided not by renouncing the politics of human rights, but only through a cosmopolitan transformation of the state of nature into a legal order' (IO 201).

Do Habermas's alternative models of the relationship between the rule of law and democracy and of international relations answer the Schmittian challenge? In what follows, we review a few important critical challenges they have faced.

The Paradoxes of Constitutional Democracy

The paradoxes of constitutional democracy have been much discussed in recent years. Much of the discussion has centred on a puzzle described by Frank Michelman (1996: 308) concerning how a constitutional founding can be legitimate by democratic standards. The puzzle arises from the fact that democratic endorsement must be attained in order for a constitutional settlement to be legitimate. But the procedures for that democratic endorsement themselves require democratic endorsement. The procedures for this democratic endorsement must again be democratically endorsed. And so on in an infinite regress. For Michelman, this result suggests that the principles of constitutional law cannot logically be made subject to democratic decision.

Michelman claims that this paradox can be resolved if and only if it happens that 'virtually all the country's people . . . [accept] a critical mass of substantive first principles of right government' (Michelman 1999: 50). However, as Michelman himself notes, there is the further problem that even the general acceptance of foundational principles or norms cannot stop the regress, since the principles and norms to which appeal is made will themselves be subject to 'reasonable interpretive pluralism' (Michelman 1998: 91). That is to say, even if everyone agrees on the substantive first principles of right government, these principles can be understood and applied in divergent ways. It appears, then, that there is a dilemma or paradox afflicting attempts to provide a democratic legitimation for a constitutional system. As Christopher Zurn helpfully puts it:

> Appeals to substantialist founding truths cannot get us out of the bootstrapping paradoxes as long as we honestly acknowledge persistent reasonable pluralism and the need for mechanisms putting a temporary end to debate. [But] proceduralist approaches [such as Habermas's] cannot get us out either, since we can always subject our currently accepted decision procedures to challenge and investigation for their constitutional and democratic worth. (Zurn 2010: 213)

In response to Michelman's objections, Habermas has revisited and revised his account of democratic legitimacy. He still rejects the idea that the constitutional structure of a political association can be justified by appeal to a set of 'substantialist founding truths'. But now he also recognises that neither can it be justified by appeal to the democratic credentials of the founding event, since evidently these credentials can always be subject to challenge, as Michelman observes (CD 774). How then is it possible for a constitutional arrangement to be legitimate from a democratic point of view?

Habermas proposes to resolve the dilemma by understanding a constitution not as a fixed inheritance but as a 'project that makes the founding act into an ongoing process of constitution-making that continues across generations' (CD 768). The task of justifying any given constitutional democracy does not lie in the past but in the future. The relationship between democracy and constitutionalism must be worked out over time by 'tapping' the 'normative substance' of the system of rights in a 'self-correcting learning process' (CD 774). This process is a 'politically autonomous elaboration' of the *formal* system of rights *in law*. It is a fallible, revisable and ongoing project facing every political community to grasp more fully the formal system of rights and what it demands of citizens, and to embody these rights in the legal norms and democratic practices of the society. We should not expect to reach a determinant endpoint at which the political self-organisation of society will be perfected. But we can expect there to be a learning process in which democratic deficiencies of the constitutional system are identified and remedied, and in which social life is democratised through revisions of the system of rights.

This model implies that the constitution should not be viewed as a means for citizens of the past to control the citizens of the present and future. The constitution cannot be taken to represent the 'true' will of the people. Equally, however, it cannot be said that the 'true' will of the people resides in the present, in the current state of popular opinion. Both the constitution and public opinion are elements in a constantly mobile constellation. In this way, Habermas sees his deliberative theory of democracy and law as being equally committed to both popular will (democracy) and rights (the rule of law). Neither is prior or superior to the other; both are essential and 'co-original' components in the unfolding process of self-legislation (CD 767).

Habermas's approach, if it is theoretically coherent, not only addresses Michelman's dilemma; it also promises to disarm one of Schmitt's most worrying claims, namely that 'the political' stands outside the constraints of deliberative rationality. According to Andreas Kalyvas, Habermas's writings on the paradox of constitutional democracy have contributed something unique and of lasting value on this point. Namely, the insight that acts of constitution-making can be 'as principled and consistent as normal politics even if they operate in an indeterminate and unstable environment where formal, legal constraints have been weakened by an audacious, disruptive constituent power, reclaiming its, primordial, instituting powers' (Kalyvas 2005: 243–4). The people discover that their extra-legal 'constituent power' must itself embody (or at least approximate) principles of democratic practice if it is to claim legitimacy for itself. And these principles are not handed down like divine law but are 'immanent' in the sense that they characterise the very practice of acting together with others to reach agreement. In other words, it is the pragmatics of communicative agreement itself that provides a normative framework for the people's exercise of their 'constituent power'. This rescues the unavoidable exercise of 'constituent power' from the pure decisionism that Schmitt attributes to it.

But has Habermas succeeded in showing that the paradox of constitutionalism and democracy can be resolved? Even sympathetic readers such as Christopher Zurn and Ciaran Cronin have found some obvious inconsistencies in Habermas's account. For instance, Habermas insists that contemporary citizens must be able to see themselves as sharing the 'same standards' as the founders and that they must judge the project of democracy from the 'same perspective' (CD 775). But why should the standards of the founders enjoy such a determinative status? This seems to presuppose an unnecessarily high view of founders (Zurn 2010: 220). What's more, it is probably false to say that, for example, contemporary American or French citizens share the same intuitive understanding of the democratic project as the founders of their constitutions did in the late eighteenth century (Cronin 2006: 364). But this need not be seen as a problem. Zurn and Cronin argue that Habermas shouldn't be troubled by discontinuities with the past and that he would be better off adopting a more consistently future-oriented account of democratic legitimacy. Kevin Olson (2007) agrees. An existing constitution should be considered legitimate, he proposes, if it has the 'ability to produce conditions allowing full political inclusion at some point in the future' (Olson 2007: 332). This view, which Olson calls 'dynamic constitutionalism', has the advantage that it (realistically) does not lead us to judge a constitution to be illegitimate just because it is not fully satisfactory in its current form – provided that it is structured in such a way as to make it possible for citizens to shape it according to democratic processes.

Pluralism, Hegemony and Deep Disagreement

Other challenges to Habermas's procedural model of democracy have focused on more basic assumptions. 'Agonistic' democrats such as Chantal Mouffe and Bonnie Honig have questioned whether it is possible in principle for 'the political' to be accommodated by a 'procedural' model of democracy. According to Honig, there exists an unresolvable paradox in democratic politics, a paradox which arises because of the difference between what Rousseau called the 'general will' and the 'will of all'. Only the 'general will' bears the mark of legitimacy. But no articulation of the 'general will' can ever hope to achieve acceptance by all:

> The general will can never be really equally in everyone's interest nor really equally willed by everyone. More to the point, given the vicissitudes of legislative processes, there is always some divergence between what people will, as authors, and what emerges as law over them, as subjects. (Honig 2007: 5)

For Honig, there is no way to square this circle. At no point, neither in some original founding act nor in some anticipated future, can self-government be achieved as such. Hence, 'our cherished ideals – law, the people, general will, deliberation – are implicated in that to which deliberative democratic theory opposes them: violence, multitude, the will of all, decision' (Honig 2007: 8).

Similarly, according to Mouffe, there is an ineliminable tension between democracy and liberal constitutionalism; the demand for self-rule and the demand for law-rule are essentially at odds. This is because the actual demands of a people will necessarily exclude other possible demands, thus contravening the standard of inclusion of all as equal citizens. In practice, every process of deliberation must be resolved through a moment of 'decision' which is 'hegemonic' – that is, through a decision that excludes other possible (and rationally defensible) outcomes (Mouffe 2000: 105). The political systems that we participate in and observe are only ever the outcome of such temporary 'hegemonic' resolutions of the collision between the twin 'logics' of democracy and liberalism (Mouffe 1999: 43–4).

In Mouffe's view, the appropriate response to this observation is not to seek a 'principled' resolution to the tension between democracy and constitutionalism, even in some ideal future, since anticipated consensus is always fictitious and ideological. Instead, we should simply insist that all parties in a democratic polity must take responsibility for their exclusions and ensure that the contestation of consensus remains alive: 'A well-functioning democracy calls for a vibrant clash of democratic political positions', a 'struggle between adversaries' (Mouffe 2000: 103–4). Likewise, Honig argues that we should not try to resolve the conflict between the 'general will' and the 'will of all'. Instead, we should acknowledge that each captures an aspect of political life. 'The best a democratic politics can do', Honig argues, is to 'set the material conditions of shared living in such a way as to relieve the propensity of these two [e.g. the 'general will' and the 'will of all'] to diverge and to harden into oppositional relation' (Honig 2007: 8). For Mouffe and Honig, to recognise an irreconcilable conflict at the heart of political life (that which Schmitt referred to as 'the political') is not to endanger democracy, as Habermas fears, but to acknowledge the very condition of its existence.

Zurn plausibly argues that the anxieties of Mouffe and Honig about the 'closure' of democratic contestation in Habermas are misplaced. Habermas's model is not static as they suggest but dynamic, not fully 'reconciled' but only oriented by the ideal of reconciliation (Zurn 2010: 216). Similarly, Cronin maintains that Habermas's account presents not so much an attempt to 'reconcile' constitutionalism and democracy as an expectation that they can come into 'productive interrelation over time' (Cronin 2006: 368n22). Habermas accepts that the institutional elaboration of the two 'logics' of democracy and constitutionalism (both of which he sees as requirements for democratic legitimacy) will be a site of permanent conflict; and this is exactly what one should expect under conditions of fallibility. On this reading, Habermas's position is not so far from that of Mouffe or Honig after all.

Nonetheless, Habermas's position does differ from Mouffe and Honig in its claim that the legitimacy of the democratic system as a whole – in all its 'agonistic' messiness – rests on the procedural credentials of the decision-making process itself. We value the liberal-democratic paradigm of inclusion and ongoing political contestation, as Mouffe and Honig do, precisely because political institutions that reflect these norms and practices lend legitimacy to the legal arrangements that result from them, notwithstanding the fact of ongoing disagreements about the content and application of law. Contrary to Schmitt's model of sovereignty, not just any decision-making procedure will satisfy the demands of public reason. To satisfy these demands, the decision-making procedure will have to be inclusive and democratically organised (see Chapter 5.2). There is a world of difference between the delusional pronouncements of a dictator and the democratically informed and accountable procedures of a modern government. This is why we are not and should not be Schmittians.

Having said that, it is worth stressing that Habermas's discourse theory of democracy does not assume that all disagreements within a political society are resolvable (see Chapter 1.2). (This is especially true at the level of international politics, as we shall discuss below.) Disagreements at the level of 'ethical' reasoning will persist so long as there is a diversity of cultures and of personalities. Similarly, disagreements at the level of 'moral' reasoning will persist because the discursive process is fallible and revisable, even on questions that admit only one correct answer. Contrary to what is often said, therefore, Habermas is not among those who believe that democratic deliberation should ideally aim at consensus in all matters. Even so, Habermas does think it is possible for legitimate lawmaking to occur within such pluralistic societies. Laws can prove acceptable to a diversity of social groups that disagree with each other on substantive 'moral' and 'ethical' matters, provided that the laws represent a settlement that is based on an inclusive consideration of the interests of all and that respects the rights of all. The acceptability of the law thus rests on the virtues of the procedure of decision-making.

Nonetheless, it might be objected that such a model of legitimacy is 'hegemonic' at another level. Is it not the case that the procedures of decision-making and dispute resolution are themselves a cultural product of the Western tradition and that these exclude other possible bases of legitimation for political institutions? For his part, Habermas recognises that, of course, the model of constitutional democracy he defends is the product of a historical learning process and that that learning process is infused with the ethical and religious assumptions of Western culture and Judeo-Christian theology (see Chapter 3). Nonetheless, he argues that the formal system of rights, which is derived from the pragmatic presuppositions of argumentation itself, reflect a set of legitimacy constraints that are unavoidably at work within the development of (any) political culture itself. Habermas does not assume that democratic practices have an immutable form; they will be subject to evolution and learning like all aspects of the 'project' of constitutional democracy. Still, Habermas clearly assumes that questions of procedural fairness rest on a universalist basis, and that agreement on such questions is attainable in principle (IO 99).

Exclusionary Dynamics in Deliberative Politics

An important challenge to Habermas's faith in the legitimacy-conferring power of deliberative procedures comes from critics who argue that the deliberative procedures he appeals to can never *in practice* provide a neutral ground for political disagreement. For instance, Nancy Fraser (1992) and Iris Marion Young (2000: 37–40) argue that certain social groups are effectively excluded or silenced by the assumption that democratic discourse must take the form of critical argumentation. Habermas's image of democratic discourse, they argue, reflects the cultural norms of the white, male, educated circles to which he belongs. His model of argumentation serves to reinforce existing social inequalities by insisting that these culturally specific features of speech be treated as essential features of deliberative practice.[2]

If this were the extent of the problem, however, it seems as though Habermas's deliberative model could be saved by appropriate modifications. Young herself, for instance, proposes that a more truly inclusive democratic practice could be created if we embrace a broader suite of communicative practices, including greeting rituals, storytelling, rhetoric and emotional displays (Young 2000: 52–80). Of course, Young's recommendations need not be seen as the last word on the matter. But, they illustrate why criticisms of the kind we are discussing need not take us beyond the Habermasian deliberative paradigm. If we can learn to deliberate differently, modifying our expectations of what deliberation should look like in order to overcome barriers to equal participation, then it seems that the cultural biases of Habermas's deliberative model can be corrected and that the deliberative model would not need to be abandoned. However, there are deeper problems.

In her essay, 'Activist challenges to deliberative democracy' (2001), Young identifies four general kinds of obstacles that citizens oriented towards deliberative participation might face in real-world situations:

1. In some situations, not all who are affected by deliberations and decision-making are granted leave to participate, or are represented, in those processes. The deliberations and decision-making take place between elites behind closed doors, or they take place in public but citizens are only able to participate as 'observers'.
2. In contexts where rights of participation in deliberative processes

are granted to all affected (or to their representatives), even this is not necessarily sufficient to secure the effective participation of all. Notably, social inequalities can advantage those who are wealthier, those who belong to culturally respected groups, those who are more articulate according to dominant norms of public speech, and those who are well connected.
3. Even when all affected are able to participate *effectively* as equals in situations of deliberation and decision-making, decision-making bodies can possess limited authority to decide and act as they think best, and thus they face the task of choosing among a constrained and inadequate set of alternatives.
4. Finally, in rare instances where all of these structural inequalities and incapacities are absent or adequately remedied, even then the achievement of a free and un-coerced agreement among deliberating individuals can serve to reinforce the interests of dominant groups if the agreement is reached under the influence of hegemonic discourses whose premises and terms are uncritically accepted by participants.

Of course, Habermas would not be surprised to learn that such deviations from the ideals of the deliberative model occur, and he would agree with Young that these violations need to be criticised and overcome. This is precisely what the critical potential of public discourse allows for, he would say. However, Young's key point is that exclusionary dynamics will *always* occur if there are distinctions between 'formal' and 'informal' deliberative contexts and if there are differentials of power within the social order. If we grant the plausible assumption that such features of political life are ineradicable, then we must conclude that there will always be situations in which deliberative engagement will prove to be impossible, futile or self-defeating.

Because the avenue of 'deliberative persuasion' is often unavailable or unfruitful, Young argues that participants in democratic politics must be able to avail themselves of the resources of critique and disruption to oppose flawed deliberative processes – even if it means breaking with the spirit of mutual respect and cooperation that is the hallmark of the 'deliberative stance'. In these instances, if political disagreement is still to be pursued non-violently, then it can only be pursued in 'non-deliberative' modes:

> Under these circumstances of structural inequality and exclusive power, [the activist claims,] good citizens should be protesting outside these

meetings, calling public attention to the assumptions made in them, the control exercised, and the resulting limitations or wrongs of their outcomes. They should use the power of shame and exposure to pressure deliberators to widen their agenda and include attention to more interests. As long as the proceedings exercise exclusive power for the sake of the interests of elites and against the interests of most citizens, then politically engaged citizens who care about justice and environmental preservation are justified even in taking actions aimed at preventing or disrupting the deliberations. (Young 2001: 677)

Thus, Young concludes, we ought to reject the recommendation that citizens should only engage with each other deliberatively. Rather, we ought to regard the 'activist stance' as a fully legitimate and reasonable option alongside the 'deliberative stance'. Both deliberative and activist stances should be accepted as 'responsible' forms of 'democratic communication,' which we may rightfully utilise as seems necessary in the struggle for justice (Young 2001: 688).

Have these conclusions led us beyond the deliberative paradigm? It is debatable. If the deliberative paradigm is defined in strictly egalitarian and cooperative terms as Habermas tends to do, then they would mark a departure from the paradigm. However, if we take a more inclusive view of how actors participate in the theatre of public discourse, then we can see Young's observations as an invitation to revise and expand our view of the deliberative paradigm so that it envelops some of the more 'unruly' practices of political contestation (see Russell 2016).

The Epistemic Reliability of Public Deliberation

The issues raised by Young primarily concern the dynamics of power in the 'strong' public spheres of formal deliberation and decision-making. If we critically reflect on the rational potential of public discourse in 'weak' public spheres of informal communication, different and more troubling questions arise. For instance, is it plausible to believe that audiences of mass media engage in anything approaching a critical assessment of the messages they receive? And, if they do not (or do not reliably), where does this leave a political theory for which the communicative generation of power in and through public discourse is fundamental to democratic legitimacy?

In the past two decades, empirical evidence has emerged that has cast doubt on the assumption that group deliberation has advantages over other methods of decision-making. Cass Sunstein (2000), in particular, has argued that group deliberation is prone to a number of identifiable epistemic defects. Three examples of apparent defects that have been experimentally shown to afflict deliberating groups are the following:

1. *'Informational cascades'*: In a social setting, individuals are liable to defer to the belief of others. As each individual takes a cue from the other, this makes it seem to other members of the group that the belief has a high level of support and hence should be presumed to be acceptable. In this way, a belief can gain momentum simply through a weakly motivated series of assumptions on the part of individuals. The result is that a belief is adopted throughout a social network with very little rational basis, simply because it is believed by others.
2. *'The law of group polarisation'*: A well-attested body of evidence shows that, if deliberation occurs among like-minded individuals, the very process of seeking to reason about one's views with others leads participants to hold their views even more strongly. The group tends to pool reasons for the view they already hold without subjecting that view to any real criticism. At the same time, the group's critical faculties are mobilised to identify reasons not to accept the views of others outside the group with whom they disagree. The result is that when like-minded people deliberate with one another about what to believe, they tend to come to believe there are more or better reasons to hold the view they hold than they previously thought, and that those who think otherwise are not only mistaken but unreasonable.
3. *'Rhetorical asymmetry'*: There appear to be some situations in which certain kinds of reasons have a rhetorical advantage over others. For instance, in deliberations concerning the appropriate penalty for drug-related offences or the appropriate punitive damages for white-collar crime, it appears that deliberation tends to favour arguments for increasing penalties, such that a deliberating group will tend to arrive at a stiffer penalty than the group members individually favoured prior to the deliberation.

David Estlund (2009) has argued that the empirical data cited by Sunstein do not really speaks against the value of deliberation. For instance, Sunstein cites a study that found that deliberative groups 'performed better than their average member, but not as well as their best member' in solving a variety of brainteasers (Sunstein 2006: 60). Is this really a sign of failure on the part of the group? Estlund notes that from the perspective of the group, this is a good result, indicating that group deliberation was the best procedure to follow, unless the group had some means at its disposal to identify who the best member was. In cases where the best member is able to show that they have a solution to a problem, then the empirical evidence shows that groups will quickly and reliably defer to that member. Again, this seems to be a sign of the rationality of the group, even though it is not the group that generates the correct solution *per se*. Even when it comes to the much-discussed phenomenon of group polarisation, Estlund argues, the evidence is more mixed (and hopeful) than Sunstein's presentation might suggest. As Sunstein himself (2006: 65) admits, deliberative groups 'move toward the majority far more often when they are correct than when they are wrong', shifting more dramatically towards correct rather than incorrect answers. In other words, the majority is influential when it is wrong, but it is even more influential when it is right (Estlund 2009: 23). In short, Sunstein's own evidence can be interpreted as providing a reasonably impressive defence of the epistemic value of group deliberation.

The more serious challenge to Habermas's 'epistemic' model of democracy stems from the widely noted pathologies of public discourse that appear to be endemic in the contemporary media environment. The media environment today is more fragmented and siloed than ever before, predictably leading networks of like-minded individuals towards a more polarised stance (Sunstein 2017). There is also evidence that the predictive algorithms utilised, for example, by search engines and social media further amplify this effect (Alfano, Carter and Cheong forthcoming). In addition, social media providers report that fake profiles and fake content are constantly being channelled into their services (Levy 2017). These distinctive challenges facing public deliberation in the contemporary context do not stem from the psychological biases of human reasoning *per se*, nor from the incapacity of human beings to reach rationally justifiable judgements through dialogue with each other. They stem rather from the way in which communication flows are channelled in contemporary media environments and from the ways in which these media environments are susceptible to manipulation.

It could be countered that a strength of Habermas's model of deliberative democracy is that it does not naïvely look to the 'weak' public sphere of mass communication to generate justifiable beliefs and policy positions. In fact, Habermas gives a relatively modest role to the informal public sphere. He expects that it will be able to keep political communication active, to steer it and filter it; but he does not believe it has the resources or organisational capacity necessary to systematically weigh reasons and focus discussions to the point of forming a judgement. The latter functions are performed by the 'strong' public spheres of governmental institutions (see Chapter 5.3). What's more, Habermas has always voiced a rather cautious view about the potentiality for emancipation through rational public discourse given the undermining effects of capitalism and social injustice.

Even so, it is evidently essential to Habermas's two-track model of deliberative politics that public discourse has a *rationalising* role to play in the system of democratic opinion- and will-formation. And it is precisely this claim that has come to appear increasingly dubious in the age of 'post-truth' politics and 'fake news'. Habermas could plausibly point out that we have no choice but to make use of the resources of communicative rationality in order to critically judge the truth and justifiability of claims made in the public sphere (see Chapter 2). This seems to me to be indisputable. All the same, problems of trust and polarisation in media-based communications are the new frontier of deliberative theory. And Habermas's theoretical reflections on political communication in media society have done little to come to grips with the epistemic dimensions of the challenge.

The Democratic Deficit in Habermas's Cosmopolitanism

Does Habermas's cosmopolitan model succeed in charting a course between the Scylla of cultural imperialism and the Charybdis of *realpolitik* in international relations? Critics have raised a number of concerns about Habermas's approach.

As we have noted, Habermas has become increasingly sceptical about the prospects of institutionalising rights of democratic participation at the global level (Chapter 5.5). The arguments he gives for this scepticism have struck some readers as 'unexpectedly Schmittian' (Fine and Smith 2003: 474). There may be empirical reasons to think that global democracy is a non-starter. But it is not clear that global democracy is in fact conceptually incoherent. In any case, it is clear that Habermas has judged that the only plausible way forward is to embrace a more 'liberal' model, in which a cosmopolitan order is implemented from above by a set of global political institutions without a 'formal democratic mandate' (Fine and Smith 2003: 475). Retreating from the goal of democratisation at the global level,

Habermas's work on regional and global governance takes on a merely 'defensive' stance, aiming only to preserve existing sites of democracy (Scheuerman 2008: 153).

However, Habermas continues to maintain that the constitutionalisation of international law will not be a 'civilising process' unless the new legal instruments created by international organisations can claim legitimacy for themselves – that is, the kind of legitimacy that comes from democratically generated law (LT 56). What's more, he insists that a democratic basis of legitimacy is required at the transnational and global level in order to avoid 'sociopathological side-effects'; global governance will remain technocratic and beset by legitimation problems so long as it is not democratised (PC 84). Habermas thus sits in an unresolved position where he cannot offer a democratic legitimation for his cosmopolitanism, yet he is still theoretically committed to the need for such a legitimation.

In recent work, Habermas has placed greater emphasis on the concept of human dignity as a basis of legitimation for the global political order (CEU 71–100). But this shift in emphasis is problematic for several reasons. First, Habermas claims that 'moral outrage' at 'egregious human rights violations' is a normative reaction common to all world cultures (DW 143). But while this may be true of those of us who are products of the Western tradition, Habermas himself accepts that citizens of developing nations may not have come to form the same normative expectations (DW 165). Second, as a consequence, the 'civilising process' of implementing and protecting human rights cannot be a 'bottom-up' process that occurs within states that lack human rights. It falls to those powerful 'developed' nations for whom human rights are 'uncontroversial' to undertake this work, and to this extent 'the civilizing force of law begins to feel uncomfortably imperialistic' (Roele 2014: 208). Thus, non-Western nations are excluded from both the generation of the legal norms to which they are subject and the implementation of those norms. In short, although Habermas's strategy for justifying and implementing human rights is supposed to be an antidote to the hegemony of the West, and he renounces the 'unilateral imposition [of human rights] at gunpoint', it appears that his own model requires just this. Indeed, it comes dangerously close to the 'moralisation' of global politics that Schmitt cautioned against.

Even if the framework of human rights were uncontroversial, there are problems with entrusting their interpretation and application to a political entity such as Habermas envisages. Habermas argues that so long as it restricts itself to the judicial rather than political matters, namely decisions that concern issues of fundamental human rights, then the United Nations can avoid making decisions in areas where its legitimacy would be questionable. This means also that there is little need for world citizens to engage in the complex processes of political opinion- and will-formation. However, human rights decisions are always political or at least have political dimensions. As Scheuerman (2008: 162) notes, matters of interstate conflict and human rights interventions are among the most controversial and fundamental of political questions. While prohibitions on genocide and war are widely accepted, there is no unanimity on what these prohibitions entail in given cases. Indeed, it is precisely for this reason that states are reluctant to give over jurisdiction to the United Nations and the International Criminal Court to declare acts of war to be legal or illegal.

The type of cosmopolitanism that Habermas advocates for has been criticised also for its thin 'liberal' understanding of human rights. While Habermas argues that at the national (and even regional) level the whole suite of liberal, political and social rights must be given legal expression, he claims that to attempt to implement rights of political participation and social rights at the global level would be to 'overtax' the global political system (BNR 323). Human rights, he argues, should be treated as analogous to classical liberal rights; they are merely 'negative' rights. But, again, this is an odd departure from the position that Habermas takes elsewhere about the necessary supplementation of civil and political rights with social rights (see Chapter 5.2) (Ingram 2009). Several critics have argued that Habermas should follow his own reasoning and accept that the legitimacy of global institutions of law and politics will be radically weakened if they do not apply human rights law to problems, say, of global economic inequality and poverty (Lafont 2008; Flynn 2009).

Relatedly, Habermas argues that matters of 'global domestic policy' must be entrusted to processes of intergovernmental negotiation and to the oversight of bodies that are responsible to monitor and regulate matters of international concern. Without any plausible account of how these mechanisms can be democratised or how they can be arranged to counterbalance the vast asymmetries of bargaining power, Habermas's position amounts to little more than a qualified endorsement of the current systems of international decision-making – the very systems that have brought us economic globalisation as we know it (Scheuerman 2008: 164–5).

European Cosmopolitanism as Vanguard for Humanity?

Habermas's sincere concern for the future of Europe is obviously connected with his citizenship and his personal motivation to see Europe realise the promise of its own heritage. But Habermas clearly also views Europe as the pacesetter for the world when it comes to forging institutional frameworks of peace and justice (see Chapter 4). As Fine and Smith (2003: 483) remark:

> There is a sense in which Habermas presents Europe as the universal nation of our day, alone capable of conserving the democratic achievements of the nation-state – civil rights, social welfare, education and leisure – and of extending them beyond the limits of the nation.

Does Habermas's faith in Europe risk 'turning Europe into a vehicle for a new form of transnational chauvinism rather than into a vehicle for cosmopolitan ideas and solidarity' as Fine and Smith claim?

Gurminder Bhambra certainly believes it does. Habermas portrays European civilisation as a product of an internal learning process, e.g. through the pacification of the wars of religion. The project of cosmopolitanism means translating the learnings of Europe into new and wider contexts. But this is problematic for at least two reasons. First, Habermas seems to ignore the way in which the European project is also a colonial project, intimately connected with the Global South, and not merely a set of institutional structures that might be replicated elsewhere.

> The articulation of cosmopolitanism as a specifically European phenomenon rests on a particular understanding of European history that evades acknowledging European domination over much of the world as significant to that history. It also disavows examining the consequences of that domination for the contemporary multicultural constitution of European societies. (Bhambra 2016: 193)

If Habermas wanted to develop a critical theory of globalisation, he would have to face squarely this facet of European history. A consequence of this first feature of Habermas's work is that he does not anticipate that institutional models of inclusion and democracy might be found outside of Europe.

Second, and relatedly, Habermas has a tendency to understand the notion of the 'postcolonial' only in terms of the social and political transformations taking place in formerly colonised countries. There is no appreciation that colonising countries will also have to undergo a de-colonising transformation. This presents a deep normative and political challenge: 'insofar as the cosmopolitan project of Europe does not come to terms with its colonial past and postcolonial present, it establishes a form of neocolonial cosmopolitanism that legitimizes neocolonial policies both within and outside Europe' (Bhambra 2016: 189).

Navid Hassanzadeh concurs. Habermas's cosmopolitanism is presented in such a way that it assumes 'that the political culture and history of Europe place it in a special position with regard to the principles underlying constitutional patriotism' (Hassanzadeh 2015: 439). Evidence of the one-sidedness of Habermas's political reflections can be found in the fact that he has not engaged in any substantive way with non-Western traditions to discover what we might learn about better or different ways to solve the social and political problems caused by globalisation. Indeed, Hassanzadeh (2015: 444) observes, he might discover that the phenomenon of globalisation itself looks quite different from the standpoint of other peoples and places.

Not only should these deficits lead us to suspect that Habermas's cosmopolitan vision is insufficiently critical and theoretically underdeveloped, but according to Pheng Cheah (2006) they also mean that his vision is unfeasible. It is unfeasible, first, because it presumes to universalise the 'cosmopolitan virtues' of northern states and features of the northern constitutional welfare state without adequately appreciating the repressive features of these same values and institutions. Second, it is unfeasible because it implicitly requires that all states undergo a process of economic 'modernisation' in order to be able to provide social welfare according to the blueprint of northern states. But economic modernisation according to the dominant neoliberal model has, in many cases, come at the expense of the welfare of citizens in developing countries. Third, it is unfeasible because northern countries have a vested interest in continuing to extract economic benefits from the Global South, and Habermas's vision offers no plausible path towards overcoming this conflict of interest and remedying the underlying problem of global economic inequality. In short, 'global economic inequality is simultaneously the material condition of possibility of democratic legitimation in the North Atlantic and that which hampers its achievement in the postcolonial South' (Cheah 2006: 494).

For his part, Habermas readily acknowledges that economic and social modernisation have opened up developing nations to new forms of predation and oppression. However, he argues that these injustices can only be redressed through more adequate forms of law and through more robust legal and political institutions. Rights are the solution to these problems, not the cause of them. Nonetheless, Habermas admits that the conceptual and institutional solutions that the West has developed as answers to the challenges of modernity may not be 'the only one[s] or even the best one[s]' (PC 128). And, while Habermas has by no means been an exemplar in this respect, he does assert that intercultural dialogue is essential for enabling each of us to come to an awareness of our 'blind spots' (PC 129). In this spirit, we should be content to treat Habermas's cosmopolitan vision as a fallible contribution to an ongoing conversation that will have to be truly global in its inclusivity. Such a conversation has barely begun.

Conclusion

This final point returns us once again to the guiding motif of Habermas's political philosophy: the inescapability of the need for communication and an orientation towards mutual understanding. Paradoxically, even the advocates of radical difference and irreducible plurality must articulate their defence of difference and plurality in a language that seeks the understanding and rational acceptance of interlocutors. The desire for mutual understanding and the need to justify ourselves pulls us inexorably back into the whirlpool of discourse – and democracy. Habermas's theory of constitutional democracy and his cosmopolitanism are contestable in their specifics. Nonetheless, Habermas's enduring legacy is that he has brought the practice of argumentation to the centre of political theory. Largely as a result of Habermas's influence, it is now generally acknowledged that a 'deliberative turn' has taken place in contemporary political theory. Democracy implies discourse, the reciprocal exchange of reasons among speaking beings. To this extent, we are all Habermasians.

Notes

1. On this basis, Habermas argues minority groups within states can be afforded equal rights as citizens (IO 203–36). For a discussion of Habermas's views on multiculturalism, see Baxter (2011: 208–22).

2. Postcolonial theorists have similarly criticised Habermas's model of deliberation for universalising conventions of Western political discourse to the exclusion of other styles of communication. See, for instance, Hassanzadeh (2015: 439–41).

References

Alfano, Mark, Joseph Adam Carter and Marc Cheong. (forthcoming). 'Technological seduction and self-radicalization'. *Journal of the American Philosophical Association*.

Allen, Amy. (2007). 'Systematically distorted subjectivity? Habermas and the critique of power'. *Philosophy & Social Criticism* 33(5): 641–50.

Allen, Amy. (2008). *The Politics of Our Selves: Power, Autonomy, and Gender in Contemporary Critical Theory*. New York: Columbia University Press.

Allen, Amy. (2009). 'Discourse, power, and subjectivation: The Foucault/Habermas debate reconsidered'. *The Philosophical Forum* 40(1): 1–28.

Allen, Amy. (2010). 'Recognizing domination: Recognition and power in Honneth's critical theory'. *Journal of Power* 3(1): 21–32.

Allen, Amy. (2016). *The End of Progress*. New York: Columbia University Press.

Allen, Amy. (2017). 'How not to critique the critique of progress: A reply to Payrow Shabani'. *Journal of Value Inquiry* 51: 681–7.

Allen, Amy, Rainer Forst and Mark Haugaard. (2014). 'Power and reason, justice and domination: A conversation'. *Journal of Political Power* 7(1): 7–33.

Amin, Samir. (2009). *Eurocentrism: Modernity, Religion and Democracy* (2nd edn). New York: Monthly Review Press.

Anderson, Elizabeth. (2012). 'Epistemic justice as a virtue of social institutions'. *Social Epistemology: A Journal of Knowledge, Culture and Policy* 26(2): 163–73.

Arendt, Hannah. (1958). *The Human Condition*. Chicago, IL: The University of Chicago Press.

Arendt, Hannah. (1963). *On Revolution*. New York: Viking Press.

Arendt, Hannah. (1970). *On Violence*. New York: Harcourt.

Arendt, Hannah. (1977). *Between Past and Future*. New York: Penguin Books.

Ashenden, Samantha and David Owen (eds). (1999). *Foucault contra Habermas: Recasting the Dialogue between Genealogy and Critical Theory*. London: Sage Publications.

Barry, Brian. (2002). 'Capitalists rule OK? Some puzzles about power'. *Politics, Philosophy, and Economics* 1(2): 155–84.

Baynes, Kenneth. (2002). 'Freedom and recognition in Hegel and Habermas'. *Philosophy & Social Criticism* 28(1): 1–17.
Baynes, Kenneth. (2016). *Habermas*. London and New York: Routledge.
Baxter, Hugh. (2011). *Habermas: The Theory of Law and Democracy*. Stanford, CA: Stanford University Press.
Bernstein, Jay. (1995). *Recovering Ethical Life: Jürgen Habermas and the Future of Critical Theory*. New York: Routledge.
Bernstein, Richard J. (2010). *The Pragmatic Turn*. Malden, MA: Polity.
Bhambra, Gurminder K. (2016). 'Wither Europe? Postcolonial versus neo-colonial cosmopolitanism'. *Interventions* 18(2): 187–202.
Böckenförde, E. W. (1991). *State, Society and Liberty: Studies in Political Theory and Constitutional Law*, trans. J. A. Underwood. New York: St Martin's Press.
Bohman, James. (1986). 'Formal pragmatics and social criticism: The philosophy of language and the critique of ideology in Habermas' theory of communicative action'. *Philosophy & Social Criticism* 11(4): 331–53.
Brandom, Robert. (1994) *Making It Explicit: Reasoning, Representing, and Discursive Commitment*. Cambridge, MA: Harvard University Press.
Breen, Keith. (2007). 'Work and emancipatory practice: Towards a recovery of human beings' productive capacities'. *Res Publica* 13(4): 381–414.
Brown, Carol. (1981). 'Mothers, fathers and children: From private to public patriarchy'. In Lydia Sargent (ed.), *Women and Revolution* (pp. 239–67). Boston, MA: South End Press.
Brownstein, Michael and Jennifer Saul (eds). (2016). *Implicit Bias and Philosophy*, 2 vols. Oxford: Oxford University Press.
Butler, Judith. (1995). 'Contingent foundations: Feminism and the question of "postmodernism"'. In Seyla Benhabib, Judith Butler, Drucilla Cornell and Nancy Fraser, *Feminist Contentions. A Philosophical Exchange* (pp. 35–58). New York: Routledge.
Butler, Judith. (1997). *The Psychic Life of Power: Theories in Subjection*. Palo Alto, CA: Stanford University Press.
Chakrabarty, Dipesh. (2002). *Habitations of Modernity: Essays in the Wake of Subaltern Studies*. Chicago and London: The University of Chicago Press.
Chambers, Simone. (2009). 'Who shall judge? Hobbes, Locke, and Kant on the construction of public reason'. *Ethics & Global Politics* 2(4): 349–68.
Cheah, Pheng. (2006). 'Cosmopolitanism'. *Theory, Culture & Society* 23(2–3): 486–96.
Cohen, Jean L. (1995). 'Critical social theory and feminist critiques: The debate with Jürgen Habermas'. In Johanna Meehan (ed.), *Feminists Read Habermas* (pp. 57–90). New York: Routledge.
Coleman, James S. (1963). 'Comment on "On the concept of influence"'. *Public Opinion Quarterly* 27(1): 63–82.
Cox, Robert W. (1997). 'Democracy in hard times: Economic globalisation

and the limits to liberal democracy'. In A. McGrew (ed.), *The Transformation of Democracy?* Cambridge: Polity.

Cronin, Ciaran. (2006). 'On the possibility of a democratic constitutional founding: Habermas and Michelman in dialogue'. *Ratio Juris* 19(3): 343–69.

Cudd, Ann E. (2006). *Analyzing Oppression*. New York: Oxford University Press.

Dahl, Robert. (1957). 'The concept of power'. *Behavioral Science* 2: 201–15.

Darwall, Stephen. (2006). *The Second Person Standpoint: Morality, Respect, and Accountability*. Cambridge, MA: Harvard University Press.

Daukas, Nancy. (2006). 'Epistemic trust and social location'. *Episteme: A Journal of Social Epistemology* 3(1): 109–24.

Delanty, Gerard. (2006). 'Modernity and the escape from Eurocentrism'. In Gerard Delanty (ed.), *Handbook of Contemporary European Social Theory* (pp. 266–78). London: Routledge.

Dews, Peter (ed.). (1986). *Habermas: Autonomy & Solidarity*. London: Verso.

Dotson, Kristie. (2011). 'Tracking epistemic violence, tracking practices of silencing'. *Hypatia: A Journal of Feminist Philosophy* 26(2): 236–57.

Dussel, Enrique. (1993). 'Eurocentrism and modernity'. *boundary 2* 20(3): 65–76.

Eisenstadt, S. N. (2001). 'The civilizational dimension of modernity'. *International Sociology* 16(3): 320–40.

Eley, Geoff. (1992). 'Nations, publics, and political cultures: Placing Habermas in the nineteenth century'. In C. Calhoun (ed.), *Habermas and the Public Sphere* (pp. 289–349). Cambridge, MA: MIT Press.

Estlund, David. (2009). 'On Sunstein's "Infotopia"'. *Theoria: A Journal of Social and Political Theory* 56(119): 14–29.

Fine, Robert and Will Smith. (2003). 'Jürgen Habermas's theory of cosmopolitanism'. *Constellations* 10(3): 469–87.

Finlayson, James Gordon and Fabian Freyenhagen (eds). (2011). *Habermas and Rawls: Disputing the Political*. New York: Routledge.

Flikschuh, Katrin. (2008). 'Reason, right, and revolution: Kant and Locke'. *Philosophy & Public Affairs* 36(4): 375–404.

Flynn, Jeffrey. (2009). 'Human rights, transnational solidarity, and duties to the global poor'. *Constellations* 16(1): 59–77.

Flynn, Jeffrey. (2014a). 'Truth, objectivity and experience after the pragmatic turn'. In Judith Green (ed.), *Richard J. Bernstein and the Pragmatist Turn in Contemporary Philosophy* (pp. 230–60). New York: Palgrave.

Flynn, Jeffrey. (2014b). 'System and lifeworld in Habermas' theory of democracy'. *Philosophy & Social Criticism* 40(2): 205–14.

Forst, Rainer. (2002). *Contexts of Justice*, trans. John M. M. Farrell. Berkeley, CA: University of California Press.

REFERENCES

Forst, Rainer. (2012). *The Right to Justification*, trans. Jeffrey Flynn. New York: Columbia University Press.

Forst, Rainer. (2015). 'Noumenal power'. *The Journal of Political Philosophy* 23(2): 111–27.

Foucault, Michel. (1973). *The Birth of the Clinic*, trans. Allan Sheridan. New York: Pantheon Books.

Foucault, Michel. (1977). *Discipline and Punish*, trans. Alan Sheridan. New York: Pantheon Books.

Foucault, Michel. (1978). *History of Sexuality, Volume 1: An Introduction*, trans. Robert Hurley. New York: Pantheon Books.

Foucault, Michel. (1983). 'The subject and power'. In Hubert Dreyfus and Paul Rabinow (eds), *Michel Foucault: Beyond Structuralism and Hermeneutics* (2nd edn). Chicago, IL: Chicago University Press.

Foucault, Michel. (1984). *The Foucault Reader*, ed. Paul Rabinow. New York: Pantheon Books.

Foucault, Michel. (1988). 'The ethic of care for the self as a practice of freedom: An interview with Michel Foucault on January 20, 1984'. In James Bernauer and David Rasmussen (eds), *The Final Foucault* (pp. 1–20). Cambridge, MA: MIT Press.

Foucault, Michel. (2006). *History of Madness*, ed. Jean Khalfa, trans. Jonathan Murphy and Jean Khalfa. New York: Routledge.

Fraser, Nancy. (1985). 'What's critical about critical theory? The case of Habermas and gender'. *New German Critique* 35: 97–131.

Fraser, Nancy. (1989). 'Foucault on modern power: Empirical insights and normative confusions'. In *Unruly Practices: Power, Discourse, and Gender in Contemporary Social Theory* (pp. 17–34). Minneapolis, MN: The University of Minnesota Press.

Fraser, Nancy. (1992). 'Rethinking the public sphere: A contribution to the critique of actually existing democracy'. In C. Calhoun (ed.), *Habermas and the Public Sphere* (pp. 109–42). Cambridge, MA: MIT Press.

Fraser, Nancy. (2003). 'Social justice in the age of identity politics: Redistribution, recognition, and participation'. In Nancy Fraser and Axel Honneth, *Redistribution or Recognition? A Political-Philosophical Exchange*. London: Verso.

Fricker, Miranda. (2007). *Epistemic Injustice: Power and the Ethics of Knowing*. Oxford: Oxford University Press.

Gadamer, Hans-Georg. (2007). 'The universality of the hermeneutical problem'. In Richard E. Palmer (ed.), *The Gadamer Reader*. Chicago, IL: Northwestern University Press.

Giddens, Anthony. (1968). '"Power" in the recent writings of Talcot Parsons'. *Sociology* 2(3): 257–72.

Günther, Klaus. (1996). 'Communicative freedom, communicative power, and jurisgenesis'. *Cardozo Law Review* 17: 1035–58.

Haslanger, Sally. (2015). 'Social structure, narrative and explanation'. *Canadian Journal of Philosophy* 45(1): 1–15.

Hassanzadeh, Navid. (2015). 'Post-nationalism and Western modernity: Beyond the limits of the "European-wide public sphere"'. *Constellations* 22(3): 435–46.

Hegel, G. W. F. (1991a). *The Encyclopedia Logic: Part 1 of the Encyclopaedia of Philosophical Sciences*, trans T. F. Geraets, W. A. Suchting, and H. S. Harris. Indianapolis, IN: Hackett.

Hegel, G. W. F. (1991b). *Elements of the Philosophy of Right*, ed. Allen W. Wood, trans. H. B. Nisbet. Cambridge: Cambridge University Press.

Heidegger, Martin. (1962). *Being and Time*, trans. John Macquarie and Edward Robinson. New York: Harper & Row.

Held, David. (2002). 'Crisis tendencies, legitimation and the state'. In David M. Rasmussen and James Swindal (eds), *Jürgen Habermas*, vol. 2 (pp. 215–30). London: SAGE Publications.

Hobbes, Thomas. (1994). *Leviathan*. Indianapolis, IN: Hackett.

Honig, Bonnie. (2007). 'Between decision and deliberation: Political paradox in democratic theory'. *American Political Science Review* 101(1): 1–17.

Honneth, Axel. (1991). *The Critique of Power*. Cambridge, MA: MIT Press.

Honneth, Axel. (2010). *The Pathologies of Individual Freedom: Hegel's Social Theory*, trans. Ladislaus Löb. Princeton, NJ: Princeton University Press.

Honneth, Axel. (2014). *Freedom's Right: The Social Foundations of Democratic Life*, trans. Joseph Ganahl. Cambridge: Polity.

Honneth, Axel. (2017a). *The Idea of Socialism*, trans. Joseph Ganahl. Cambridge: Polity.

Honneth, Axel. (2017b). 'Three, not two, concepts of liberty: A proposal to enlarge our moral self-understanding'. In Rachel Zuchert and James Kreines (eds), *Hegel on Philosophy in History* (pp. 177–92). Cambridge: Cambridge University Press.

Ingram, David. (2005). 'Foucault and Habermas'. In Gary Gutting (ed.), *The Cambridge Companion to Foucault* (pp. 240–83). Cambridge: Cambridge University Press.

Ingram, David. (2009). 'Of sweatshops and subsistence: Habermas on human rights'. *Ethics & Global Politics* 2(3): 193–217.

Iser, Mattias. (2013). 'Recognition'. Edward N. Zalta (ed.), *The Stanford Encyclopedia of Philosophy*, <https://plato.stanford.edu/archives/fall2013/entries/recognition/>.

Ivison, Duncan. (1997). 'The secret history of public reason: Hobbes to Rawls'. *History of Political Thought* 18(1): 125–47.

Jackson, Ben. (2013). 'Social democracy and democratic socialism'. In Michael Freeden, Lyman Tower Sargent and Marc Stears (eds), *The Oxford Handbook of Political Ideologies* (pp. 348–63). Oxford: Oxford University Press.

Joas, Hans. (1991). 'The unhappy marriage of hermeneutics and functionalism'. In Axel Honneth and Hans Joas (eds), *Communicative Action* (pp. 97–118). Cambridge, MA: MIT Press.

Jütten, Timo. (2011). 'The colonization thesis: Habermas on reification'. *International Journal of Philosophical Studies* 19(5): 701–27.

Jütten, Timo. (2013). 'Habermas and markets'. *Constellations* 20(4): 587–603.

Kalyvas, Andreas. (2005). 'Popular sovereignty, democracy, and the constituent power'. *Constellations* 12(2): 223–44.

Kant, Immanuel. (1996a). *Practical Philosophy*, ed. and trans. Mary J. Gregor. Cambridge: Cambridge University Press.

Kant, Immanuel. (1996b). *Religion and Rational Theology*, ed. and trans. Allen W. Wood and George di Giovanni. Cambridge: Cambridge University Press.

Kant, Immanuel. (1998). *Critique of Pure Reason*, ed. and trans. Paul Guyer and Allen Wood. Cambridge: Cambridge University Press.

Kelly, Michael (ed.). (1994). *Critique and Power: Recasting the Foucault/Habermas Debate*. Cambridge, MA: MIT Press.

Kunda, Ziva. (1990). 'The case for motivated reasoning'. *Psychological Bulletin* 108(3): 480–98.

Laden, Anthony Simon. (2012). *Reasoning: A Social Picture*. Oxford: Oxford University Press.

Lafont, Cristina. (2008). 'Alternate visions of a new global order: What should cosmopolitans hope for?' *Ethics & Global Politics* 1(1–2): 1–20.

Landes, Joan B. (1995). 'The public and the private sphere: A feminist reconsideration'. In Johanna Meehan (ed.), *Feminists Read Habermas* (pp. 91–116). New York: Routledge.

Levine, Steven. (2010). 'Habermas, Kantian pragmatism and truth'. *Philosophy & Social Criticism* 36(6): 677–95.

Levy, Neil. (2017). 'The bad news about fake news'. *Social Epistemology Review and Reply Collective* 6(8): 20–36.

Locke, John. (1980). *Second Treatise of Government*, ed. C. B. Macpherson. Indianapolis, IN: Hackett.

Lovett, Frank. (2012). 'Power'. In Robert E. Goodin, Philip Pettit and Thomas W. Pogge (eds), *A Companion to Contemporary Political Philosophy* (pp. 709–18). Oxford and Cambridge, MA: Wiley-Blackwell.

Lukács, Georg. (1971). *History and Class Consciousness*, trans. Rodney Livingstone. Cambridge, MA: MIT Press.

McCarthy, Thomas. (1990). 'The critique of impure reason: Foucault and the Frankfurt School'. *Political Theory* 18: 365–400.

McCarthy, Thomas. (1991). 'Complexity and democracy: Or the seducements of systems theory'. In Axel Honneth and Hans Joas (eds), *Communicative Action* (pp. 119–40). Cambridge, MA: MIT Press.

McCarthy, Thomas. (2009). *Race, Empire, and the Idea of Human Development*. New York: Cambridge University Press.

Marshall, T. H. (1950). *Citizenship and Social Class*. Cambridge: Cambridge University Press.

Marx, Karl. (1990). *Capital: A Critique of Political Economy*. London: Penguin.

Mason, Rebecca. (2011). 'Two kinds of unknowing'. *Hypatia: A Journal of Feminist Philosophy* 26(2): 294–307.

Michelman, Frank. (1996). 'Review of Jürgen Habermas, "Between Facts and Norms"'. *Journal of Philosophy* 93: 307–15.

Michelman, Frank. (1998). 'Constitutional authorship'. In L. Alexander (ed.), *Constitutionalism: Philosophical Foundations* (pp. 64–98). Cambridge: Cambridge University Press.

Michelman, Frank. (1999). *Brennan and Democracy*. Princeton, NJ: Princeton University Press.

Moran, Richard. (2005). 'Getting told and being believed'. *Philosophers' Imprint* 5: 1–29.

Mouffe, Chantal. (1999). 'Carl Schmitt and the paradox of liberal democracy'. In Chantal Mouffe (ed.), *The Challenge of Carl Schmitt*. New York: Verso.

Mouffe, Chantal. (2000). *The Democratic Paradox*. New York: Verso.

Mouzelis, Nicos. (1999). 'Modernity: A non-European conceptualization'. *British Journal of Sociology* 50(1): 141–59.

Müller-Doohm, Stefan. (2016). *Habermas: A Biography*. Cambridge: Polity.

Neuhouser, Frederick. (2000). *Foundations of Hegel's Social Theory: Actualizing Freedom*. Cambridge, MA: Harvard University Press.

Noonan, Jeff. (2005). 'Modernization, rights, and democratic society: The limits of Habermas's democratic theory'. *Res Publica* 11(2): 101–23.

Olson, Kevin. (2007). 'Paradoxes of constitutional democracy'. *American Journal of Political Science* 51(2): 330–43.

Olson, Kevin. (2011). 'Legitimate speech and hegemonic idiom: The limits of deliberative democracy in the diversity of its voices'. *Political Studies* 59: 527–46.

Pateman, Carole. (1988). 'The fraternal social contract'. In J. Keane (ed.), *Civil Society and the State: New European Perspectives* (pp. 101–28). London: Verso Books.

Pettit, Philip. (1997). *Republicanism: A Theory of Freedom and Government*. Oxford: Clarendon Press and New York: Oxford University Press.

Pettit, Philip. (2013). 'Two republican traditions'. In Andreas Niederberger and Philipp Schink (eds), *Republican Democracy: Liberty, Law and Politics* (pp. 169–204). Edinburgh: Edinburgh University Press.

Piketty, Thomas. (2014). *Capital in the Twenty-First Century*. Cambridge, MA: Harvard University Press.

Pippin, Robert. (2008). *Hegel's Practical Philosophy: Rational Agency as Ethical Life*. Cambridge: Cambridge University Press.

Post, Gaines. (1964). *Studies in Medieval Legal Thought: Pubilc Law and the State 1100–1322*. Princeton, NJ: Princeton University Press.

Postema, Gerald. (1995). 'Public practical reason: An archeology'. *Social Philosophy and Policy* 12(1): 43–86.

Rawls, John. (1971). *A Theory of Justice*. Cambridge, MA: Harvard University Press.

Rawls, John. (1995). 'Reply to Habermas'. *Journal of Philosophy* 92(3): 132–80.

Rawls, John. (2005). *Political Liberalism* (2nd edn). New York: Columbia University Press.

Roele, Isobel. (2014). 'The vicious circles of Habermas' cosmopolitics'. *Law and Critique* 25: 199–229.

Rousseau, Jean-Jacques. (1968). *The Social Contract*, trans. Maurice Cranston. New York: Penguin Books.

Russell, Matheson. (2016). 'Polemical speech and the struggle for recognition'. *Parrhesia: A Journal of Critical Philosophy* 26: 157–75.

Russell, Matheson. (2017). 'Habermas and the "presupposition" of the common objective world'. *Metodo* 5(1): 171–203.

Russell, Matheson and Andrew Montin. (2015). 'The rationality of political disagreement: Rancière's critique of Habermas'. *Constellations* 22(4): 543–54.

Said, Edward. (1994). *Culture and Imperialism*. London: Vintage Books.

Scanlon, Thomas. (1998). *What We Owe to Each Other*. Cambridge, MA: Harvard University Press.

Scheuerman, William E. (2008). *Frankfurt School Perspectives on Globalization, Democracy, and the Law*. New York: Routledge.

Scheuerman, William E. (2011). 'Jürgen Habermas: Postwar German political debates and the making of a critical theorist'. In C. Zuckert (ed.), *Political Philosophy in the 20th Century: Authors and Arguments* (pp. 238–51). Cambridge: Cambridge University Press.

Scheuerman, William E. (2013). 'Capitalism, law, and social criticism'. *Constellations* 20(4): 571–86.

Schmitt, Carl. (2005). *Political Theology. Four Chapters on the Concept of Sovereignty*, trans. G. Schwab. Chicago, IL: University of Chicago Press.

Schmitt, Carl. (2007). *The Concept of the Political. Expanded Edition*, trans. G. Schwab. Chicago, IL: University of Chicago Press.

Schmitt, Carl. (2008). *Constitutional Theory*, trans. J. Seitzer. Durham, NC: Duke University Press.

Sitton, John F. (1998). 'Disembodied capitalism: Habermas's conception of the economy'. *Sociological Forum* 13(1): 61–83.

Spivak, Gayatri Chakravorty. (1987). *In Other Worlds: Essays in Cultural Politics*. New York: Methuen.

Sunstein, Cass. (2000). 'Deliberative trouble: Why groups go to extremes'. *The Yale Law Journal* 110(1): 71–119.
Sunstein, Cass. (2006). *Infotopia: How Many Minds Produce Knowledge*. New York: Oxford University Press.
Sunstein, Cass. (2017). *Republic: Divided Democracy in the Age of Social Media*. Princeton, NJ: Princeton University Press.
Tully, James. (2009). 'On law, democracy, and imperialism'. In *Public Philosophy in A New Key*, vol. 2 (pp. 127–65). Cambridge: Cambridge University Press.
Vatter, Miguel. (2008). 'The idea of public reason and the reason of state: Schmitt and Rawls on the political'. *Political Theory* 36: 239–71.
Weber, Max. (1978). *Economy and Society: An Outline of Interpretive Sociology*, vol. 1, ed. Günther Roth and Claus Wittich. Berkeley, CA: University of California Press.
Young, Iris Marion. (2000). *Inclusion and Democracy*. Oxford: Oxford University Press.
Young, Iris Marion. (2001). 'Activist challenges to deliberative democracy'. *Political Theory* 29(5): 670–90.
Zurn, Christopher. (2010). 'The logic of legitimacy: Bootstrapping paradoxes of constitutional democracy'. *Legal Theory* 16: 191–227.

Index

absolutist state, 62–3, 125–7
administrative state, 14, 55–7, 62–3, 64, 66, 74–5, 76, 80–1, 83, 86, 87, 102–3, 103–7, 143
agency, 6, 26–7, 39
agonism, 183–4
Allen, A., 45–8, 51, 52n, 113, 115–20, 122n
Arendt, H., 19, 30, 31–5, 37n, 100n, 148
argumentation *see* discourse
authoritarianism, 174–7
autonomy, 17–18, 27
  private, 60, 67, 71, 75, 84, 126, 129, 134, 135–6, 142, 148–9, 155–6
  public, 71, 75, 76, 134, 136, 149, 156
  vs freedom of choice, 22–4

banking and finance, 61, 88–9, 109, 170
bargaining, 12–13, 29, 149, 170–1, 193
Baxter, H., 104–6
Bhambra, G. K., 194–5
Bourdieu, P., 53n
Brown, C., 111
Bulter, J., 39, 45–6
bureaucracy, 2, 10, 57, 62–3, 79, 80, 82, 85, 89, 107, 109, 160, 162, 164

capital flight, 92
capitalism, 2, 4, 44, 61–2, 63, 67, 72, 76–82, 85–8, 104, 107–10, 112, 191
  global, 90, 92, 94, 170
  see also market economy
Chakrabarty, D., 119–20
Cheah, P., 195
citizenship, 67, 68–9, 84, 90, 167–8, 172n
  conceptions of, 148–9
  world, 167–8, 169, 193

civil society, 60–2, 63, 67, 80, 82, 84, 146–7, 148, 151, 171, 177
class conflict, 76–7, 108–9
coercion, 15–16, 29–30, 40, 42, 45, 47–8, 51, 103, 110, 151, 168
  via law, 57–8, 63, 66, 141, 179
Cohen, J., 110–11
Cold War, 87, 96
colonialism, 61, 101, 112–15, 115–16, 121n, 194–5, 197n
commodification, 79–80, 85, 91, 107–8, 110
communication
  flows of, 74, 82–3, 130, 145–7
  systematically distorted, 42–5, 48–52
communicative action, 7–11, 16, 26, 102
communitarianism, 149
consent, principle of, 124–30
constituent power, 174, 182
constitution making, 126, 134, 138–40, 154, 162–5, 178, 180–2
constitutional patriotism, 160, 195
constitutional state, 64, 85, 87, 94, 99n, 141–3, 150
  historical development of, 54, 62–6, 68, 75–6, 77
  justifications for, 127
  tasks of, 141, 148, 150, 155
  see also democracy: constitutional
constitutional world society, 167–8, 170
cosmopolitanism, 87, 94, 97–9, 161, 167–9, 171, 175, 179, 191–6
courts, 58, 64, 118, 133, 142–3, 145, 172
critical theory, 3, 107, 109–10, 115–16, 121n, 194
  normative foundations of, 115–19
Cronin, C., 182, 184

culture
  commodification of, 110
  political, 93, 146, 151, 154, 160, 166, 185, 195
  popular, 69, 73, 90–1, 110

Dahl, R., 28, 37n
decision-making, 29, 34, 57, 76, 105, 125–6, 141–7, 151–2, 157, 174–6, 178, 182, 183–5, 193
Delanty, G., 120
deliberation, 50, 84, 128, 131–2, 141–2, 152, 181, 188–91
deliberative democracy, 24, 50, 87, 129–30, 131–3, 140, 147–50, 159, 175, 177, 181–2, 183–5, 196
  epistemic reliability of, 132–3, 188–91
  exclusionary dynamics in, 186–8
  two-track model of, 129, 143–7, 150, 172n, 191
democracy, 2, 21, 39, 67, 83, 87, 98, 99, 105–6, 116–17, 123, 133, 139, 146, 148, 185
  constitutional, 123, 138–40, 141, 180–2, 183–5
  freedom and, 21
  history of, 68–9, 75–6, 111–12
  models of, 139–40, 148–50
  principle of, 130–4, 136–7, 149, 154, 173n
  procedural model of see deliberative democracy
  see also consent, principle of; deliberative democracy; social democracy
democratic principle, the see democracy, principle of
dialogue, cross-cultural, 51, 119, 196
disagreement, 10–11, 17, 126, 150, 183–5, 186–7
  modernity and, 60–1, 65–6, 179
  reasonable, 33, 158
discourse, 14–17, 19–21, 24, 25, 35, 40–2, 45, 49, 53n, 114, 118–19, 122n, 147, 152–4, 186, 196, 197n
  ethical, 27, 132, 149
  hegemonic, 49–52, 187
  legal, 132
  moral, 117, 127, 131–2
  political, 33–5, 61, 71, 73–4, 87, 111, 149, 151–2, 157–60, 186–8

  pragmatic, 132
  religious, 156–8
discourse principle, the, 117–18, 131–6, 154
domination, 2, 5, 15, 29, 33, 34, 37n, 40–1, 42–3, 45–9, 52n, 82–4, 98, 101, 110–12, 121, 137, 141, 177, 194

economic policy, 77–9, 88, 91–2, 162–3, 165, 195
economy see market economy
Eisenstadt, S. N., 120
elections see voting
enemies, 175–8
environmental issues, 88, 91, 170, 172n
equality, 2, 5, 15, 64, 70, 73, 93, 114, 123–9, 134–40, 146, 150, 151–2, 155–60, 164–5, 168, 175, 177, 179, 183, 196n
Estlund, D., 189–90
Eurocentrism, 112–15, 119–20
Europe, 1–2, 59–60, 64, 67, 68–70, 72, 73, 90, 94–5, 112–16, 120, 162–7, 176, 194–5
European Union, 1, 87, 161–7, 168
exploitation, 63, 77, 81, 107–8, 110, 112–14

fake news, 191
feminism see gender
finance see banking and finance
Fine, R., 191, 194
Forst, R., 11, 37n, 50, 122n
Foucault, M., 38–41, 46–8, 52n, 53n, 80, 84
Fraser, N., 102, 110–11, 138, 144, 186
freedom
  communicative, 24–7
  individual, 21–4
  social, 18–21
  see also autonomy
French Revolution, 67, 68–9

Gadamer, H.-G., 10
gender, 43, 46–8, 89, 110–12, 155
general will, 128–30, 147, 183–4
Global financial crisis, 92, 109, 162
Global South, 88, 194–5
globalisation, 78, 87–90, 91–3, 99, 109, 160–1, 166–7, 193–5; see also political integration: global
Günther, K., 32–3

INDEX

Hassanzadeh, N., 195
Hegel, G. W. F., 19, 23, 36n, 122n
Heidegger, M., 6
Hobbes, T., 62, 125–9, 175
Honig, B., 183–4
Honneth, A., 18–21, 36n, 101–2, 122n
human rights, 95, 114–15, 158, 161, 169–71, 172, 178–9, 192–3
humanism, 87, 175–6
humanitarian intervention, 98, 176

identity
  collective, 68, 69, 156
  loss of, 81–2
  personal, 9, 23–4, 89–90
  socialisation and, 10, 45–9
  see also national consciousness
ideology, 34–5, 42–5, 50, 73, 113, 120, 176, 183
illocutionary obligations, 25–6, 32–3, 40
imperialism, 98, 112–13, 115, 119, 169, 176, 192
inclusion, 113, 142, 146, 154–5, 159–60, 182, 183–5, 194
inequality, 43–4, 52, 85, 90, 93, 109–10, 137, 147, 166, 186–7, 193, 195
influence, 11, 29, 31, 34, 40, 74, 82, 87, 104–5, 146, 170
injustice, 85, 130, 170, 191, 196
  epistemic, 53n
  structural, 44
International Criminal Court, 96–7, 172, 193
international law, 94–9, 167–72, 193
international relations, 88, 94–9, 169, 170–2, 176–9, 185, 191–3

Joas, H., 102
judicial authority, 57–60, 95, 125, 142–3, 151, 171, 172, 193; *see also* courts
juridification, 54–5, 64, 75, 77, 85, 94, 99n, 105, 110, 121n
jus ad bellum, 94–5
justice, 55, 114, 131, 148, 151, 168, 179, 188
  distributive, 137, 169
  global, 172
  natural, 131
  principles of, 150–4
  secular, 159
  social, 77
  standards of, 163
justification vs application, 142
Jütten, T., 108

Kalyvas, A., 181–2
Kant, I., 113, 122n, 127–30, 133, 135
  on cosmopolitanism, 94, 99, 167–8
  on freedom, 21–3
King Jr, M. L., 158

labour, 61–3, 79, 80, 85–6, 88–9, 93, 107–9
  women's, 110
labour movement, 76–7
law, 17, 66, 105–6
  janus-faced, 48, 106
  labour, 77
  morality and, 56, 65–6, 131–2
  natural, 61, 130–1, 134
  private or civil, 63, 67
  public, 63, 67
  sacred, 57–61
  stabilising function of, 33, 56, 65–6, 130
  see also international law; juridification; legitimacy of law; rule of law
League of Nations, 94–5
learning processes, 7, 15, 44, 51, 99, 114, 116, 118–20, 137, 158, 160, 181, 185, 194
Lefort, C., 148
legal positivism, 130–1
legislative authority, 58, 124–9, 132–3, 139, 141–3, 165, 169–70, 176
legitimacy, 33–5, 55, 58–9, 62, 64, 102–3, 124, 126–9, 133–4, 138, 140–7
  post-conventional basis of, 59–61, 66, 68, 75, 178
  religious basis of, 57–9
legitimacy of law, 60–1, 66, 75, 106, 126, 129, 130–3, 138–40, 146, 149, 184, 192–3
legitimation problems, 54–5, 76–87, 92–3, 96, 99, 163, 192
liberalism, 67, 69–72, 98, 129, 137, 139–40, 148–9, 150–6, 159, 175, 179, 183–4, 191, 193; *see also* rights: liberal
  political, 151–4
liberty *see* freedom

209

lifeworld, 9–10, 16, 20, 24
  colonisation of, 80–2, 83, 86, 89–90, 110, 146
  system and, 13–14, 101–3
  uncoupling of system and, 62, 101, 103, 104
Locke, J., 127–9
Lukács, G., 80–1, 100n

McCarthy, T., 102, 113
majority rule, 39, 142, 172
market economy, 4, 13–4, 19, 29, 61–2, 63, 66, 72, 74–5, 76–9, 80–1, 83, 85–6, 87–9, 102–3, 104, 107–9, 110–11, 126, 137
  global, 88–93, 96, 109, 160–1, 163, 166
Marshall, T. H., 77
Marx, K., 19, 43–4, 63, 72, 80, 85–6, 107–8, 114, 156
Marxism, 2, 43–4, 85–7, 107–9
mass media, 30–1, 71, 73, 75, 145–6, 188, 190
Michelman, F., 180–1
modern consciousness, 16–17, 65–6, 114, 116, 118, 120, 159
morality, 5, 56, 139, 178–9
  post-conventional, 65–6, 111, 118
Mouffe, C., 183–4
Mouzelis, N., 120
multiculturalism, 155, 194; see also inclusion
mutual understanding see communicative action

nation-state, 68–70, 76, 78, 154, 177–8, 194
  cosmopolitanism and, 167–9, 171
  globalisation and, 87–9, 90–4, 99
  transnational democracy and, 160–3
national consciousness, 67–9, 90–1, 99, 166, 178
nationalism, 68–70, 90, 160, 163, 177–8
neo-conservatism see neo-liberalism
neo-liberalism, 78–9, 92, 100n, 137
Neuhouser, F., 18, 36n

Olson, K., 182

parliament, 64, 74, 99n, 142–3, 145, 166
  world, 169–70, 171

parliamentary principle, the, 142
Parsons, T., 30, 31, 104, 121n
Pateman, C., 111
people, the, 31, 67, 68–9, 72, 127–9, 138–9, 147, 174–5, 177–8, 181–3
pluralism, 33, 118, 126, 130–1, 149, 150–4, 155, 177, 180, 185
  religious, 59–61, 62, 68, 150, 155–9
  political, the, 59, 150–4, 175–8, 181, 183–4
political integration
  global, 94–9, 161, 166–72, 191–3
  transnational, 94, 160–6, 167, 192–3
political organisation, stages of, 55–64, 67–75, 76–7, 94–9
political participation, 67, 75–6, 93, 123, 136–8, 143–4, 147, 149, 156, 165, 186–8, 193
political parties, 34, 74–5, 79, 83, 92, 144, 161, 173n
popular sovereignty see sovereignty: popular
postcolonial theory, 112–13, 115–16, 121, 176, 194–5, 197n
postmetaphysical thinking, 6–7, 17, 49–52, 114, 116–17, 119, 154, 159
postnational constellation, 87–94
post-secular society, 158–9
post-truth, 191
power, 2–3, 28–31, 104
  administrative, 29–30, 34, 56–7, 74, 83–5, 105–6, 141, 143
  communicative, 28, 30, 31–5, 73, 80, 82–3, 104–5, 140, 146–7
  cultural or symbolic, 43, 45
  economic, 28, 74
  illegitimate, 33–4, 83–4, 150
  media, 30–1, 74, 84
  political, 31, 34, 54–5, 56–9, 60, 71–2, 80, 82, 98, 105–6, 140, 141
  social, 28–9, 31, 33, 43–4, 56–7, 82–3, 141
power-over vs power-with, 5, 28–30
private sphere, 60, 61, 63–4; see also autonomy: private
progress, historical, 108, 113–16, 119–20, 176–7
psychology
  adaptive preference formation, 44
  implicit bias, 44
  motivated reasoning, 49
public accountability, 72, 75, 118, 129, 143, 146, 163, 171, 185

INDEX

public opinion, 31, 71–4, 87, 126, 140, 145, 147, 149–50, 177, 181, 191
public reason, 73, 124, 129, 136, 151–3, 175, 184; *see also* public sphere: religion in
public sphere, 67, 71, 87
  contemporary, 73–5, 144–6
  history of, 70–3
  religion in, 154–9
  vs private sphere, 63, 111
  weak vs strong, 144–5, 188, 190–1

Rancière, J., 53n
rationalisation, societal, 18, 65, 85, 114, 115–18, 119–20, 141, 191
rationality *see* reason
Rawls, J., 7, 123, 134, 150–4, 157, 169
reason, 7, 38, 114–17
  communicative, 5–7, 44–5, 47, 49, 51
  group *see* deliberation
  motivating force of, 16, 32–3, 48
  pragmatic, moral and ethical uses of, 22–3, 127, 132, 154, 185
  procedural conception of *see* postmetaphysical thinking
  strategic, 13–14
  see also deliberation; public reason
reasonableness, 150, 152–3, 155, 157, 180
reasons
  public vs private, 12–13
  religious and non-religious, 154–9
recognition, 20, 24, 26–7, 36n, 151
Reformation, 59–60
reification, 80–1, 85, 121n
religious belief, 88, 90
representation, 59, 67–8, 124, 142, 143, 152, 168, 171
republicanism, 69, 128–9, 139–40, 148–9, 154; *see also* rights: political
rights, 75, 77, 133–8
  liberal, 64, 67, 76, 134–7
  political, 67, 71, 136–7
  social, 77, 136–8
  see also human rights
rights against the state, 142
rights of private autonomy *see* rights: liberal
rights of public autonomy *see* rights: political
Rousseau, J.-J., 127–30, 147, 183

rule of law, 3, 67, 85, 99n, 130, 140–1, 150, 177–8, 181
  global, 161, 169, 171, 175

Scheuerman, W., 104, 174, 192–3
Schmitt, C., 125, 174–9, 181–2, 184, 191–2
secularisation, 59–61, 118
secularity, 68, 155–9
self-realisation, 23, 27, 46
separation of church and state, 60, 155–7
separation of powers, 141, 143
Sitton, J. F., 108
Smith, W., 191, 194
social contract, 5, 61–2, 125–8
social democracy, 2, 85–7
social movements, 69–70, 76, 111, 144, 158–9
social pathologies, 10, 79, 81–2, 85, 109, 192
social stability, 55–6
social systems, 13–14, 83, 101–3
  self-programming, 34, 83, 106, 108–9, 141, 143
  see also administrative state; market economy
solidarity
  civic, 158, 166
  social, 5, 9, 16, 17–18, 20, 65, 68, 78, 80, 81–2, 85–6, 90, 91–3, 102, 148, 153, 158, 166, 168–9, 194
sovereignty, 62–3, 147–8, 163, 174–8, 184
  popular, 69, 127–30, 138–9, 140, 143–4, 147–8, 152, 161, 164, 174, 177
  principle of, 124–5
speech acts, 8–14, 24–7, 40; *see also* illocutionary obligations
state of emergency, 175
steering media (power and money), 11–14, 16, 61–2, 76, 86, 102, 104–5
steering problems, 77–8, 83–4, 85–6, 107
strategic action, 11–14, 24, 42, 102
Sunstein, C., 188–90
systems *see* social systems

taxation, 77–8, 82, 90–2
technocracy, 163–4, 192
third way politics, 161

trade negotiations, 97, 163, 170
truth, 6, 8, 15, 35n, 40–2, 50–2, 118, 129, 148, 191
  metaphysical, 175
  moral, 153

United Nations, 95–7, 161, 168–72, 193
United States of America, 95–6, 96–9, 165

validity, 6, 35n; *see also* truth
validity claims, 7–8, 20, 26, 32, 36n, 51, 104, 118
Vatter, M., 124
violence, 12, 28–9, 33, 40–4, 46, 98, 110, 113
  state, 63, 141, 151, 168, 170, 172, 175, 177, 183
  structural, 35, 44, 52
voting, 34, 72, 142, 143–7, 151, 155, 173n

war, 94–7, 125, 161, 163, 169, 176, 193–4
war crimes, 95–6, 193
war on terror, 97
Weber, M., 28, 30, 37n, 55, 80
Weithmann, P., 173n
welfare state 76–7, 83–4, 90, 93–4, 109–11, 161–3, 194–5
  crises tendencies of, 77–80, 93
Wolterstorff, N., 173n
women *see* gender
work *see* labour
working class *see* labour movement
world-relation, 6, 24
World Trade Organization, 97, 170
World War I, 94
World War II, 1–2, 95, 96, 161

Young, I. M., 186–8

Zurn, C., 180, 182, 184

EU representative:
Easy Access System Europe
Mustamäe tee 50, 10621 Tallinn, Estonia
Gpsr.requests@easproject.com

www.ingramcontent.com/pod-product-compliance
Lightning Source LLC
Chambersburg PA
CBHW061713300426
44115CB00014B/2670